Ian Botham, England's greatest post-war all-rounder, burst on to the international cricket scene in 1977 and immediately made an impact by force of personality, size of frame, and sheer ability. His early successes on the field and his headstrong, ebullient manner combined to make him an exhilarating sportsman and a threat to the gentlemanly traditions in the game.

But it was not all success. He became disillusioned at his inability as captain to imbue his team-mates with some of his daredevilry and aggression and was dogged for years by a back injury. He was also hounded by the tabloid press and constantly at odds with the England management. This is the Botham uncovered here – a gifted man whose boundless loyalty, warmth and generosity were continually compromised by a media whirl of accusation, indiscretion, hot-temperedness and indiscipline.

Dave Bowler has written biographies of various pop groups, as well as the acclaimed *Shanks*, the authorised biography of Bill Shankly, also available from Orion.

NO SURRENDER

The Life and Times of Ian Botham

Dave Bowler

ORION

An Orion Paperback
First published in Great Britain by Orion in 1997
This paperback edition published in 1998 by
Orion Books Ltd,
Orion House, 5 Upper St Martin's Lane,
London WC2H 9EA

Copyright © 1997 Dave Bowler

A CIP catalogue record for this book is available
from the British Library

ISBN: 0 75281 637 3

Typeset by Selwood Systems, Midsomer Norton

Printed in Great Britain by
Clays Ltd, St Ives plc

To Mom and Dad
My best friends

And for Denise
A mountain moving deep within
Always
David

CONTENTS

ACKNOWLEDGEMENTS

There are a number of people without whom this book could not have been written. Chief among them are Tanja Howarth and Mark Hayward and everyone at Orion Books. Thanks too to Bryan Dray. And Carrie – show them this at school.

I'd also like to thank David Frith for his help and encouragement both with this book and in the past. Thanks also to Phil Neale, Tom Graveney, Dennis Breakwell and Ted Dexter for their offers of assistance.

Finally thanks to Denise who had to put up with me while I wrote this, and to Mom and Dad for introducing me to Edgbaston a long time ago.

AUTHOR'S NOTE

The following is not strict biography, nor does it follow any obvious chronological pattern. More than enough such books are already available about Ian Botham, and in the wake of his own autobiography it is impossible to justify such a narrow reading of his life through the simple facts and figures.

Instead, *No Surrender* is an attempt to look at Botham as he is revealed by his relationships with other people and agencies. In studying his reaction to the county game, his contacts with the media, his arguments with the TCCB, I believe that it is possible to learn more about this surprisingly complex individual than it is by simply reliving the events of the Oval in 1982. Ian Botham is the most important cricketer of the post-Packer years. In understanding his story, perhaps we can better understand the way the game has developed over the last twenty years.

This thematic approach means that there must inevitably be a degree of cross-over from one chapter to another. Every effort has been made to reduce any such repetition to the bare minimum.

A little rebellion now and then
is a good thing.

Thomas Jefferson, 1787

INTRODUCTION

The Art of the Impossible

To the end of the English season in 1996, more than 2000 individuals had represented one or more countries at Test match level since play began in the inaugural Test at the Melbourne Cricket Ground in March 1877. From Old Trafford to the SCG, from Basin Reserve to Sabina Park, a galaxy of talent has registered a catalogue of mighty deeds. Their memory has been handed down through the generations via the pages of *Wisden Cricketers' Almanack*, yet their achievements raise barely a flicker of interest among those not committed to the game. Among those hundreds of fine cricketers, few have done more than graze the consciousness of the outside world. W.G., Jack Hobbs, the Don, Denis Compton, Garfield Sobers, Fred Trueman, Dennis Lillee, Brian Lara, these are among the select handful who have managed to thrill even those who otherwise have no understanding of, nor interest in, the game of cricket. To that elite group must be added the name of Ian Terence Botham.

In his prime, year in, year out, it was Ian Botham who

provided the most memorable moments of the season: a stunning spell of swing bowling at Lord's to unhinge the Pakistanis in 1978; an explosive acceleration towards the Test match double in 1979; *his* summer of 1981; a murderous double hundred against the overwhelmed Indians in 1982; bludgeoning the punch-drunk Aussies into submission in 1985 with a fusillade of boundaries and bouncers. These, rather than the staggering facts and figures that he amassed along the way, are the enduring images of one of the most remarkable careers the game has witnessed.

Yet there has always been more to Botham than just cricket. No sporting field, however huge, could contain so generous or mighty a spirit and it was surely inevitable that his larger than life personality would spill from the game and out into the real world. To become an icon, as Botham most assuredly has, you have to be much more than just a highly gifted sporting superstar. The majority of those giants already listed were more than mere players. Grace was as much a grand Victorian impresario and showman as a cricketer; likewise there was Compton the Brylcreem boy, epitomising ideals of post-war elegance and joie de vivre, Sobers the smiling, happy-go-lucky gambler, the face of the sunshine islands, Trueman the bluff caricature of Yorkshire bloody-mindedness, Lillee the perennial rebel without a cause. In those cases, forces beyond the individual's control took a guiding hand, irresistibly dragging them to a position where what they did became somehow less important than what they represented. It's not unique to cricket, of course, for you could say much the same about Chaplin, Valentino, Presley, Monroe, Lennon, Warhol, Madonna, Gascoigne, Cobain, Cantona, though those unfortunates have had to deal with far greater fame on a far wider scale. Among cricket's greats, perhaps only

Bradman and now, to a lesser extent, the record-breaking Lara achieved their international renown thanks solely to their efforts on the field, cricketing equivalents of Pele, Babe Ruth or Jack Nicklaus.

As the media has grown since the war, so has the public's demand for the extraordinary, the legendary. It is an appetite that mere sporting prowess cannot satisfy, an appetite increasingly fed by controversy, scandal and salacious gossip. A hundred before lunch at Lord's may get you into the papers, but it won't keep you there. To stay in the limelight, and thereby maximise your earning potential, you need to be able to do a bit more than handle a slab of willow. To maintain a high profile in the face of fierce and constantly renewing competition, you must become a 'celebrity', a 'personality'. It's not a new phenomenon but it's an increasingly important one as the press fights to keep its hold on the audience's ever dwindling attention. Today's celebrities are like buses. Missed one? Never mind, there'll be another one along in a minute. It's good for newspaper sales, bad for the individuals who are used, discarded and sometimes destroyed in the process.

Football has always been ahead of cricket in that respect, simply because it is the national game with a far stronger hold on the hearts of the population. In modern terms, George Best was probably the first sporting superstar. Utterly uncalculating, Best became an icon by accident rather than via the Machiavellian scheming of some shadowy agent. He was one of the most potent symbols of the 1960s not simply because he was a footballing genius, but because he caught the popular mood. Freed from the slavery of the maximum wage, footballers suddenly became wealthy, at least in comparison with the working man. George enjoyed that new financial freedom to the full, while taller and taller tales saw him surrounded by booze, birds and boutiques. Best's legend is still far stronger than that of comparable team-mates Denis Law and Bobby Charlton because he was seen as more than a young man who could do extravagant things with a football. Where Charlton was a nice but dull, archetypal 'I know my place' 1950s man, Best was the footballing Beatle, the long-haired maverick who bought his gear in Carnaby Street, the flawed genius who had the world at his feet but kicked it into touch. Best provided the stories and the excitement that the public wanted and his reward was to become inextricably linked with his decade – think of the 1960s in England, and Georgie's there. History will show that Ian Botham caught the public mood equally well in the 1980s.

Much of the Botham legend has been a function of his immaculate timing. He arrived on the scene just as England's premier all-rounder Tony Greig was being turned into the pantomime villain and lured away by Packer's lucre. The Packer schism allowed Botham to make his mark on the international scene against relatively poor opposition, gobbling cheap runs and wickets on the way. His post-captaincy rehabilitation in 1981 coincided with the royal wedding, a time when British flag-waving was at its height. His brash rampage through the 1980s provided personification of the laddish loadsamoney culture, Porsche-driving city boys and buttock-baring brickies alike enshrining him as some kind of patron saint. The later, often lean, years saw him maintain his place in the England side long after he should have been dropped, an automatic selection simply because there was no other viable alternative for the all-rounder berth.

Ian Botham is such a huge character that everyone can take something from him that he or she can enjoy or admire, be it a thumping drive back over the bowler's head, a cheeky aside to Bill Beaumont on *A Question of Sport*, the generosity he's consistently shown to leukaemia sufferers or his refusal to be ground down by the wheels of the Establishment. It is equally inevitable that everyone finds something in him that drives them to distraction – a boorishness that has occasionally bordered on thuggery, the inanities of his media persona, the stubborn refusal to accept the passing of time and the dimming of his powers, the inability to turn the other cheek in the face of insults, imagined or real.

To trawl through Botham's life day by day is a futile exercise. More than enough ink has already been spilt on that score – the dozens of filing cabinets currently buckling beneath the weight of Beefy-related clippings in assorted newspaper libraries across the country testify to that. What needs to be established are his claims to greatness, his place among the quartet of superb all-rounders that dominated the 1980s, the uses to which he put his huge abilities, the legacy he left to English cricket, and the way in which his rise and fall has mirrored that of the English game as a whole. Equally, his treatment at the hands of the media needs to be assessed for Botham represents the bridge between the relatively deferential treatment meted out to Best in the 1960s and the vilification of Gazza in the 1990s. Did Botham manipulate the media or was he controlled by it? How did living his life in the glare of the media spotlight affect other members of the England team? Ian Botham's story needs to be looked at from a different angle than the merely chronological.

Simon Hughes, his colleague at Durham, best summed up the dilemma that faces anyone attempting to write about Ian Botham in his book *From Minor To Major*: 'It is hard for anyone else really to relate to him. He has such a powerful aura that sweeps past, leaving everything else in its wake. Pressmen who privately ridicule him daren't do so in print. Rightly so too. They are wary of writs arriving on their desk and mindful also, perhaps, of a remark of Dr Johnson: "A fly, Sir, may sting a stately horse, and make him wince; but one is but an insect, and the other is a horse still."' To some, including perhaps Botham himself if his autobiography is any guide, Ian Botham is at the very least the greatest *English* cricketer that ever drew breath and almost certainly the world's finest all-rounder bar none. For his supporters, any hint of criticism of the great man is heresy, vindictive claptrap that is rooted solely in jealousy. Elsewhere, revisionists are making the case that Botham was, as E.W. Swanton remarked, at best 'a mixed blessing', that his greatest performances were reserved for inferior opposition, that he was never the colossus he was portrayed as being, and that his off the field exploits damaged the game.

From a personal standpoint, the arrival of Ian Botham at the crease, with either bat or ball, was a source of great pleasure and no little excitement. Having followed cricket for twenty-five years, I can think of no player who provided greater value for money, none who has played the game with such visible enjoyment, nor one who has had the capacity to thrill and disappoint in equally dramatic measure. To see Botham seize a game at whatever level and bend its course according to his whim was a regular, but nonetheless remarkable, feature of the sporting life. As David Frith, founding editor of *Wisden Cricket Monthly*, points out, 'for force of personality, he ranks with only one other all-rounder since the war, and that's Keith Miller'. To see Botham at his peak was to see the game of cricket come alive, to enjoy it at its vibrant best. Even so, so haphazard were his performances post-1982, it is hard to rate Botham accurately and there are a number of other players who can lay claim to his crown as the premier all-rounder of the modern era. Domestically, too, players such as Gooch, Gatting, Brearley, Willis and Gower would have their supporters in any election to find England's most valuable player of the Botham years. What none can rival is the relationship that Botham enjoyed with the British public: Botham put more bums on seats than anyone else, and for that achievement alone English cricket should be eternally grateful.

What follows is a look at the key elements of Botham's life. It is ordered thematically though for those that require a jog to the memory, a chronology is included in the appendix. The facts and fictions of Botham's life are already a matter of public record, but they provide just a part of the tale, showering us with conflicting evidence. It seems that what is now required is a degree of objectivity and a wider perspective on the man's life and times. I hope that the following chapters will contribute towards a better understanding of England's most famous cricketer.

CHAPTER ONE

May You Live In Interesting Times

The County Game

Cricketers achieve greatness in the Test arena. International matches are the be all and end all of the game. A ground like Edgbaston can be packed to overflowing for a dull, one-sided Test match occasion, yet the following week a far more absorbing duel in the County Championship can be played out before a couple of hundred spectators. One of the great Championship games of modern times between Warwickshire and Northamptonshire in 1995 struggled to attract more than a couple of thousand paying spectators to Edgbaston over its four see-sawing days.

Whatever the differences in profile between county and international matches county cricket is the bedrock of the English game. Future Test talents are forged in its arenas, and valuable experience gained in what is still, despite claims to the contrary, a competitive environment for most of the season. This is where a player grows towards greatness. If a young man cannot make his mark domestically, the call will never come from the English selectors.

Naturally, some people make a bigger and quicker impact; most build gradually over three or four years, registering 1000 runs in a season, then 1200, 1600, 2000, accompanied by a slowly increasing average and an 'A' tour or two, before graduating to full honours. This is the path followed by the likes of Graham Thorpe and Dominic Cork in the last few years. Some explode onto the domestic scene, demanding a place in the England side – Graham Gooch had played fewer than twenty first class games before representing his country. Surprisingly, although Ian Botham made a big splash in his first full season with Somerset, he belongs to the former category, a player who built incrementally on his strengths over three seasons.

Botham was always likely to end up with Somerset. Born in Heswall, Cheshire on 24 November 1955, he had a peripatetic childhood. His father Les was serving in the Fleet Air Arm and so Botham the toddler spent his time in Londonderry before the family returned to his native county. Within a year or so Ian, Les, mother Marie and younger sister Dale had moved to Yeovil and put down some roots. Botham senior was working for Westland Helicopters and the family were happy to settle in the very heart of the West Country. Ian went to a small private school before moving on to Milford Juniors for the autumn term of 1962, where he was introduced to football and cricket. An enthusiastic child, he made the school teams well in advance of his age, holding his own among the older boys. It was clear that Ian Botham was something a little out of the ordinary. A love of sport ran in the family: his father played most games during his stint in the Fleet Air Arm and his mother was a keen cricketer, captaining the VAD nursing service during 1946.

For some kids, the prospect of going to a larger secondary

school is a daunting one. Not for Botham, who approached his transfer to Buckler's Mead with relish, admitting in his autobiography that 'my sheer bloody-mindedness about getting my own way was well established'. He already knew what he wanted to do with his life and nothing was going to stop him. Big for his age, he was able to dominate his classmates on the sports field, while his monumental desire to win helped him compete against older boys. This was all the proof he needed to show that a life in professional sport was waiting for him. The only choice was between football and cricket. Crystal Palace had offered him terms and several other clubs were carefully monitoring his development. His father counselled that he was a far better cricketer than footballer, and so the die was cast.

Nowadays, the call is to catch our kids at a young age and instil the basics of a sport in them before they can develop bad habits. The success of Australia's cricket academy suggests that there's a lot in this, as does the Ajax philosophy in football, where promising seven-year-olds are invited to play for the club's numerous junior sides. Even so, vast amounts of coaching can drive promising youngsters away from their love of sport. Turn the sports field into an extension of the classroom and enthusiasm quickly wanes. Kids want to play sport, not learn about it – Botham was the prime example. He worked on his game by playing matches anywhere and everywhere, be it a representative game for the school or an impromptu net in the back garden with his sisters bowling to him.

Already he was a big character. At home, his sisters lived in fear of being the butt of another of his practical jokes, and at school he was the centre of attention, at least where games were concerned. He was the best sportsman of his year and was very popular with his classmates as a consequence. Some of his teachers were harder to win over, driven to distraction by his refusal to knuckle down to school work. A precocious child, Botham couldn't see the need for diplomas and certificates. He'd make his mark on life with a cricket bat and ball. Having a Geography 'O' level wasn't much help when you wanted to get into a county cricket side. Though not a disruptive influence on his school, his absolute sense of assurance was unnerving for those who represented the education system, teachers who had seen many like him fail to make the sporting grade with no qualifications to fall back on. Botham continued to follow his own particular path. As he developed physically, his sporting prowess grew at a commensurate rate. Sport was all that interested him, winning all that mattered, his interest in girls first pricked only when he found one who could actually run faster than him.

Before he was fifteen, he suffered his first real cricketing set-back. Having won selection for the South West in the English Schools Under Fifteen Festival to be held in Liverpool, and having bowled well to a meticulously set field, Botham felt sure that the five wickets he'd claimed would merit selection for the England Schools side that would go on to play the Public Schools XI. Instead, his father told him that he'd overheard one selector commenting that 'it was a fluke'. This first injustice was perhaps a pivotal moment in his career. It still burned brightly enough for him to write twenty-three years later that 'whenever I managed to achieve anything on the cricket field, it gave me the greatest satisfaction to remember those blinkered observers and wonder what they were doing with their lives at that moment'. Just as important was the selectors' conclusion that Botham was primarily a batsman, not an all-rounder, reasoning that his bowling wasn't up to scratch. While this desire to prove himself was a vibrant part of the young Botham who made his mark in international cricket, it became a handicap later on when he was determined to show that he was a great bowler long after those days had passed.

That failure in Liverpool was swiftly consigned to the history books when later that same year he was accepted on to the groundstaff at Lord's. On the recommendation of Somerset he had a trial there in August 1971 and was invited back the following year. With his confidence still intact despite the snub he'd received from the Schools selectors, Botham went about his new job with relish. At Lord's he got to bowl at members of the MCC in the nets, something that helped build his formidable stamina. Given that he found some MCC members supercilious and full of airs – as well as being poor tippers – it also helped feed the fires of his hostility towards batsmen. Cricket aside, Botham had a riotous time now that he was unleashed on the big city, away from home for the first time. He shared digs with the young South African Rodney Ontong, who went on to play county cricket for Glamorgan. The two worked hard at Lord's, but away from the ground they made up for time lost during the day with most evenings spent wrapped around a pint or two.

A second year at Lord's was planned for 1973, but Botham had broken into Somerset's Second XI by then. In the under twenty-five county competition, he made a name for himself by taking three Glamorgan wickets in the final over when they'd required just eight to win. Participating in the Minor Counties Championship, Somerset Seconds came in second behind Shropshire. Botham averaged almost thirty-one from his ten innings, though his bowling was unremarkable at this stage – nine wickets at thirty-two. Based on those performances, few had much faith in his talent; many of his Somerset contemporaries felt that he was a useful cricketer but hardly an explosive one. Writing in *It Sort Of Clicks*, Peter Roebuck noted that 'at the age of sixteen [in 1972], no one I know predicted that Botham would break through ... he might be a useful belter down the order but you couldn't play that way in county cricket'. Having said that, given Somerset's slender resources, it was seemingly just a matter of time before he made the leap into the first team. He even managed to get into their one day side at the end of 1973.

However, it was in 1974 that Botham made his break-through, under the wing of Brian Close. Botham, once again, timed his arrival to perfection. After years as a backwoods side, as a team that enjoyed its cricket but was never competing for honours, Brian Close had begun to forge a club that played good aggressive cricket and was acquiring the winning habit. Though Close never managed to lead the county to a trophy, he was the pivotal figure in helping the club land its first ever trophies in 1979 when Somerset clinched both the John Player League and the Gillette Cup. Somerset were clearly a maturing side when Botham joined their ranks. They had old stagers such as Close, Graham Burgess and Derek Taylor on hand to provide experience and discipline on the field for youngsters like Botham who were making their claims to the future of the county.

Just as Botham had lived life to the full in the company of Rodney Ontong at Lord's, he was soon adopting a similar attitude with spinner Dennis Breakwell. In 1973, the two shared a flat that seemed little better than a squat. So dismal were their surroundings, they spent most of their spare time in the local pubs and clubs, putting off the inevitable moment when they had to return home to a sleeping bag on the floor and a couple of cockroaches for company. As the two moved up the pecking order at Somerset, Botham's salary increasing to £500 for 1974, the pair moved out to share a flat next door to the county ground with the club's newest import, Vivian Richards. Richards was no slouch as a socialiser either and the three enjoyed one another's company. The bond between Botham and Richards was especially strong. The two were inseparable mates at county level, sharing a similar passionate belief in their cricketing destinies. Within a few years both were thrust towards superstardom by their efforts on the field; away from the game they could talk and share each other's problems, knowing that they were two of the few men in the world who could really understand the pressures involved. As the two most famous cricketers of their generation, it was probably as well for them both that they were able to spend so much time in each other's presence.

It was Richards who first made his mark on the world scene, his batting in England in 1976 verging on the Bradmanesque. Scoring two double hundreds in the four Tests he played, he established himself as the greatest batsman in the world with extraordinary ease. With an arrogant demeanour on the field, off it he took the plaudits modestly but with a sense that they were his due, the reward for a lot of hard work. Richards had grown up playing cricket on the beaches of Antigua without the inherent advantages of comparative wealth that Botham, like the vast majority of his fellow countrymen, took for granted. Richards took little for granted, and though he was always willing to go out for a drink with the boys, he always looked after himself physically and mentally.

Botham was a little less circumspect, noting that while Richards slept with his bat by his side, he slept with a bottle of gin.

Brian Close instilled a Yorkshire-style professionalism in the side. In addition, he was a part of the staff who had groomed a new generation of players, men like Botham, Roebuck, Rose, Slocombe and Marks. The talents of these young men were complemented and enhanced by the phenomenal batting skills and absolute confidence of Vivian Richards, probably *the* county cricketer of the 1970s. Yet, as *Wisden* pointed out, in 1974 it was Botham who 'showed star quality ... his successful fight to win the Benson & Hedges quarter final at Taunton showed technical abilities underlined by courage and temperament of the highest order'. It was that game on 12 June that established Botham in the minds of the cricketing public. Hampshire had scored a moderate 182 (Botham two for thirty-three from his eleven overs) but Somerset collapsed to 113 for 8 with fifteen overs left. Botham, coming in at number nine, had just Hallam Moseley and Bob Clapp for company, neither of whom could rank among the adequates with a bat. With Somerset scarcely any closer to their target, West Indian paceman Andy Roberts, one of the quickest bowlers in the world, came on, ostensibly to finish the game. Within moments, Botham took a fierce blow in the mouth from a Roberts bouncer. The all-rounder spat out a couple of broken teeth, had a glass of water, and then proceeded to thrash the living daylights out of an astonished Hampshire attack. Victory came when Botham hammered yet another boundary to clinch the game by one wicket with an over to spare, finishing with forty-five not out and the Gold Award as man of the match. That sort of display was headline news across the country, though as he was firmly informed by some seasoned Somerset pros, he was famous today, nobody again tomorrow. That was good advice, for the rest of the season was a comparative anti-climax, although he did enough to catch the eye of *Wisden* editor Norman Preston. In his notes to the 1975 almanack, he took the unusual step of commending him to the selectors: 'I would particularly like to see Botham given a chance while he is young and enthusiastic.'

Botham returned for 1975 as an established player but failed to make such a powerful impact. He suffered from second season syndrome: players who are an unknown quantity in their debut season are soon worked out by their fellow professionals. Botham's bowling was solid if unspectacular – 'a useful seam bowler of increasing pace', according to *Wisden* – and his batting was intermittently brilliant but largely disappointing. At this stage, Botham was all promise with little delivery. Of that season, Close felt that 'he tried to make things happen and things don't always happen in cricket'.

Botham would never agree with what he would see as defeatism. He would play county cricket the way he played Schools cricket, hurling the ball down, staring out opposing batsmen and belting the leather off the ball. That was what had worked in Yeovil, it would work at Lord's, Taunton and Headingley too. That blinding confidence carried him through two fairly ordinary years, statistically speaking. What *did* make its mark was his competitive spirit, his willingness to bowl all day, his desire to win every individual battle, every game in which he took part. Brian Close was a wily enough captain to recognise that such a temperament was rare indeed. Cricket is a mind game as much as a physical one and many have failed simply because they cannot cope with the pressure out on the pitch – Mark Ramprakash, for example, was summarily dismissed from the England scene by Ray Illingworth since he believed that here was another fine player who couldn't handle the Test match spotlight. Close saw that Botham would never be lacking in confidence or faith in his ability and that the only danger was of overestimating his own talents. Writing in his 1978 autobiography, Close also pointed out that 'he is the ideal type for the present-day game, a natural all-rounder . . . experience and time will teach him to temper his aggression with a little patience: an exciting prospect for the future'.

In spite of Close's belief in him, had Somerset had more players on call, perhaps it might have taken Botham a little longer to win a regular place in the side. Part of Botham's problem as well as his attraction was that his game was built largely on belligerence in those early days. As a nineteen-year-old he was fit, but against older men he was not always strong enough to get away with some of his more extravagant play. By 1976 he had matured physically and was starting to look more like the man mountain that terrorised opponents for the next few years. His figures reflect this passage from strapping adolescent to full manhood. Bowling a yard or two quicker, he took sixty Championship wickets at twenty-seven. More significantly, with Viv Richards touring with the West Indians, Botham seized the opportunity his absence offered. Underlining a lesson that few learned in his career, Botham was at his best when accepting responsibility for the team. Taking the burden of replacing Viv's runs on himself, he began to bat at number four, passed 1000 first class runs for the season, and scored his maiden hundred, a blistering 167 not out at Trent Bridge where he hammered the Nottinghamshire attack into the ground, hitting six sixes and twenty fours.

Thanks to that knock, Somerset successfully chased what had seemed a stiff target of 301 to win with plenty of time to spare. Unlike the Benson & Hedges game with Hampshire two years before, this was no false dawn. Ian Botham had arrived. *Wisden* felt that over the season he 'played a large number of exciting attacking innings, and if many subsided in over-ambition, he frequently showed the ability to harness his enormous talent to building a large innings'. Their summary closed with one of the great understatements: 'at twenty, he will surely get many further chances to advance in the game'.

Although he managed a place in the England side for the one day internationals at the end of 1976, he was disappointed to miss out on the chance of touring India under Tony Greig in 1976/77. Perhaps that was a blessing in disguise, for instead he wintered in Australia under a Whitbread sponsorship scheme, though he admitted to sulking for days on end when the chance to visit India had been denied him. That Australian trip broadened his experience, though his actual playing returns were quite meagre; because of the way the scholarship was organised, he spent more time surfing than playing cricket on his visit. Off the field he was able to make a name for himself, in typical Botham fashion, via an unedifying brawl with Ian Chappell in a Sydney bar.

When he got back to Taunton for the 1977 season, he was hotly tipped as the coming man in English cricket, his new popularity following the Chappell incident doing him no harm with a press always on the look-out for someone to provide stories. Once Tony Greig's involvement with Packer was announced in the first weeks of the season, all eyes turned to Botham as his natural successor in the England team. Raising his game to meet these new circumstances, he proceeded to demonstrate that he had the temperament to withstand any sporting pressures. His early season performances were impressive: five wickets in a rain-ruined game against Glamorgan; a half century against Nottinghamshire; and five wickets and scores of fifty-nine and thirty-nine not out against the touring Australians. Although he wasted a week carrying the drinks during the one day internationals, when the call finally came from the England selectors for him to join the party at Trent Bridge for the Third Test, Botham was ready. Unrecognisable from the bucolic character who had first got his chance under Brian Close, his all round game had responded to the disciplines of county cricket while his aggressive character and utter faith in his abilities remained undimmed. They were the classic components of the Test match temperament.

For a lot of players, once they've broken into the England side county cricket can seem like a chore. Often there's a lot of discontent among county members that their England star seems unable to put the same effort into his bread and butter job – Bob Willis and David Gower often stood accused of that failing. Initially, at least, Botham had no trouble putting everything into his game at Somerset. Perhaps he was fortunate that Somerset were living through exciting times, always in the running for trophies. Even so, his regular absences from the side over the next few years meant that Somerset were never really in any position to challenge for the County Championship. In 1977, he managed to play in twelve of the twenty-two fixtures, in 1978 he played ten matches, eleven in 1979. Given that Somerset were never in the running for the three-day crown, it was hard for Botham, now used to the adrenalin that flowed during a Test match, to respond to the challenge of a cold day in Taunton in front of 150 people. The more Test cricket he played, the less enticing the Championship games became. Nevertheless, he continued to be an important member of the side, particularly in their quest for a one day title, their best chance of success. With the addition of the mighty Joel Garner, one of the finest of the limited overs bowlers, Somerset were a formidable team.

Ironically, Botham was not always the master of the one day situation. As an attacking cricketer it might seem he was ideally suited to its peculiar demands, but as the game evolved domestically it was often the more cautious, canny cricketers who came out on top. As a bowler, the young Botham was so determined to take wickets, so keen to experiment, that he could be costly; in limited overs cricket, eleven overs bowled for twenty without taking a wicket is eminently preferable to eleven overs bowled for sixty, even if the latter spell contains two or three scalps. That was anathema to his way of thinking. Though he did manage to bowl some miserly spells, he was fortunate that his profligacy at one end was balanced by the economy of Garner at the other. The fact that Garner would rarely concede more than a couple of runs per over gave Botham a little extra licence to bowl aggressively and look to pick up wickets, leeway he rarely got with England.

Somerset, a county without any trophy, came astonishingly close to breaking their duck throughout the 1970s. In 1978 they cruised to the Gillette Cup Final where they met unfancied Sussex, a side they'd trounced by 102 runs in the Benson & Hedges Cup earlier in the year. Having seen Brian Rose take fourteen off Imran's opening over, Somerset collapsed. Richards reached forty-four, a comparative failure by his standards, and it was left to Botham to nurse the side to a reasonable total of 207, another example of his willingness to take on responsibility. His eighty was the Somerset mainstay but no one was able to offer him enough assistance. When he bowled, his twelve overs cost sixty-five, and though he got rid of Imran and Barclay, Sussex romped home. The following day Somerset had the chance to atone. Back at Taunton, they needed only a tie (or a no result) from their game against Essex to take the John Player League. Set 190 to win, they batted with unaccustomed indecision. Botham top scored with forty-five as his team fell short by just two runs. Somerset had paid for their caution at the death, their determination to win – or rather, their fear of defeat – overcoming their natural inclination to excite and entertain. Botham was to remember the pain of those defeats for a long time. His resolve that he would not lose sheepishly again in future surely contributed to his downfall as England captain, notably in his dismissal at the hands of Viv Richards in Trinidad. The utter determination to take the fight to the opposition, recklessly on occasion, was a trait he rarely managed to subdue.

Richards and Botham reaped the benefits from playing in a side and in a location that offered them a kind of relaxation away from the pressures of playing for a side like Surrey, Yorkshire or Middlesex, where expectation was high. Though they still put on some good displays in the Championship, their efforts were concentrated on one day cricket, a format in which Somerset could be expected to compete with the best. If the crowd and committee indulged their occasional three-day failings because of this, they also revelled in the marketable nature of their two superstars. There were Botham T-shirts, Richards posters, Somerset hats and the like providing a lucrative sideline for a county that had never had any financial clout in the past. In addition, by 1980 membership subscriptions alone raised £100,000 surpassing the 1978 record of £45,000. Such records continued to fall for a number of years. The club found itself presented with a commercially sustainable future, no longer dictated to by the penny-pinching needs of the pre-Botham and Richards era.

Their two West Indian stars were wholly committed to the club, and it showed in 1979 when they returned to make amends for the failures of the previous year. This time around there was to be no mistake. Although their assault on the Benson & Hedges Cup ended in ignominy – they were disqualified when captain Brian Rose declared their innings closed after one over in a group match in order to protect their run rate, within the laws of the game but outside its spirit – they moved serenely on to the Gillette Cup Final. Botham took three for fifteen and Garner five for eleven to brush Kent aside in the quarter-finals, while four more Garner wickets and a powerful ninety from Peter Denning beat Middlesex in the semis. Against Northamptonshire in the final Somerset were in complete control from the outset, winning by forty-five runs. Richards scored a peerless hundred and Botham came in to bludgeon twenty-seven in a partnership of forty-one that lasted just seven overs, to take their score out of reach. The following day, Somerset travelled to Trent Bridge needing to beat Nottinghamshire to take the John Player League. With just 185 to defend, Botham nipped out Hassan early on and returned to finish the game by trapping Mike Bore lbw. After 104 years without a trophy, the club had won two in two days. Having finally broken their duck, Somerset looked poised to dominate the one day domestic agenda for the next five years and more. Their side was a nice balance of the explosive – Botham and Richards –

the thoughtful – Roebuck, Marks and Rose – and the experienced – Burgess and Taylor. As players like Botham continued to mature, the side could only get better.

That disqualification from the Benson & Hedges Cup was a defining moment, for it showed just how desperately Somerset wanted to win, how much it now mattered to them. As Peter Roebuck noted in *It Sort Of Clicks*, 'like Viv and Vic [Marks], perhaps even Joel, Ian is more emotionally committed to the county than he'd care to admit'. Yet being England's brightest star meant that Botham had to lead a schizophrenic existence: most of his thoughts inevitably focused on the national side. This was never more true than in 1980 when he was elevated to the England captaincy. Often his performances for the county seemed to be little more than reactions to his troubles elsewhere. Heaving that mighty sledgehammer bat, he set out his credentials for the captaincy by flaying Warwickshire for 126 in 109 minutes and then celebrated his new status by taking 228 off Gloucestershire in four minutes over three hours with ten sixes and twenty-seven fours. As the season progressed and the level of criticism grew, Somerset's opponents felt the weight of his frustration. His innings were often brief, but always furious – ninety-four in eighty minutes against Worcestershire, for example. Even so, he topped Somerset's Championship averages with 875 runs at 62.5, but there were no new trophies as the side lost Richards and Garner to the touring West Indians and Rose and Botham to England. Even when Botham did play for the county, he was so hampered by a serious back injury that he rarely bowled in anger.

The next year, 1981, was another season of reaction for the all-rounder. By now, the writing was on the wall as far as the England captaincy was concerned. The Chinese water torture dripped on until after the Second Test at Lord's in the first week of July. In the game before that inevitable demotion, having all but decided to relinquish the captaincy, Botham had plundered 123 in 137 minutes from Glamorgan. Once he had announced his intentions after his pair at the Lord's Test, he relaxed by picking up three for twenty-three in the Benson & Hedges semi-final against Kent and then took six for ninety and played what *Wisden* called 'a dazzling innings' of seventy-two against Sussex. The rest of the summer was his in England colours, but with Somerset it was anti-climactic once the Benson & Hedges Cup was won. Understandably drained by his efforts in the Tests, he fired only intermittently. When he did, it was glorious, but mentally he often seemed to be elsewhere.

The next couple of seasons followed the same pattern. In 1982, the Benson & Hedges Cup was retained with ease, Botham taking two for nineteen as Somerset restricted Nottinghamshire to 130, but consistency eluded them. He cracked 131 in sixty-five minutes to clinch an unlikely win against Warwickshire – his hundred came off fifty-six balls – but sixth was all they could manage in the Championship. The following summer, Botham captained the side intelligently in Rose's absence, playing a match-winning innings in the NatWest semi-final win over Middlesex, guiding his side home with disciplined strokeplay, then repeating his excellent leadership in victory in the final. Still he seemed reluctant to bowl – 119 overs in ten games wasn't hard labour. By now, Somerset were looking purely to the one day game for success, apparently dismissing any hopes of a serious tilt at the title. There was a suspicion that Somerset were beginning a transitional phase. Perhaps some members of the trophy-winning teams weren't as hungry as they had been and needed fresh challenges. Certainly County Championship encounters no longer lit as bright a fire of ambition as once they had; though racked by injury, tenth place was the poorest result for some time. Over a couple of seasons, some of the senior players had begun to look jaded, exhausted by the sheer volume of cricket they had played around the world. By 1985, Botham for one was tiring of the daily grind of the game and was in need of fresh momentum. As he demonstrated with his eighty sixes in that summer the county game did not stretch him; he no longer needed it as his power base and he often treated it with a withering contempt.

Much has been made in recent times of the frailty of the Championship game while there have been many recommendations that our top performers should be rested from them at the behest of the England management – Graeme Hick and Mike Atherton were involved in minor skirmishes on that point in 1996. It's significant that the only time a side can guarantee to field a full-strength outfit is in the Benson & Hedges and NatWest games. These are scheduled specifically so that they do not clash with Test matches, an indication of the priorities within the English game: money comes before quality.

It has to be accepted that the County Championship is economically unviable. It's unlikely that it ever will be again, for any game that unfolds during the day in the midst of the working week is doomed to failure, though more adventurous pricing could attract pensioners, children and those not currently working. Even so, any such increases in revenue would inevitably be minimal. It is the one day games, great occasions such as a NatWest semi-final, that get the punters through the gates. The Sunday League has become something of an institution, a regular family day out for many. One day cricket is a vital part of the programme and it can help the overall development of some players; good players can succeed in any form of cricket. Any batsman that can hit powerfully and selectively will do well. A bowler that can maintain a good length and line under pressure will prove invaluable. Even so, the conventional wisdom is that the one day game can stunt professional growth and lead to technical problems when under the microscope of the five-day game. Certainly the 1996 Indian tourists, starved of Test cricket, seemed at sea in the first of the three Test series. If that is so, then perhaps our top players need to play more Championship cricket and fewer one day games. One day matches would continue to thrive with or without their presence simply because they offer the package people require: like a good play, a limited overs game has a beginning, middle and an end, all in one day. In contrast, if you can only spare the time to see one day of a county game, you will hopefully see some good cricket but not in its full context. Without context, a dogged defensive innings or a spell of express pace bowling is interesting but largely meaningless. Nevertheless, this is the form of the game in which players must excel if they want to make a go of Test cricket. Botham had to make his runs and take his wickets all over the country before he made the Test side. Perhaps once a player reaches the England team, he should be excused the exhausting one day duties instead of Championship chores, for a tight one day game is infinitely more taxing.

Botham was close to burn-out on a number of occasions. If he'd been spared the hurly burly of a Sunday afternoon, perhaps he would have stayed fitter for longer. There are adverse financial implications for the individuals involved which would have to be addressed, but this is not an insurmountable problem given the substantial rewards available to an England regular. In addition, for those players who replace the England star there is the chance to play in matches which often mean more to the club, certainly in terms of pressure. This would help selectors to see whether an up and coming individual can cope with the tension that is the very stuff of Test matches. The down side to this is that young talents who are attempting to find their way in the game can find it hard dealing with the changing requirements of first class and one day cricket. Yet good players – the ones who are going to become top quality Test stars – can cope with either. Ian Botham did.

However, this does not address the central problem. Should these England players be excused county commitments? Net practice is still considered a vital part of honing skills. If that's true, the corollary to good practice is better match play. Therefore, should not Test players be required to play *more* County Championship cricket? The difficulty there lies in motivation. If a player has just scored a hundred to win a Test at the Oval, where's the attraction in returning to an unimportant Championship game against Glamorgan in Cardiff? If you happen to be an Ian Botham, that doesn't necessarily matter. As Phil Neale, his captain at Worcester, pointed out, 'Ian always wanted to win, whether it was a big game or not. He just wanted to win.' Some of his international colleagues have shown less commitment to their respective counties, and had Botham not been reinvigorated by his move to Worcester, perhaps he too would have lost interest in the domestic scene.

One argument against county cricket, and a strong one too, is that a player needs to be fresh in order to give full expression to his ability. There is a lot to be said for this, but it ignores the fact that quick bowlers like Allan Donald and Courtney Walsh seem to manage the trick. Similarly, if a batsman makes nought in his only innings of a Test and then goes two weeks before playing another innings, again in a Test match, he could justifiably complain of feeling rusty and out of touch. What the experience of players like Ian Botham teaches us is that good players will take what they want from the county game and that no one can prevent them from doing so. If a good cricketer has a point to prove – Botham post-captaincy, Gower in 1992 – he will do so conclusively. If he is secure in the England team, he will treat county opposition accordingly. If the mood takes him, he'll hammer the bowling to all four corners of the ground in a masterly exhibition of strokeplay. On another day, there'll be a few quick runs and a swift return to the dressing room. Some, those from the Boycott school of thought, will treat each county game as though their lives, or at least their averages, depend on it. Others, on the eve of a Test, for example, might look for a confidence-boosting net out in the middle, or might spend the afternoon studiously trying to avoid the captain's eye and an exhausting spell of bowling into the wind. This is not to say that these players are not committed to their county, but rather that no individual can be a world-beater every day. It is impossible for some to maintain the necessary level of intensity away from the Test match arena.

There's a belief that English cricket is now too soft – certainly Botham believes that to be the case. Since the days of Botham's prime, the international schedule has become more punishing. Tours last longer, there are more matches crammed in, and, with the growth in satellite television, players are under the microscope more than ever. That must put a lot of mental as well as physical pressure upon a Test team, particularly its captain, more even than when Botham was under attack through the 1980s. That's not going to change. If anything, the pressure to win will intensify. Mark Taylor has been a very successful leader and yet, having won the first two Tests of the 1996/97 series against the West Indies, once he ceased to score his customary heap of runs and Australia lost out in the one day games and the Third Test, his position was apparently under on-going threat. To grasp the rewards that are on offer, a professional cricketer will have to harden himself to these pressures, be they rightly or wrongly applied. Some suggest that to instil such steel we split the Championship into two divisions, playing just eight four-day games a year. Though that is a model similar to the Sheffield Shield in Australia, which has been producing top class Test cricketers in abundance recently, it's one that would have significant drawbacks here. The theory is that if there are only eight games to be played, that's a maximum of sixteen innings in which to bat or bowl, and each opportunity is therefore precious. In the current domestic format, it is argued, an up and coming player is less focused as he knows he'll get another chance tomorrow. But does that hold true? No player actually likes getting out or being hammered all round the ground to take one for eighty from twenty overs. Each player has a high level of pride – if they don't, they don't last long in the county game.

Even if we agree that a reduction to eight games might help players physically, will it improve their game? A prerequisite is decent surfaces on which to play and there are precious few of those around the country. So many games are finishing well inside three days because of pitches that favour the bowlers that the players aren't getting the opportunity to play properly. Another problem is the

English weather. In Australia, the chances are a four-day game won't be too badly affected by rain or poor light. In a wet summer with just eight first class games, a top order batsman might be lucky to play nine or ten innings, while a front-line bowler might manage just 200 overs. This is scarcely enough for them to hone their skills. Botham became a top flight bowler by sending down 2126 overs in his first four seasons; given his aversion to what he saw as meaningless net practice, it was vital that he got through so much work out in the middle. Bowlers learn how to bowl by bowling. And pity the poor spinners in damp weather on seaming pitches.

Combative cricket makes for combative cricketers; the improvement seen in both Nick Knight and Ashley Giles after moving to Warwickshire is proof of that. Although Ian Botham had enough competitive spirit for a whole team, it was sharpened by the dressing room environment in which he developed and by the level of cricket he played. If Brian Close was the foremost of the Somerset personalities, Botham also learned much from Vivian Richards. In his book *The Enemy Within*, Alastair McLellan makes the telling point that 'if Vic Marks and Peter Roebuck were the brains of Somerset's impressive late 1970s and early 1980s team, and Ian Botham was the sinew, then Viv Richards was the heart'. Perhaps this is where English cricket has lost its edge in recent years. Since the number of overseas players per county was reduced to just one (in most cases) from 1987, English cricket has hardly been awash with wonderful new talent. Yet overseas cricketers were, supposedly, inhibiting Englishmen. Just look at some of the Englishmen who came through between 1968, when the overseas contingent first made their mark, and 1987, when change was effected. Among the batsmen there are players such as Gooch, Randall, Gatting and Gower, among the bowlers the likes of Willis, Hendrick, Emburey, Edmonds and Dilley. Then, of course, there is Ian Botham. Any one of those players would walk into the current England side, selectoral eccentricity excepted.

These were the players who came through when the competition from the foreign players was at its stiffest. Rather than stifling the development of English talent, the presence of great players from around the world seems to have provided an incentive. Only the very best English talent broke through, and then went on to do well on the international stage. They had to be determined, bloody-minded, confident and, more than anything else, good. Very good. If the English game is weak now, it is because a couple of places that could be filled by talented Australians, Pakistanis or South Africans are being filled by mediocre Englishmen. In addition, how could any potential Test match cricketer be harmed by spending a year or two playing with and against Wasim Akram, Dean Jones, Allan Border, Viv Richards, Michael Holding, Richard Hadlee, Waqar Younis, Allan Donald or David Boon? Didn't Botham come to prominence by taking on and beating Andy Roberts? If a youngster is good enough, he'll get into the side. The best way to improve the quality of county cricket is to make it fiercely competitive by the re-introduction of another overseas player per team, always providing that said player is of top Test match standard – quality thresholds would need to be introduced. We need to produce more young Bothams, Gowers and Gattings, cricketers with the hunger, the desire and the determination to do well, men who are not awestruck when they come across Courtney Walsh in Kingston or Shane Warne in Sydney.

It was the presence, or rather the sacking, of the overseas players that brought Botham's time with Somerset to a close, though it was a parting of the ways that was always coming. Captain in 1984 and 1985, Botham was determined to maintain Somerset's glory years as a springboard for another assault on the England captaincy, yet so often was he away on England duty, he managed to play just twenty-two of Somerset's forty-eight Championship games. Without the necessary continuity, it was almost impossible for him to lead the side in any coherent fashion. In 1984, Martin Crowe, replacement for the touring Richards, was a huge success and Marks, Roebuck and Popplewell showed marked improvements, but Somerset came seventh in the Championship, thirteenth in the Sunday League, and were quarter-finalists in the Benson & Hedges and NatWest competitions. These were miserable performances for a county used to success. The following year, Rose, Roebuck, Wyatt, Felton and Garner all suffered serious injuries; twenty-four men represented the team in the Championship. The club slumped to bottom of the Championship, tenth in the John Player League, fell at the first hurdle in the Benson & Hedges, and made the quarter-finals of the NatWest. Unable to turn the tide, Botham seemed more interested in hitting a record number of sixes than in galvanising his team to better things. Perhaps the presence of Richards inhibited him as captain, possibly he felt that his six-hitting translated into leadership from the front – he did average one hundred in the Championship after all. More likely he was simply taking out his anger on the opposing bowlers in the absence of the communication skills necessary to motivate youngsters who were in awe of him.

Botham's spell as captain ended in failure and he relin-

quished the captaincy for 1986, Peter Roebuck taking over.
Tellingly, Botham then accepted a one-, rather than two-
year playing contract. In their joint book, *It Sort Of Clicks*,
Roebuck pointed out that

> he had a vision of a beautiful world at Somerset, where he
> and his mates, arriving in eccentric clothes to upset the
> fuddy-duddies, would laugh and drink the nights away, and
> then storm around defeating all the conventional types with
> their managers and their serious faces. He wanted his team
> to play by his own lights, with an anarchic, daredevil spirit.
> Above all, he wanted Somerset to do well ... but Ian could
> not communicate his vision, he wanted it simply to happen.
> Nor did he show his younger team-mates that he wanted
> his team to do well ... they saw his anarchism not as
> hilarious but as destructive.

He missed much of the 1986 season because of the ban
which followed his *Mail on Sunday* revelations that he
had smoked pot. Once he returned with form that was
'thunderous even by his standards', according to *Wisden*,
it was clear that things were not as they once were. In his
'County Cricket' column in *Wisden Cricket Monthly*, David
Foot, that seasoned observer of the West Country cricketing
scene who had collaborated with Viv Richards on his
autobiography, had been hinting that a time of reckoning
was coming for the club. In his summary of the season in
the October 1986 issue, he noted, 'ordinary players, lesser
mortals, have confided that there have been too many
disruptive elements. The cult of the personality has worked
rather cruelly against them.' A small club by county standards, Somerset was no longer big enough to handle men
who had become internationally famous. Had he played

for Surrey, Botham might have had some anonymity in the capital city, but in Taunton he was a whale in a garden pond.

The events that cloaked Somerset in darkness for some months differ according to which side is doing the telling. They were brought to a head by the thorny issue of the overseas player. A change in the rules for domestic cricket meant that each county would be able to field only one overseas player, an exception was made if a player was contracted prior to 1979. That meant that both Richards and Garner could still play in the same Somerset team for as long as they wished. So far, so good. However, Somerset's fortunes, so buoyant in the early 1980s, had taken a tumble over the previous couple of years. Garner had fallen foul of the stresses and strains to which all quick bowlers are prey and had missed a lot of games. Richards, though still the world's leading batsman – the fastest ever Test hundred in Antigua in April 1986 was proof of that – seemed stale with Somerset, and could not raise himself to the heights with such regularity, though perhaps he too was affected by events off the field. Certainly the Somerset chairman had asked him earlier in the season whether or not he might feel it was time to give county cricket a rest. In the background there was New Zealander Martin Crowe, who had made such an impact in his year with the county in 1984 scoring 1900 runs and taking forty-four wickets, positively Bothamesque. In addition, *Wisden* noted that 'his mature influence and general deportment rounded out a wonderful introduction to county cricket'.

David Foot revealed further disquiet in his November 1986 column in *Wisden Cricket Monthly*: 'Somerset ended the season one from the bottom. It was a wretched season. A summer which opened with a vibrant enthusiasm under a new captain became distorted by controversy. The media's attention for Botham must have been disruptive for many of the young pros. One told me, "All I want to do is play cricket in a normal atmosphere. I'm sick of this personality cult."' Inevitably Botham's return to the side after his drugs ban caught the headlines. TV, radio and newspapers swamped Somerset's games to report on the rehabilitation of England's all-rounder; the attention was more intense since England were in the process of losing to India and then New Zealand on home soil. For Botham, the publicity was a mixed blessing. He revelled in the limelight but resented the intrusion. And the Somerset dressing room was no longer the haven it had been. Five years earlier it was full of men with whom he had grown up. Now there was just Roebuck – with whom he was soon to fall out – Marks, Garner and Richards. Somerset were rebuilding and the new boys were understandably cowed by sharing a dressing room with these legends whose great abilities allowed them to cruise through the county games. Many suggest that a divide grew between Botham's gang and the newer players, players not used to his idiosyncrasies, his disdain for practice, and so on. For his part, Botham found it hard to understand anyone who was not as robust as himself, who could not burn the candle at both ends and still clatter a century before lunch the following day.

In *It Sort Of Clicks*, there's a revealing passage that shows the gulf between Botham and mere mortals. Roebuck writes: 'In 1985, he gambled … with Somerset plagued by injuries he summoned a lager-drinking friend of his to play against Glamorgan. Luck did not smile upon this gamble, for the friend (one of the best players in club cricket) tore a muscle before or during the game – it was not clear which, though he had been lying on the physiotherapist's table before taking to the field – and was a virtual passenger in a match which was lost on its last ball. [This was] a devastating blow to Ian's standing in the team.' As Roebuck added, had this typical gamble worked, Botham would have been hailed a genius, yet they seldom did. As a county captain he was willing to take a chance, but these so often relied on others to pull off the kind of audacious stunt of which only he was capable. Brian Close's axiom that he wouldn't ask any player to do something that he wouldn't do did not work for Botham – his whole career had been built around doing things that nobody else could. Ironically, by now he was better suited to the demands of captaining England where experienced players could, or were at least more likely to be able to, do the extraordinary. At Somerset, younger players in the team apparently felt his leadership was at best insensitive to their particular needs, at worst simply wilful; these new talents, lesser players perhaps than colleagues such as Marks or Roebuck, needed discipline, not maverick leadership. Given the pressure that Botham was under following the drug stories emanating from the 1983/84 New Zealand tour, it was understandable if subconsciously he did not always concentrate fully on the plight of his youthful charges. The fact that he lived in North Yorkshire during his tenure as captain could hardly have helped – as Bob Willis had pointed out in his 1978 *Diary Of A Cricket Season*, 'My only fear for him is that his interminable chasing up and down the country may eventually get him down. I could do it at twenty-two, but I couldn't now.' Willis was twenty-nine when he wrote those words. In 1984 when he ascended to the Somerset captaincy, Botham was twenty-eight. Even he must have been prey to fatigue.

When the Somerset crown passed to Roebuck and

Botham then had to sit on the sidelines because of suspension, his authority dwindled still further, yet as far as the press were concerned, Somerset was still Bothamshire. In the dressing room things were a little different. As Botham's position weakened, so too did that of Viv Richards. The two had long been inseparable, forming the most potent of cricketing double acts. The first rumours of Botham's possible defection from Somerset apparently arose in the middle of the summer as soon as he had returned from his ban – Roebuck's official history of Somerset, *From Sammy To Jimmy*, bears that out. That can only have undermined Richards further; if Botham left, he would lose his closest, most powerful ally as well as his loyal friend. While Joel Garner was fit and firing, Somerset would employ both him and Richards, but Garner was approaching the end of the road, leaving Viv exposed to the winds of change. As Botham pointed out in his autobiography, Garner only wanted to play for one more season. Effectively, that meant the committee had a straight choice between Crowe and Richards for the overseas berth, a position further complicated by Richards' inevitable absence in 1988 when he would be with the West Indian tourists.

The matter was brought to a head when Martin Crowe was approached by Essex to replace Allan Border as their overseas player for 1987. If Somerset did not act now, they would lose Crowe and still have to cast around to replace Richards in 1988. Although Botham confirms in his book that Richards had already been told he was to be offered a contract for 1987, he was called into the Somerset offices – while Botham was away and becoming the greatest wicket taker in Test history at the Oval – to be told his services were no longer required. It is this that is the most damaging reflection on the club, that they should renege on their promise. In cricketing terms, the decision between Richards and Crowe was a hairline one given Richards' forthcoming international commitments and the contrast between the club's rejuvenation in 1984 and the decline in 1985 and 1986. In Crowe's favour was his rapport with the youngsters at the club. Roebuck writes of him forming 'the youngsters into a club which met every Thursday at the Nag's Head in Taunton, wore blazers to matches and worked hard in the nets. Crowe is a magnificent coach because he has built his own game as an architect builds a house. To the apprentices he was an example and a help. Without his influence in 1985 they were much less successful.' It helped that Crowe was not a legend when he first arrived in Somerset, thus making it easier for him to fit in. Giant personalities such as Richards and Botham are often unaware of the fact that their very presence makes others feel uneasy. On the field, that gives them an edge; off it, it can make life awkward. Players like these need to make an effort to relax their team-mates, particularly if they are new to the dressing room. All too frequently older heads and the new men form separate cliques. With Somerset needing fresh direction to clamber up the Championship table, Crowe seemed the sort of player who might break down the barriers that existed. As a cricketer he was on the threshold of a glittering career. At the start of the 1987 season, he would be just twenty-four while Richards would be thirty-five. Clearly Richards had more left to offer, but how much more? After a gruelling tour with West Indies in 1988, would he fancy another season of county cricket in 1989 when he'd be thirty-seven? With Crowe, Somerset looked assured of having available for the next three years a top class batsman who could also bowl a few useful overs. With Richards, there would be some uncertainty. On those grounds, Martin Crowe looked the better option, hard though it would be to dispense with the services of a man who had done so much to turn Somerset into a successful county. As Richards pointed out, it had been his runs that had built the new pavilion at Taunton.

Botham's stance was a little melodramatic. Certainly loyalty is to be valued and one can hardly criticise a man for the admirable trait of standing by his friends through thick and thin, but Botham and Richards were both experienced enough to know that professional sport is a ruthless business where the cliché that you're only as good as your last game holds true. As international captains, each knew that he had to have the very best side for the job out on the field. Once a player has reached the end of his useful life or is out of form he has to be replaced, otherwise the side is lost by dint of loyalty to one particular individual. That is the nature of the game, survival of the fittest. Those rational considerations went out the window as Botham blustered. It was natural that he should be desperately upset that his close friend had been let down by the club after they had offered him assurances of his retention. That was appalling behaviour, undeserving of any sympathy. Since both Richards and Botham are highly principled figures, perennial believers in the value of a handshake, both would be angered and wounded by Somerset's duplicity. Nevertheless, Botham's decision to pin a 'Judas' note above Roebuck's peg in the dressing room was pathetically juvenile, although he still states that he was proud of his actions. He followed that up with the bitter statement that 'I hope Somerset don't win anything for another hundred years. For what they did to Viv that would be fair.'

Roebuck's part in the drama is, like that of most others,

clouded in mystery. Certainly as an incoming captain he would have wanted to stamp his authority on the side, not easy if the dressing room was packed with superstars. As Botham argues in his book, perhaps Roebuck was at the root of it all, keen to get Richards and Garner out of the way, happy to work with Crowe and determined to isolate himself from criticism within the side. Perhaps, too, Roebuck was a poor choice to replace Botham given that in his book *It Never Rains ...* he had portrayed himself as mildly depressive and extremely introspective, not ideal captaincy credentials. In *From Sammy to Jimmy*, he admits that he might have handled the situation better, but insists that the breach was between the committee and the players concerned. He had no real sympathy for either.

The rights and wrongs of the affair could fill a book of their own. It is Botham's part in it all which should concern us here. If we accept the declamations of all concerned at face value, Botham emerges as an extremely loyal man given to childish demonstrations of that devotion. We might also ask whether he should have been more loyal to the club as a whole, the people who paid his wages and who had given him his break, rather than to two of his colleagues. Given his relationship with the authorities in every form, that was always unlikely. Botham's persuasive riposte would be that Somerset's actions meant they had forfeited the right to his support. They had breached the code of ethics by which he lived, a code which meant he acted first in defence of his friends and thought of the consequences much later. As later chapters will show, this was not the first example of such conduct. Such rash disregard for self-interest allowed him to prosper at the crease; it did not always benefit him in life beyond the boundary.

Further questions remain unanswered. Did Botham really make threats in 1985 to leave after the 1986 season and, as some stories suggest, promise to take Richards with him? If that is the case, Somerset's actions were justifiable – they were acting to safeguard the future of the club. Was the Richards affair part of a wider agenda to rid the club of the triumvirate that was too big for some of their colleagues? The cricket committee must have known where Botham stood in relation to his friend, must have known he would quit if Richards was pushed out. Botham was so close to Richards that, even had he not been generally unsettled anyway, he would certainly have followed him out the door. In that case, why did Somerset want rid of him? The sad truth is that a personality like Botham is so big that in the media age he's simply too large for a county like Somerset to accommodate. In the West Country there is no top flight football team to deflect attention away from the cricket. The cricket is the focus of local sporting life. Botham, by definition, had to be at the very centre of it all. Initially, that was a bonus, helping the county shed its unfashionable image and capture some silverware. As time wore on and Botham became as renowned for his off the field activities, the media spotlight went from being tiresome to embarrassing, and finally to disruptive. This was not all the fault of Botham himself, but neither could he dismiss it. Whatever happened on the field, all the tabloid media saw was what Botham had done.

It was sad to hear that this great team man had been involved in the irrevocable breakdown of team spirit. At the special general meeting called by the club to discuss the Richards departure, Nigel Popplewell, speaking for the club, won the day. Popplewell had retired after 1985 and his speech was a devastating critique of the dressing room atmosphere. He told the gathered throng that through his final season the atmosphere in the side had been 'dreadful', while the commitment of Richards and Garner 'was different to everybody else's', adding that they expected maximum effort from everyone else but only contributed when it suited them. Given that Richards managed to average 76.5 in 1985 and scored 322 against Warwickshire that seems harsh, but it does reflect the breakdown between the two factions in the dressing room.

Botham's indignation was real, there's no question of that. At the same time, the turn of events acted in his favour. By now, it was obvious that for all concerned it would be better if a change were made; Botham had already intimated that much after the leadership passed to Roebuck. Without the captaincy to sustain him, he needed fresh momentum. Ian Botham was the archetypal Somerset cricketer. He played the game with a smile on his face, looked like he was enjoying his work. With those powerful shoulders and mighty forearms, he could swing the bat like the most agricultural of belters, though he was clearly no mere slogger. Botham was in the line of Woods, Wellard and Gimblett, huge hitters who entertained the Somerset public and became a vibrant part of the local folklore. In the long term that probably did Botham a disservice, for it made it easy to characterise him as just another yokel. For journalists not disposed to him, it was a short step from yokel to yob, and he was often portrayed as a thick hooligan with a bat. He might not have shown a lot of common sense on occasion, but Botham is anything but stupid. Nor is he without his cultural interests. The brash beerboy was a nice 1980s cartoon, but it hid much of what was real about Botham. By now, such idle journalism was becoming a pain in the neck and, on occasion, was threatening to turn his life upside down. Had he had a different public image, one more like that of David Gower for example, the scandal sheets would have been hard put to hang anything on him. As it was, Botham's public persona suggested he was capable of anything.

That he wanted to turn things around in both his personal and professional life was clear. He allowed his 1986 joint venture with Peter Roebuck, the book *It Sort Of Clicks*, to be described as 'part of Ian's campaign to rebuild his reputation'. Having tried to draw a line under the drug allegations with his *Mail on Sunday* confessions, perhaps it was time for a new cricketing start too. He'd decided that the England tour in 1986/87 would be his last, choosing thereafter to winter in Queensland instead. Maybe this was the right time to pull up the roots on the domestic front. His hand was forced by Richards' sacking, but for Botham, it was all for the best. Had Richards stayed at Somerset, however, Botham might have too. Although he needed a change of scene and relished the chance to sign a more lucrative contract than that on offer at Taunton, he was comfortable there, the more so when he could exchange stories with Richards. The two men were a team and a powerful one, even if their best days were behind them. The two greats of their generation, they were a mutual support group. As the eye dimmed, each could reassure the other that he was still a giant; while neither was capable of the regular destruction of old, in each other's company they were still the greatest and would prove it. In spite of the threats, it's hard to imagine that Botham would have gone if Richards had not been torn away from Somerset.

Botham's passionate defence of his colleague did his image no harm either. As the wheels of the Somerset establishment tried to grind these free spirits into the dust,

Botham was staunch in his support. That was his natural stance, he could do nothing but respond to Richards' plight, but it certainly played well to the cameras. In addition, it gave him the opportunity to leave Somerset as a hero rather than being branded as a traitor for walking out, a charge he would otherwise have found hard to refute having received a club record benefit of £90,822 from the 1984 season. Botham did not engineer these circumstances, nor did he deliberately look to profit from them, but for the first time in a while, events happened to fall in his favour.

Even so, had he imagined that every county in the country was desperate for his signature, he would have been wrong. A number of clubs were put off by his reputation, with Warwickshire pulling out of the hunt following a lot of unrest among the membership. His eventual employers, Worcestershire, were equally troubled by the prospect of having Botham on board, though the fears were soothed by the presence of Duncan Fearnley. Fearnley was Botham's bat manufacturer and had had a cordial relationship with him for a number of years. As chairman of the club, he was in a position to allay some of the more outlandish concerns that were expressed about Botham. In the final analysis, though, Phil Neale was the Worcestershire captain and, consequently, the man whose opinion was most important. It was he who would need to integrate Botham into the dressing room, he who would have to get the best from him. He never had any doubts that Botham could play a huge part in the development of Worcestershire's cricket: 'We'd been developing well as a side from the early 1980s when we'd become a young side very quickly, right through to 1985, 1986 when we were a decent side but kept losing semi-finals. We didn't quite have the final ingredient to make us winners. The ability was there, it was more a question of self belief and knowing how to win. When it became clear that Ian might be available, I was very definite that he was right for us.' Neale and his Worcestershire team had already had the proof that Botham was still a considerable county cricketer if the motivation was there:

We were the first team to play Somerset after his ban had finished, so we had two months to contemplate his come-back! He duly came back at Weston-Super-Mare, scored 104 not out in sixty-six balls, and he smacked us all around the ground and then that evening he received a cheque for about £900,000 for his John o' Groats to Land's End walk! It was around then that we first picked up the vibes that he might be available, that he wasn't happy at Somerset. I came back to Worcestershire and told everyone we should go for him. There was some anti feeling initially. Some supporters felt that Ian would be a disruptive element in a settled dressing room, and eighty or so people signed a petition against him; another twenty would have meant a special general meeting which costs the club a fortune. I put something in the local paper saying that as far as the players were concerned, we were looking forward to having him, we didn't think there'd be a problem and we wanted a top player in our midst. Duncan Fearnley and Mike Jones went off to Australia to complete the signing and came back with Graham Dilley as well which was a real coup. So for the 1987 season, we were raring to go with top quality men in the side.

The Worcestershire deal was made public in Australia on 10 January during the final Test of the Ashes tour. Though no details were revealed, it's fair to say that

Botham's financial package was far better at Worcestershire than it had ever been at Somerset. And so it should have been. He was the greatest crowd pleaser of the age and deserved to share in the profits that were made off his back. Worcestershire's membership went up and, in a move not unrelated to his arrival, they announced a £100,000 sponsorship agreement with the Carphone Group and another 'lucrative' deal with the Midlands Electricity Board. Without Botham, it's unlikely that that would have happened. Some have complained that men like Botham, Gower and Gooch were too well rewarded and that it dulled their hunger. This is surely a fallacious argument. As the rewards escalate, the motivation to stay at the very top becomes greater. Are Clint Eastwood and Martin Scorsese making poorer movies now that they're wealthy men? Great sportsmen want to stay at the top for egotistical as much as financial reasons. They need to prove that they're the best, not merely the wealthiest. If their youthful tunnel-visioned approach to the sport changes, it's more to do with a widening range of interests than the cash, something that is true of most of us as we get older. *Wisden* made it clear that it felt Botham was worth every penny Worcestershire had invested in him:

A new era dawned at New Road in 1987 as Worcestershire, inspired almost inevitably by Ian Botham, captured their first trophy for thirteen years by becoming the first winners of the Refuge Assurance League. Much of their improvement on the previous season in the Sunday competition, when they finished sixteenth, could be credited to the England all-rounder. His arrival from Somerset amid a blaze of publicity, had not met with the approval of all the members, nor with the unanimous backing of the committee. But come the final

Sunday of the season when for the first time since the days of Bradman the County Ground gates were locked behind a capacity crowd, there was no longer any doubting the wisdom of luring Botham to Worcester.

Although the side slipped to ninth in the Championship, Botham having an ordinary season with bat and ball, that summer was all about utilising the new optimism around the ground and winning that first trophy. A brilliant knock by Surrey's David Smith defeated them in the Benson & Hedges quarter-finals and good bowling from Lever and Topley saw Essex through in the NatWest second round on a seamer's paradise, so Worcestershire placed all their eggs in the Sunday basket. Needing to win the last game at home to Northamptonshire to take the trophy, they obliged, romping home by nine wickets as Botham scored sixty-one and took two wickets. It was a fairytale ending to the season, but no more than one had come to expect from Botham. Interestingly, Neale had encouraged Botham to try a new role on Sundays:

Ian opened the innings for us. He didn't play outrageously, Tim Curtis often kept pace with him, but the two of them and Graeme Hick all got 500 runs on a Sunday. In the last four games when we needed to go out and win the trophy, Ian and Tim kept putting on century partnerships to see us through. Ian's form once we got close was very consistent and that was what we needed as a side, someone to show us how to win trophies. We'd brought Ian here as a move to prove to the players that we meant business. With a player of his stature at the club, they started to believe in themselves and in the club. Winning the first trophy is always the hardest, you have to acquire that winning habit.

His role on Sundays was huge and it provided the breakthrough.

Botham was a revelation for many. It wasn't simply his form that was crucial, it was also his presence in the team. Young players at Worcestershire were delighted to see him join them. Where at Somerset the deeds of the recent past weighed heavy on the up and coming professionals, Worcester had little to live up to. They wanted to win and Botham showed them how to do that. Keen to build on the efforts of the previous year, it was especially sad when his 1988 season ended almost before it had begun. On 20 May, that eight-year-old back injury finally needed proper treatment. Botham entered hospital for an operation to fuse two vertebrae. Even so, such was the belief engendered by the previous year's exploits, Worcestershire managed to retain the Refuge Assurance title, finished beaten finalists in the NatWest, and then took the County Championship, beating Kent by one point. Neale recalls that 'Ian gave his County Championship medal away. I don't know whether it was because he felt he hadn't played enough games because of his injury or whether it was just a mark of respect for Jack Turner, the pavilion attendant, but he gave it to him, and Jack was absolutely thrilled, over the moon about that.' Having never won a Championship medal and with no guarantee of doing so in the future, that was a mighty gesture. It was indicative of Botham's commitment to his newly adopted home, where he spent some of his happiest and most productive years as a county cricketer.

Having been out of the game for twelve months, 1989 was a crucial year for him, as Neale recalls: 'He came back and he wanted to stamp his presence on another Championship-winning side. He also had to prove that he was fully fit. He had slightly limited mobility but he used his experience instead and bowled in a different fashion. He still hit the wicket hard because he had a good action and he was so strong, but he became a very good bowler on our wickets which were good for seamers at the time.' That season was his best with the ball for some years: he claimed fifty-one victims at twenty-two. His batting was poor, seemingly affected by an injury sustained in June when a delivery from Glamorgan's Steve Barwick left him with a depressed fracture of the right cheekbone. As *Wisden* noted, his 'modest 357 runs at an average of 18.78 ... must have counted against him when the selectors were choosing the England team for the West Indies'. Nevertheless, Botham fulfilled an ambition by playing an active part in wrapping up the County Championship with a game to spare. Interestingly, crucial parts had been played by men such as Stuart Lampitt and Martin Weston who had seemed most under threat from Botham's arrival at New Road. Instead, they had drawn inspiration from him and had become very good county cricketers. Botham took particular delight in this, using it as ample evidence that the effect of his presence in a dressing room was not as malign as his detractors would suggest.

Once Botham had missed the trip to West Indies in 1989/90, his career gradually began to wind down as it became clear he would never again dominate the international stage. Injury restricted him and a number of team-mates throughout a less successful campaign in 1990. It's a theme that recurs, but Botham has a very low boredom threshold. So great are his gifts that he treats them too lightly, takes them for granted, and if they are not stretched to the utmost he cannot function, cannot lay his hands on his genius; that is why he and he alone of the cricketers from his era could have rescued England at Headingley in 1981. It was a nice challenge, something to be faced. By 1990, life at Worcestershire had become cosy. He'd done what he went there to do. They were now a formidable county, yet without the adrenalin rush of regular Test cricket, that was not enough for Botham. An excellent season with both bat and ball in 1991 helped see Worcestershire home in the Benson & Hedges Cup and the Refuge Assurance Cup, but that was that. An irresistible challenge was waiting in the wings. Having been less than warm in their welcome in 1987, Worcestershire's members were disappointed that he was now ready to leave before the end of his contract. Phil Neale was realistic however:

> We had him for five years and I think he'd always given his best for Worcestershire. He'd changed a lot of people's opinions about him – yes, there's a lively side to him, but in his commitment to his cricket and to Worcestershire, he showed there was a lot more to him than what you read in the papers. I think by 1991 he felt the international scene had gone, and he always wanted fresh challenges. Durham seemed interesting to him. It was taking him closer to his home and it was very exciting to launch a new county, the first time it'd been done in seventy years or so. We couldn't stand in his way – he'd given us five good years and it was time for the next stage of his career. We had players like Stuart Lampitt who were ready to play regularly and so it was right for all concerned.

Leaving without acrimony was the right way for his Worcestershire odyssey to end. Sadly, as he conceded, going to Durham was one of the worst decisions he ever made. Perhaps in his 1981 splendour Botham might have arrived at Chester-le-Street, galvanised the ragbag of seasoned professionals and utter novices with his own brilliance, and propelled Durham to the summit single-handed. Well though Botham played at times – a blistering century off ninety-eight balls on his first class debut – he couldn't turn the tide. Even that hundred came in a losing cause and Durham, predictably, finished bottom of the table. Early season promise degenerated into injury and the latter stages of the season saw Botham absent – he didn't play in any of the final four games. Wearied and battle-scarred, it was sad to see him in a team going nowhere, unable to change its course as he had so easily in his youth. His disenchantment was increased by the fact that he thought he was going to Durham to captain the side, only to find that David Graveney had already been appointed. Botham also felt that Director of Cricket Geoff Cook did not want him on board, though whether this was an example of Botham's deeply rooted establishment-related paranoia is hard to tell.

In *It Sort Of Clicks*, Roebuck avers that Botham 'is a man with a life to lead, believing that it is better to burn out than to fade away. Nothing would be more horrible to him than playing as a grumpy old professional of thirty-eight.' At thirty-seven years and eight months, grumpy or not, Ian Botham finally drew stumps. It had been his intention to retire at the end of the 1993 season, but with the Australians touring he'd hoped for one final fling at the old enemy. Once it became clear that he had no hope of breaking into the England team, the fragility of the ambition that had kept him going was exposed. When Australia played Durham at the university in July, Botham's resolve finally collapsed and he announced his retirement. It was fitting that he bowed out against the Australians, sad that perhaps he had continued beyond his useful sporting life.

In his autobiography, Botham complained that his glorious finale was turned into a damp squib. On the field, there was no one to blame but himself. His self belief had been his trump card a decade earlier, now it made him look rather ridiculous. A public slanging match with England chairman of selectors Ted Dexter was unedifying, his final performance for Durham described in *Wisden* as 'flippant'. Better by far to forget those final days and recall the days when Botham was such a giant he was the unanimous choice of the people as England captain.

CHAPTER TWO

Storms

The Captaincy

Lives, careers, history can turn on just one incident. For Botham, that legendary 149 not out at Headingley in 1981 changed his life for ever. Among the many implications, it ensured that he would never again receive the call to captain his country. Having taken a mere thirty-five wickets to add to just 276 runs in a dozen games as captain, the Establishment came to the understandable, if possibly flawed, conclusion that it was no coincidence this first match without the burdens of leadership produced his first match-winning display since Bombay in 1980. Never again would Botham be considered for the captain's job for conventional wisdom had it that that would be tantamount to dropping him as a player. It's interesting, if fruitless, to speculate on the possible reaction had Botham holed out early on in that innings with one of those extravagant hoicks, or if Dilley, Old and Willis had perished quickly leaving him high and dry on forty-seven. The 1981 series might have gone begging, Botham might not have enjoyed his most famous hour, but he might have been deemed worthy of a second chance as England captain just as Gower was given further opportunities after his first stint in the job had ended in failure.

It is impossible to defend Botham's captaincy without belittling the events of Headingley, but facts have to be faced. However enormous the feat, it was achieved against very average opponents and with an enormous degree of luck – certainly it wasn't remotely in the same class as his peerless hundred at Old Trafford or his ton in Melbourne in 1979/80. Botham entered the 1981 series under a cloud of comparative failure. The previous eighteen months had been nightmarish: ten Tests without a win and none of the customary individual fireworks with bat or ball, though it is true to say that very few players produced consistently good performances against the West Indies, such was their domination of world cricket. In comparison with Clive Lloyd's men, Australia, robbed of the likes of Greg Chappell, were a poor side, further enfeebled by the internal disputes over Kim Hughes' role. Lillee and Alderman aside, the 1981 Australians were little better than the Indian and Pakistani sides Botham had trounced in previous years. It was only to be expected that a player of his stature would knock the stuffing out of them at some stage in the summer; the weaker the opposition, the more likely any player is to produce average-enhancing displays. If you are willing to accept that view, then the Australians had Headingley coming to them. If he hadn't destroyed them at Leeds, he'd have done it elsewhere sooner or later.

Once that argument is accepted, it must be conceded that, rather than the captaincy itself holding him back in the first two games of 1981, it had been selectoral uncertainty which had finally felled the giant. For the first time in years, by appointing him on a game by game basis those at the top were questioning his ability. Worse still, they were following a policy that had failed and has continued to fail time and again: Denness was given one Test in 1975 against Australia and lost it; Gower was given one game against India in 1986 and lost that; Emburey and Cowdrey suffered similar indignities against the West Indies in 1988. Selecting on a game by game basis is simply an unintelligent approach in an age when cricketers are under external scrutiny to a far greater extent than in the playing days of selectors like Bedser, May, Illingworth and Dexter. Under that spotlight, players need greater security to help their talents flourish. It was *that* intolerable pressure rather than the cares of leadership that took the edge off Botham's game, those external suspicions that required him to question his ability, technique and temperament and forced him into the agony of self doubt in the throes of which one's best form must always be elusive.

The legend of Mike Brearley is almost as potent as that which surrounds Ian Botham himself. He was the captain with 'the degree in people', as Rodney Hogg termed him, the man who could inspire England's cricketers to play above and beyond their own abilities, the shrewd tactician who could pressurise his opponents into playing false shots or bowling loosely. Even now, almost sixteen years after his last Test, England's captains are still judged against the yardstick he provided and he is being tempted back into the England set-up in some kind of counselling role. There's little doubt that Brearley was the finest English skipper of his generation. Keith Fletcher was his only real rival, and that was purely at county level. However, Brearley's primacy among all England's leaders must be questioned.

He came into the job at the right time. Having been thoroughly beaten by Lillee and Thomson in 1974/75 and then outclassed at home by the West Indies in 1976, there was an ongoing post-mortem into the state of English cricket. The national team was at its lowest ebb in years and not even an impressive win in India in 1976/77 altered that assessment, the parochial view which dismissed the Indians as a minor cricketing nation still holding sway. Nevertheless it is always hard to beat India in their own backyard and those hard-won victories, followed by a strong performance albeit in defeat at the Centenary Test in Melbourne, indicated that England were on the way back. Tony Greig had taken up the captaincy in 1975, after Mike Denness bowed to the inevitable following another massive defeat against Australia in the first of the summer's four Tests at Edgbaston. Greig has become a much maligned figure, understandably so since many felt he betrayed his position as England captain by signing for Kerry Packer and becoming one of the chief disciples of his World Series empire. That simplistic dismissal ignores the good work that he did as England skipper, rebuilding a team that had had its confidence shattered by express pace bowling. Greig instilled his own colossal self belief into the side, leading it from the front. Some of his oratory was self defeating – his avowed desire to make the West Indians grovel in 1976 was the prime example – but by the time he was stripped of the captaincy in 1977 for his role in the Packer schism, he had created a team that believed in its own abilities again, leaving Brearley to inherit a dressing room buoyed by the strongest team spirit. When set alongside the crumbling authority Greg Chappell held over the visiting Aussies riven by the Packer dispute, the relative harmony in the English camp was all the more valuable.

Once Brearley's men had steamrollered Australia into

submission and regained the Ashes, he was feted as a tactical and motivational genius, for English supporters prized that victory far more highly than the rather more worthy Indian success. The credit for the improvement in fortunes was laid squarely at Brearley's door and subsequent series victories over Pakistan, New Zealand, Australia and India merely enhanced that view. In truth, England were rarely stretched by the opposition over this period, thanks largely to Packer's circus which robbed Australia and Pakistan of their finest and most experienced performers while leaving England relatively unscathed: Amiss was replaced by the returning Boycott, Knott by Taylor, Woolmer by Gower, and Greig by Botham. It was not until peace broke out that Brearley's men were sorely tested. Easily beaten by the West Indies in the 1979 World Cup Final, India then pushed England hard in the subsequent home series before they flew out to contest a three-match series with a full strength Australia, a series in which England were comprehensively defeated by 138 runs, then by six and eight wickets. Not even a fine captain like Brearley could reverse the ultimate cricketing truism: when one side outclasses the other in every department, they will generally win. It was a lesson Ian Botham would have to learn the hard way.

A few commentators had begun to question Brearley's apparent invincibility even before the visit to Australia. In a prescient piece in *Wisden Cricket Monthly*, for example, Jim Laker had asked whether Brearley's decision to take the England side there was his first real error of judgement. Certainly he had required some persuasion before agreeing to go since he was now looking deeper into his post-cricketing career in psychoanalysis. Initially he had planned to winter in England so that he could study for this vocation but the Australian challenge was too great a temptation, the more so since there appeared to be no obvious replacement captain on the horizon. Inevitably, the technical short-comings among England's younger players were brutally exposed and thoroughly exploited by the battle-hardened Australians who looked on the matches against England as a little light relief after the mauling they had just received at the hands of the West Indies. In the face of such a yawning gulf in quality, Brearley was left to watch Canute-like as the irresistible Australian tide overwhelmed his men. Somehow, despite the reverse, Brearley's reputation remained intact. Lord's had refused to put the Ashes up for grabs since the three-game series had been slotted in at short notice as part of the peace settlement to appease Packer. The atmosphere was further soured by incidents such as Lillee's aluminium bat fiasco and the extremely hostile attitude of sections of the Australian crowd, whipped up into an anti-Pom frenzy by the aggressive new marketing of cricket instigated by Packer's Channel 9 TV station. Domestic reaction to England's defeat was generally sympathetic, and any gloomy reflections on Australia's superiority were quickly dispelled by England's emphatic victory over India in the Jubilee game in Bombay where Botham scored a century and took thirteen wickets in a virtuoso display. Normal service had been resumed.

Still regarded as one of England's greats, Brearley chose the side's return to confirm that he was to take his leave of the international stage, announcing that he was no longer available for touring duties. The selectors were then confronted with the choice of either persisting with him through the 1980 English summer or blooding a new captain. A tough decision was made harder by virtue of the fact that England were heading into the most taxing two years they'd ever faced: back to back series home and away with the West Indies, the undisputed world champions, then an Ashes summer, and finally a visit to India, resurgent since the arrival of their own great all-rounder Kapil Dev. Faced with such a daunting itinerary, it might have been sensible to invite an experienced hand such as Keith Fletcher or Roger Knight to take charge as an interim candidate, allowing the likes of Botham, Gooch, Gower and Gatting to mature and stake a claim for the role when India and Pakistan visited in 1982. If Fletcher had taken a beating as captain, there'd have been no longer-term psychological damage. Fletcher or Knight, at the end of their respective careers, were expendable. Botham was not.

The one real controversy of Brearley's reign had centred around his own form. Without a Test century to his name, Brearley was one of the many English players of recent years just short of international class. Had it not been for his excellent record as captain, it's unlikely he would have won more than a few caps. Even as he racked up the victories, there were still those who felt he was not worth his place in the team. With that uppermost in their minds, the selectors concluded that they had no desire to travel down that road again. Following the Australian model, they wanted to pick the optimum eleven and find a captain from among them. In essence, that meant the captain had to come from within the party that had gone to Australia and India. The decision then effectively made itself, particularly in the light of that Test match in Bombay. Ian Botham was the only option. The succession was decided, the heir anointed. Indeed, Boycott aside, he was probably the only player that could be relied upon to hold down his place throughout the summer.

In hindsight, the decision to hand the job to Botham in 1980 was fatally flawed from the outset. His selection was supposed to herald a bold new era, the great new superstar taking the fight to all and sundry, leading his men over the top in a glorious charge to the summit of world cricket. Those observers who detached themselves from the hype were a little more sceptical. Realistically, whoever captained England against the West Indies could only lead them to defeat. They might go down fighting, but they would go down all the same. The only question was the scale of that defeat. The West Indies were an awesome combination: a batting line-up of Greenidge, Haynes, Kallicharran, Clive Lloyd and the mighty Vivian Richards, then at his brilliant best, backed up by the four-man pace quartet of Roberts, Holding, Garner and Marshall (or Croft), a combination that was virtually unplayable. Even if the batsmen could preserve their wickets, the West Indies bowled their overs so slowly and delivered so many short-pitched balls, from which it was all but impossible to score, that no side could amass sufficient runs quickly enough to put them under any pressure.

One of the England selectors was Brian Close, Botham's mentor at Somerset. He made it perfectly clear that he didn't feel his erstwhile charge should be exposed to the ordeal of captaincy, particularly when he was the only England player who could be expected to withstand the Caribbean blast and give as good as he got. Ironically, that very pugnacity was the quality that made some feel Botham might be captaincy material at the tender age of twenty-four, and with no experience of running a side. The theory was that his up-and-at-'em approach and his vibrant, attacking personality might inspire England to beat Lloyd's men at their own game. Without such an attitude, many felt that England would simply lie down and die. That view failed to learn the lessons of Tony Greig's humiliation in 1976. Greig was every bit as combative as Botham. He was always looking to carry the fight to the West Indians, but he and his team were just not good enough. If anything, by the time they arrived in 1980 Lloyd's team was even stronger and an even greater threat than it had been. England, on the other hand, were anything but a robust unit for while Brearley had been successful in papering over the cracks, the side remained desperately short of real quality. Boycott, Underwood, Taylor, Knott and Willis were all nearing the end of distinguished careers, Randall's idiosyncratic batting was enough to remove the fingernails of the most equable of captains, the Test careers of Gatting and Gooch were in their infancy, and Gower was suffering an inevitable slump in form now that international bowlers had had a chance to probe for weaknesses in his technique. As far as the bowling went, Dilley was promising but raw, Edmonds, Miller and Emburey never threatened to dismantle the best batting sides, and Lever, Hendrick and Old were solid support players who were regularly beset by injury. The belief that people had had in Brearley left them with the idea that he was handing over a very good side which could hold its own in the best company. That erroneous impression merely added to the weight that already lay upon his young successor's shoulders.

Time and again throughout Brearley's reign, the difference between English victory and defeat had not been the captain but Ian Botham. Certainly Brearley handled his star player well, better than anyone else ever did, but it was Botham's ability that turned matches England's way. Brian Close was right to argue that Botham was too inexperienced to captain the side. He was also right when he insisted that England's most potent weapon should not be shackled by added responsibility at a time when the team would need him at his very best. Close had been recalled to the national colours to withstand the 1976 onslaught and had first hand knowledge of the threat that Holding *et al* would pose. Given his almost paternal pride in Botham's exploits, it's fair to assume that he was equally keen to shield him from the media backlash that would accompany the slightest fall-off in his performance. Even had Botham been allowed to do battle with the West Indians from the ranks, his figures would surely have taken a battering. Their batsmen were formidable, but facing their bowlers was akin to standing in the path of a juggernaut. Allied to that, Botham was not the greatest player of pace bowling. The slack over rate automatically meant that he couldn't keep the scoreboard rattling along, and his macho temperament meant that he could always be baited into taking on the leg trap, hooking with abandon however many men might be stationed in the deep. Botham's instinct was always to fight fire with fire, however foolhardy that might be. It was a characteristic that Joel Garner and Viv Richards knew only too well from their close association with him at Somerset. They knew it was the source of his strength but they felt it could also be a weakness, as was proved over the course of the summer.

A more serious problem was looming for Botham. Just at the point when he needed to be at his very best, he was laid low with the first serious injury of his career, an ailment so debilitating that at times it threatened his future in the game. Playing against Oxford University for Somerset on a bitterly cold April day he strained his back, X-rays eventually indicating a spinal deformity. With the rigorous schedule lying ahead of England's foremost cricketer, there was no way he could risk an operation which would put him out of action for a year and which might even do more harm than good. Any kind of back pain can have repercussions, seriously limiting mobility and requiring changes in lifestyle. When an athlete is struck down by the problem, its impact can be catastrophic. Botham made changes to his action which robbed him of much of his effectiveness, and he also ran up to the crease more gingerly than in the past, the consequent reduction in pace giving his opponents extra time to deal with any movement off the pitch. When he was routinely routing opponents on his way to the fastest 100 Test wickets in history, he'd often been bowling at a pace that was just fractionally short of genuinely quick while still retaining the ability to move the ball extravagantly. Now, he was more often than not confined to almost military medium, which was never seriously going to inconvenience the likes of Viv Richards. The intermittent nature of the injury made it all the harder to bear since for the duration of the summer Botham never knew just when it might flare up again, and so could never trust himself to bowl the long and incisive spells on which he'd built his reputation. He was unable to bowl more than a few overs throughout May, and when June and July were wet his workload was further reduced; inevitably, he put on weight and his back problem intensified.

Though the weather prevented him doing as much bowling as he would have liked, it would not have been impossible for him to take other forms of exercise to keep the weight off, thereby easing the pressure on his spine. Dennis Lillee survived a serious back injury that put his whole career in jeopardy thanks to a single-minded devotion to regaining fitness. If colleagues such as Bob Willis could fight off injuries by embracing a punishing schedule of road and gym work, Botham should really have been able to do likewise, the more so now that he'd been given the extra responsibility of leading the England team, but there are times when Botham can be his own worst enemy, driven along by his compulsion that he always knows best. As the summer wore on, his weight went up to around sixteen stone, fully a stone and a half more than his optimum cricketing weight. So serious were the implications that by the tail end of the season the England selectors were demanding that he got back into shape before they would even consider taking him on tour. Botham could and should have tried harder to stay in shape, whether he was fit to bowl or not. After all, as England captain he should not have found it difficult to find sufficient expert medical advice and have an appropriate fitness regime set up for him. That said, the whispering campaign against him, one that grew in intensity over the course of the summer, verged on the hysterical and did little for his state of mind. He had to withstand the most vituperative criticism of his weight and his family were subjected to some disgusting examples of press intrusion – members of the Fourth Estate, desperate to make stories out of Botham's tubbiness, stooped so low as to ask his four-year-old son Liam what his father had been eating! Faced by this awful behaviour from the media and with Botham's own stubborn refusal to discuss his problems, his family were placed under an intolerable strain. All that can be said, and it's pretty cold comfort, is that at least it made them, Kath in particular, strong enough to cope with the vicious blasts of scandal and innuendo that were to come their way in future.

His relationship with the press will be examined elsewhere, but it would be disingenuous to discuss his performance as captain without occasional reference to the treatment meted out to him in 1980, for it had a serious effect on him, his family and his form. Things had started happily enough. Bestowing the captaincy on Botham was viewed as a surprisingly enterprising move which boded well for the future, though there were early indications that not everyone was so confident when he was appointed only for the two one day internationals that preceded the Test series, scarcely time to prove anything to anyone. Once he had responded with a match-winning knock of forty-two in the second one day international at Lord's, smiting the winning runs off Joel Garner and avenging the defeat in the World Cup Final on the same ground a year earlier, it looked as though he was accepting another challenge with his customary relish. England approached the First Test at Trent Bridge in good heart, Botham having been re-appointed as leader.

Between the 1973/74 tour of the West Indies and the visit in 1989/90, England failed to win a solitary Test against the West Indies in twenty-nine attempts. Over that entire period, they never got as close as they did in that first Test match in Nottingham. Setting the West Indians 208 to win, England took wickets with sufficient regularity to suggest they might pull off a famous victory, Willis bowling with the fervour that would find its fulfilment in his glorious hour at Headingley a year later. Only opener Desmond Haynes stood firm among the West Indians, but at 180 for 7 he was joined by Andy Roberts with just Garner and Holding to come. They inched the score forward, but with twelve wanted, Roberts skied a delivery to cover. The swirling ball was tracked by David Gower, the finest outfielder in the England team. Suffering his own crisis in confidence following a battering in Australia, Gower got both hands to the ball but dropped the catch. A few moments later, the West Indies were home by two wickets, Haynes guiding them most of the way with a five-hour sixty-two. It was the first intimation that Botham's luck had deserted him. If Gower had held that catch, the likelihood is that England would have won the Test match, Botham would have maintained his status as the man with the Midas touch, and with the confidence booster that such an impressive early victory would have provided he might well have gone on to be a successful England captain for many years. Certainly he would have dispelled any doubts that captaincy would ruin him, the more so since he'd top scored with fifty-seven in the first innings in spite of having his batting helmet split by Garner, and had bowled intelligently throughout. As it was, England left Nottingham one down and with their backs turned to the wall. As the series unfolded, the West Indians hit their stride. The difference between the two sides became more apparent, but thanks to a combination of a powerful never-say-die attitude and some very wet weather, England managed to salvage each game, eventually losing the series by one match to nil, even holding the upper hand in the ruined Old Trafford Test.

Since Australia had been hammered at home the previous winter by the same combination, Botham could take much satisfaction from the fact that his England side had held on to the West Indians, comfortably avoiding the blackwashes which David Gower endured as captain. Admittedly Botham was fortunate when it came to the weather, for in a fine year at least one more game might have been lost. Even so, it is to Botham's credit that his men were not disgraced by clearly superior forces. Sadly, he was given little chance to experience any such glow of satisfaction at a job reasonably well done. After years of being feted by the media and public alike, he suddenly became public enemy number one. The reasons why the press turned on him so quickly were many and varied, some understandable, some ludicrous, some a result of Botham's own stubbornness and some the outcome of the vindictiveness which is apparently required to sell newspapers. In that regard, Botham contributed to his own downfall by writing a ghosted column for the *Sun*, a red rag to the rest of the Fleet Street bulls who were only too happy to discredit their rival's star reporter. Being a Test cricketer was still no passport to fortune in Botham's early career. In that light, one can hardly blame him for agreeing a lucrative contract with a newspaper, one which provided good money for little work. Once you enter the belly of the beast, however, it's hard to complain about tabloid excesses without looking like a hypocrite.

That said, no one should be forced to endure the ridicule that Botham had to put up with and, more particularly, no one's family should be caught in the crossfire. By the end of the year, England's inability to beat the West Indians had been portrayed as a national disaster rather than the honourable defeat that was more accurately the case. Many writers ascribed England's failings to the weight problems of the captain and his poor performances with bat and ball, John Arlott looking at both sides of the coin for *Wisden Cricket Monthly*: 'He has brought immense enthusiasm to the office of captain; he has motivated his players, won their confidence and introduced considerable enthusiasm and counter-attacking drive. It must, though, be asked if the responsibilities have affected his play.' Few journalists were as sympathetic, attacking his tactical shortcomings when compared with Grandmaster Brearley. The public took its lead from the media. By September, England's hero of the previous three years was subjected to jeers and cat-calls wherever he went. On the final Sunday of the 1980 season, John Player League champions Warwickshire played host to Botham's Somerset. Success-starved sup-porters packed Edgbaston to see Warwickshire skipper Bob Willis parade the trophy, but very quickly the afternoon degenerated into a Botham-baiting competition which was quite shameful in its intensity. Early the following summer, his wife Kath was driven from cricket grounds, close to tears at the malevolent abuse hurled at her husband. According to Botham's book *The Incredible Tests*, she lost a stone in weight, such were the anxieties of the time.

What was Botham to make of all this? A year earlier, he could do no wrong. He was the people's champion, every-one wanted to talk about him, praise him, congratulate him. By September 1980 the selectors were openly criticising him and threatening to leave him out of the team for the West Indies, the newspapers were writing off his career, and the public were enjoying the rare privilege of having ringside seats at a public execution. His crime was the simple one of losing form. Those that touch genuine greatness are expected to set up camp on the Olympian heights. Should they ever descend from those peaks, they are never forgiven, for in their fall from grace they remind us all of our own mortality. Gods should be above the fray, they should be invulnerable. In reality, those who can wield a bat or racquet with distinction are mere mortals, often encumbered by feet of clay. It is a rare cricketer indeed who has not tasted failure. Criticism on this scale was something new and it inevitably had an effect on his form and on his frame of mind. There's no question that the scale of the attacks was every bit as over the top as the praise that had been heaped upon him when he was at the peak of the game, but a Kiplingesque acceptance of and disregard for those two impostors were not part of Botham's character. The verbal assaults made their mark just as they would on any but the most thick-skinned individual. At this distance, the question is whether or not that degree of criticism was justified. Was Botham a good captain, was he promoted above his abilities, was he laid low by the cares of office?

The domestic series against the West Indies gave some grounds for optimism in spite of his relatively subdued performances. Prior to that series, he'd picked up 139 victims at just over eighteen each, a sharp contrast to the thirteen more he took in that series at a cost of thirty. Even so, his lack of prowess with the ball could largely be excused. There is nothing that restricts a quick bowler more than doubts over the durability of his back, so it's unsurprising that he bowled fewer overs at reduced pace and with less conviction than in the past. When you then remember that the West Indies' batting was stronger than that of any other country, it's clear that reports of his demise as an international bowler were premature. As a batsman he fared even less well. Starting brightly with a solid half century in the first Test at Trent Bridge, an innings which almost turned that game England's way, he lost his way subsequently, scoring just 112 more runs in his next eight innings. A series average of nineteen did not compare well with a career average of forty on his return from India. True, some colleagues such as Gower did not even survive the series, but others such as Gooch and Willey showed the necessary application and technique required to stand up to the most hostile of attacks. All too often Botham seemed to lack the patience to occupy the crease: his 169 runs came from just 270 balls, a healthy striking rate against that kind of attack. However, as Phil Edmonds wrote in *The Cricketer* during the 1985/86 tour to the West Indies, 'there can be no long-term capital in trying to hook the world's quickest bowlers consistently ... I am sure we will be far better off trying to occupy the crease and attack within a restricted framework'.

Unwilling to try to wear down the fast bowlers and accumulate runs, Botham regularly fell victim to his instinctive desire to take the fight back to Holding or Roberts, a brave but foolish approach that was destined to have sporadic success, especially on some of the unreliable pitches he was to encounter in the West Indies. In part, this was a failing in his technique, for though the quickest bowling had never held any physical fears for Botham, his game was not suited to combating it. His belligerent and whole-hearted strokeplay allowed him to destroy spinners or medium pacers and to hold his own even against those bowlers like the ageing Dennis Lillee or Geoff Lawson who were just that bit short of express pace. Botham's game was one built on domination of his opponents, not a plan suited to the West Indian attack where the ball was constantly speared in at the rib cage at 80 or 90 mph, and where there might be fewer than a dozen genuinely hittable deliveries in an hour, most of which could be delivered while Botham was at the non-striker's end. To graft for a two-hour session and return to the pavilion with just an extra sixteen or twenty runs to your name was not an approach which appealed to the young tiger, and consequently he was often frustrated into an error. He admitted as much in the book he wrote with Peter Roebuck, *It Sort Of Clicks*. Discussing his crucial innings at Sydney on the 1978/79 tour, when he scored six in an hour and a half to allow England's Derek Randall to build a match-winning total at the other end, he admitted, 'I'll never play another innings like that ... I didn't enjoy it ... I was told to stay in. It was vital. It was more a matter of time than runs. But I went too far.'

In Botham's defence, little has been made over the years of the systematic way in which the West Indians targeted the opposing captain. After his own humiliation in Australia in 1975/76, Clive Lloyd turned his men into a side that hunted together in packs, one which was quick to scent blood and devastatingly efficient going in for the kill. Lloyd was a shrewd tactician too, one who knew the value of undermining his opposite number: if the captain was worried about his own form, he was less likely to be able to give his full concentration to the well-being of the side as a whole. In turn, that could have a psychologically detrimental effect on the side as a whole – Mike Atherton's trials in Zimbabwe on the 1996/97 tour are testimony to that. Throughout their ascendancy under Lloyd, it's instructive to see how often West Indian armoury was deployed in this way. Back in 1976, though he still managed a couple of performances of note, Tony Greig was eventually brought to his knees by the uncompromising pace of Michael Holding, who defeated him and, subsequently, his team. One defiant performance at Headingley apart, Greig managed fifty-one runs in seven innings. He also picked up a mere five wickets at a cost of almost seventy each. In Australia in 1979/80, Greg Chappell withstood the initial barrage but was eventually overcome and, had it been a five- rather than three-Test series, he too might have been destroyed in the end, as he was in the three-Test rubber of 1981/82. His replacement, the much maligned Kim Hughes, was also given the full treatment over two series in 1983/84 and 1984/85 when he amassed just 294 runs in fourteen innings and was forced into tearful resignation by the pressures they exerted. It's a pattern that's been repeated time and again down the years, with captain after captain offered up as a sacrificial lamb every time the West Indies arrive.

Picking through the carnage the West Indies left strewn in their wake all over the world throughout the 1980s, it's clear they weren't always given the credit their awesome power deserved; writing a summary of England's 1980/81 tour in *Wisden*, Michael Melford claimed that 'this was not a great West Indies side'. Certainly their strength was often built on the sheer brutality of their bowling attack, and purists railed against that and their dismal over rates, yet that should not have disguised the fact that Clive Lloyd assembled a cricketing side that came closer to being genuinely invincible than any other – even Bradman's Australia lost sometimes. The West Indies became a fighting machine, one that was willing to win at all costs. The consequence of that was that opponents would lose in all circumstances until the Caribbean conveyor belt no longer produced sufficient players of the highest quality. Spectators from the boundary and in the press box seemed to believe that playing lightning quick, short-pitched bowling was, if not easy, then straightforward. Just apply the principles: get on the back foot, get into line, punish the short ball square of the wicket. That was the dictum, yet not even the finest players of the time such as Greg Chappell, Mohammad Azharuddin and Javed Miandad were able to prosper with regularity. The West Indian attack posed problems that were insurmountable, the equivalent of surviving fifteen rounds against Muhammad Ali only to find yourself immediately confronted by a fresh Joe Frazier. Viewed in that light, all their opponents could do was their best. It was never likely to be good enough, certainly not on a consistent basis.

Leading a team at home is a very different proposition from leading one overseas. At home, the job revolves solely around cricket and the eleven men selected to take the field. There are external pressures, largely media based, but essentially the job is straightforward. On tour, cricket can often be the least of the captain's worries. The England captain is seen as something akin to an ambassador for the nation. There are functions to attend, hands to shake, dignitaries to meet and greet. A captain must also be ready to deal with the local media as well as the travelling press corps, keep his eye on practice facilities, ensure that everyone is in good health, that they all know their jobs, and that everyone is pulling together. Away from home for months on end, team spirit is especially important, particularly among the two or three players who are quickly identified as the travelling reserves, those who aren't in line for the Test matches and who will consequently play little cricket. Their response to their personal disappointment is crucial, for unhappy, even jealous, tourists can quickly sour the atmosphere. It's a captain's job to keep these players content, remind them that there's always a chance they'll get back into the side, that they are an integral part of the party and share equally in its successes and failures. In short, the touring captain's job is a huge one. The only consolation for Botham was that the media scrutiny on tour was less intense than at home – at least, that was the case in 1981.

Momentum is all important in professional sport. A side that has won a game is filled with confidence, ready to win again. Particularly in a contest as short as a Test series, decided over three or five games, once one team has an ascendancy, things can easily run away from the other side. Gallant losers at the start of a series can easily become bedraggled and vanquished a couple of months later – David Gower's teams gave just that impression against the West Indies. In England, Botham's men had held on to the West Indies and had never capitulated as thoroughly as Australia had done the winter before. Yet even that was not enough for his critics. The pressures were built up off the field: he was surrounded by innuendo, battered with suggestions that he was tactically naive, that he wasn't up to the job. Even before England set off for the West Indies, they were written off as no-hopers.

Comments from beyond the dressing room can often undermine a team's spirit. In adversity, a side can either pull together or tear itself apart. The situation never quite reached that level of drama, but Botham's authority was called into question throughout the tour, with both Viv Richards and Clive Lloyd making the point that he did not always get the respect he deserved from senior professionals in the side. The finger was often pointed at Geoff Boycott in particular, the more so since the rebel tour to South Africa that took place in 1982 was first mooted in the West Indies. Boycott was a key figure in the organisation of that tour and any talk of deserting English cricket *à la* the Packer rebels would probably have emanated from his corner, doing little for morale. In fairness, Boycott still did his best on the field, averaging more than forty in the Test matches, but the 1977 Australians had shown just how dangerous it was for a touring party to divide into distinct camps; great player and fine leader though he was, Greg Chappell couldn't hold on to a team that was at war with itself. In his book *Opening Up*, Boycott reflected on Botham's captaincy: 'I would have preferred to see him groomed for a couple of years before being given the job. I would have liked him to have sown his wild oats while he could, but now he has it, I want him to succeed.' Never one to hide his lack of respect for Mike Brearley's ability as a Test batsman, Boycott added, 'Ian has the enormous advantage of being able to lead from the front; when the chips are down, players naturally look to a captain to pull them through by the strength of his performance. They like to feel they can lean on the skipper's ability and he won't let them down.' Even so, the relationship between Boycott and Botham was not the warmest, Boycott making the point that Botham rarely asked for his opinion on anything, on or off the field.

Early on in the West Indian tour, it looked as if Boycott's point about leading from the front was well made. In the first one day international which preceded the Test series, Botham had been impressive, top scoring in St Vincent with sixty from 125 all out as England lost by two runs. The fragility of England's batting was clearly a major worry, a situation worsened by the poor weather the side encountered in the first seven weeks of the tour, when they managed just seventeen days of cricket. The rain had an impact on the quality and frequency of practice, and on the mood of Botham's troops. Bored by the enforced inactivity, the tension in the camp began to grow almost from day one. In such circumstances, Botham was anything but the ideal leader. Trying to distance himself from the rest of the side in order to preserve his authority, he found it hard to lighten the atmosphere with the usual practical jokes that had been his stock in trade when he was one of the lads, while his efforts to cheer everyone up by getting his round in merely confused the issue. He was equally frustrated by those who found the tour hard going. He confessed in his autobiography that man management was not his strong suit. Some players in losing sides need a shoulder to cry on, need to be built up and told they're the best. Botham freely admitted that he could not understand why anyone should need motivating before going out to play for England. Playing for your country should be all that any sportsman desired. Botham failed to accept that each individual needed to be handled differently, something at which Brearley had been so adept. For the players, this shift in emphasis was something of a culture shock, and Chris Old suffered particularly from the change in leadership.

Botham had his differences of opinion with Graham Gooch too. Gooch was then in the early stages of the strict fitness regime which helped him stay at the top for so long. Botham's disregard for long training runs and net practice was already legendary. He felt that Gooch's dedication to physical preparation was taking the edge off his performances on the field, though according to Gooch, Botham tried to ban his jogging on the grounds that it left him too tired to socialise in the evenings. The irony was that a dozen years later, Botham would complain that Gooch was too inflexible as a captain and treated all his players in the same way, something of which he was equally guilty. Where Gooch was a disciplinarian, Botham was anything but, Gooch making the point that 'Ian's lifestyle did not sit easily with setting an example to his players ... when you are captain, you have to be able to detach yourself a bit, take a step back, not be aloof of course, but not be 110 per cent "one of the lads". Being the latter for a captain is almost impossible when, next morning, you might have to crack the whip.'

Had Botham been leading a winning side, questions

would not have been asked. As it was, things on tour lurched from bad to worse, most of the problems originating in areas beyond the captain's control. Early on, Bob Willis, his main strike bowler, and then Brian Rose, one of the batting successes of the previous summer, were forced out of the tour through injury. Though replacements were called for – Robin Jackman and Bill Athey – this still left Botham with a threadbare side. The loss of Willis was particularly serious for he was an experienced and conscientious vice captain who could have been an extremely valuable contributor to the tour off the field as well as on. Writing in *Wisden* in 1982, Mike Brearley reflected that 'in Australia, Bob Willis helped me, as vice captain, by being prepared to take a tough line with players on occasion, to share the responsibility for an unpopular decision or a critical attitude'. If someone as experienced as Brearley found Willis's presence invaluable, how useful could he have been to Botham, a man still learning the ropes?

Heading into the First Test in Port of Spain, England were already looking in poor shape. The problems were compounded by reckless selection: England took just four front-line batsmen – Boycott, Gooch, Gower and the ailing Rose – into the game. Having lost more than a day to the weather, a draw should not have been beyond their powers, allowing them to rethink their strategy for the remainder of the tour. Putting the opposition in to bat on an uncertain pitch, Botham had the dubious pleasure of watching Greenidge and Haynes amass 168 for the first wicket, but excellent bowling from Emburey saw England fight their way back into the game. Lloyd was still able to declare on an unassailable 426, but with almost half the allotted time gone England had given themselves hope. It was left to the batsmen to avoid the follow on and save the game. The defeat that followed was described by *Wisden Cricket Monthly*'s Paul Weaver as 'without honour, humiliation beyond redemption'. Henry Blofeld was equally scathing in the *Sunday Express*, asserting that Botham 'captains the side like a great big baby. His attitude is astonishingly naive and he is letting his country down.' Blofeld later complained that Botham had jostled him at Bermuda airport at the end of the tour, the captain understandably annoyed at this less than constructive critique. Even so, his willingness to meet antipathy with volatility called into question his judgement and placed a further question mark against his being the right man to lead England, given the prestige of that position.

The English resistance in Trinidad started promisingly, the first three wickets posting 110, with Gower undefeated and confident. From those heights England collapsed to 178 all out, Colin Croft picking up five wickets as the folly of packing the side with 'bits and pieces' players was exposed. Even so, with the intervention of the weather, they entered the final day with eight second innings wickets in hand, Rose and Gooch having gone early on. Even before England had started batting, Botham had pronounced the pitch a good one and had told a press conference that if England should lose the game, 'heads will roll'. With that exhortation ringing in their ears, his batsmen proceeded to fall apart again, Boycott and Gower once more trying to postpone the inevitable with scant support. Botham himself entered the fray with the score on 103 for 4. After scoring sixteen runs to follow his first innings duck, he holed out to mid-off, attempting to hit Viv Richards out of the ground. In a match where England had been put to the sword by the fastest bowling on earth, losing your wicket to a gentle off-spinner with no pretensions as a bowler was carelessness bordering on the suicidal. With that one stroke, Botham effectively ended his spell as captain. In his autobiography he tried to defend his actions, arguing that 'the ball was there to be hit'. In truth, the shot was indefensible. If it had gone for six, it wouldn't have mattered, wouldn't have loosened the West Indian grip on the game. At that stage, with England still more than a hundred short of the West Indian total, runs were irrelevant. Occupation of the crease was all that mattered. The captain above all others should have tried to resist such obvious temptation and knuckle down to the task in hand, however alien that was to his nature. As it was, England were just an hour short of saving the game when the final wicket fell, the rest of the side collapsing in the wake of their captain's wantonness.

The tour could easily have degenerated into utter disaster from there on in but, to give credit to Botham, he held things together in the face of awful, then tragic, circumstances, all of which was accompanied by a complete collapse in his own form. The first matter on the agenda was the replacement of Bob Willis who had to fly home for surgery on his knee. Robbed of his vice captain, Botham wanted Gooch to step into the vacancy but was ordered by Lord's to give the position to Geoff Miller. As a pragmatic move this was faintly ridiculous since, following his poor performance in Trinidad, Miller's chances of playing an active part in the remainder of the series were poor. Conversely, Graham Gooch was an integral part of the side. More importantly, Lord's had undermined Botham's position in his own eyes and in the eyes of the team, since he had already offered the position to Gooch and was forced to retract. This was a significant and very embarrassing episode, indicating that Botham was on borrowed time, a curt reminder for the uppity youngster of just who was in charge of English cricket. This was Botham's first really serious brush with the game's establishment, and it left a lingering taste of bitterness and mistrust that was to cloud the rest of his career, and often his judgement.

Willis had to be replaced as a bowler, too, so Surrey's Robin Jackman was summoned to the Caribbean, arriving in Guyana on 23 February. Jackman had close ties with South Africa, having wintered either there or in Zimbabwe for the previous decade. With the sporting boycott against South Africa at its height, the Guyanese government, among the fiercest critics of the apartheid regime, decided that Jackman was persona non grata, reasoning that his regular presence in South Africa constituted tacit support of Botha's policies. The England team was instructed to leave the island and Jackman was served with deportation papers on the twenty-sixth. For the next week, the future of the entire tour was in the balance with many of the tourists openly expressing their preference for a swift return home. In those circumstances, Botham and the tour management of A.C. Smith and Ken Barrington did an excellent job in keeping the players focused on the job in hand. Smith was the team's ambassador, dealing confidently and competently with government and cricketing officials, while Botham and Barrington tried to keep the players occupied. By 4 March, with the team in Barbados, the go-ahead finally arrived and the tour was saved. Having suffered vilification on a scale unseen since Jardine's Bodyline tour, spirits in the camp were unavoidably low. Botham was yet to grasp the basics of man management, which didn't help matters, but Jardine himself would have struggled to maintain discipline in the face of such insurmountable odds.

The Jackman affair was the most significant event of its

kind since Basil d'Oliveira had been refused entry to South
Africa in 1968. Since then, South Africa's isolation had
increased and official cricketing ties between it and the rest
of the world were non-existent. Even so, there had been
some unease within the cricketing family for some time,
centred around the many English professionals who worked
in South Africa during the British winter. Given that a
professional's salary pre-Kerry Packer might be little more
than £4000, it was hardly surprising that many felt the
need to augment their income in the off season. Few
employers were willing to grant an employee a five-month
sabbatical in the summer to play county cricket, so work
in this country was hard to find. A winter in South Africa
provided a financially vital lifeline to many cricketers.
Though some nations disliked what they saw as fraternising
with the enemy, they were generally willing to turn a blind
eye to it in the interests of world sport. The rationale was
that as long as these players were acting as individuals,
they had the right to ply their trade wherever they chose.
In the 1980s, many predominantly black nations came to
see that as a hypocritical stance, understandably so. The
more militant governments wanted to see such associations
actively discouraged and were willing to cause splits in the
sporting world to further their cause. Sporting boycotts,
for all sorts of political reasons, were becoming widespread – the Moscow Olympics, for example, was cheap-
ened by the absence of the Americans. Other regimes were
as keen to flex their diplomatic muscle in an attempt to
force every nation to sever its ties with nations such as
South Africa. In that sense, the Jackman affair was an
accident waiting to happen – it might have happened a
year earlier or a year later and it might have involved a
different cricketer, but it had to happen. The issue had

been festering beneath the surface for too long; it needed to come out into the open and a workable solution needed to be found.

Jackman was unfortunate that he was the victim of world politics; any sportsman who 'colluded' with the South Africans at that time was asking for trouble. From a cricketer's point of view the whole sorry mess reeked of double standards. Barclays Bank continued to have the strongest links with South Africa, businessmen of every kind could buy and sell their goods with impunity, but sportsmen weren't supposed to take the rand. That much was true, but then aping the indefensible is scarcely a valid response. Even so, South Africa was a highly emotive issue within the game, particularly among those cricketers who were just short of Test standard. A contract to coach in South Africa enabled them to keep their heads above water; if that were to be taken away from them, many might have to leave the game. Indeed, some genuinely felt that they were helping racial integration by insisting that they coach black and coloured children as well as whites. Yet how can there be normal sport in an abnormal society?

The attack on the commercial activities of the English players touched a nerve. In the wake of the Jackman affair there were genuine fears for the future of Test cricket: a real possibility had arisen that it would split on the lines of black and white nations. Ironically, the actions of the Guyanese government made South Africa all the more attractive to a number of English cricketers who were tired of the game's politics, concerned for their financial futures, and annoyed at the restrictions placed upon them. Such emotions provided a fertile breeding ground for the first rebel tour to South Africa which took place a year later. As noted, Geoffrey Boycott was actively involved in recruiting, and tentative discussions filled the idle moments of the Caribbean odyssey. Such intrigue did little for team spirit, the more so since anyone tempted to join the touring party was effectively putting money before their England career – understandable, perhaps, but hardly conducive to giving of one's best for the national side, nor to inspiring confidence in others.

Amid the Guyanese trials, perhaps the key figure in the camp had been Ken Barrington, the assistant manager. Loved and respected by all the players, he was instrumental in keeping things on an even keel and providing the support that the inexperienced skipper required. Botham apart, few realised the strain he was under, but the pervading tension was taking its toll. On the second night of the Barbados Test, 14 March, Botham received a call from A.C. Smith at around eleven o'clock to inform him that Barrington had suffered a fatal heart attack. Initially unwilling to carry on with the game, Botham and the players elected to continue since that would be in the very nature of Barrington's bulldog spirit. Unsurprisingly, they were unable to win or even save the game for him. Already in a poor position, England were brushed aside by the West Indians, Viv Richards atoning for a first innings duck with an imperious 182. England lost by 298 runs, but the game was remarkable for a couple of cameos. The best remembered is the over Michael Holding bowled to Geoff Boycott at the beginning of England's first innings. That most dependable of England's batsmen had his technique thoroughly unhinged by an over of bewildering speed on a lightning fast track. Holding tormented him with a series of perfect deliveries before Boycott swiftly departed for the sanctuary of the pavilion having failed to trouble the scorers. England were dismissed for just 122, Botham following a determined performance with the ball – he took four for seventy-seven in the West Indian total of 265 – with a defiant innings of twenty-six amid some of the most disciplined intimidation seen on a cricket field. David Frith described Botham's innings in *Wisden Cricket Monthly*: 'Botham managed a juicy cover-drive off Garner, the retort a bouncer which removed his helmet as he ducked. Garner sent down a high ration of lifters and Croft set a 7–2 off-side field for Botham who hooked him fine and then drove him royally. Soon he was hurling his bat away as a Holding bouncer almost sliced his chin open, and when he was caught behind he kicked the pitch in disgust and left with a face dark with anger.' Hard though Botham tried, his best form had deserted him at a time when even that might not have been sufficient to stem the tide. At Bridgetown, the wicket was prepared specifically for the West Indian quicks and they responded with glee. Just as he had beaten Boycott in the opening over, so Holding tortured Ian Botham. Watching from the dressing room, the colour drained from the faces of the English tail-enders. Seeing their captain, a man rightly described as the world's greatest all-rounder, floundering at the crease was a painful sight. As Botham threw his bat away, as if to say that it was impossible to bat against bowling of such hostility, they were beaten men before they got to the middle. Once Botham fell, the tail was annihilated, Bairstow, Emburey, Jackman and Dilley managing just seven runs between them.

The attacks on Botham were becoming increasingly personal, though he was fortunate to be as far from the British newspapers as he was, unable to read much of what was written. Even so, he knew the pressure was mounting. His greatest problem was the very quality that had been perceived as his greatest asset – the ability to lead from the front. With his prodigious form of the past now a fast fading memory, Botham could not inspire his troops in the way Boycott had forecast. Picking up a few tail-end wickets rather than scything through the top order, struggling for a dozen or so runs before getting out, even dropping catches in the field, this was not the great man England had come to rely on. Again, it must be emphasised that few players tasted success against the West Indies, but Botham's fall from grace was the more marked since it was so steep, so sudden, and so unexpected. Drained of his own powerful self belief, he was struggling for the first time in his career, and with the loss of Barrington he now had no one to whom he could turn for advice or reassurance.

His troubles badly affected his authority on the field. Where Brearley had been able to detach himself from his failings with the bat and retreat into the captaincy as an intellectual diversion, a refuge from personal adversity, Botham did not see cricket in the same way. Where to Brearley it was a strategic game, chess played with human pieces, for the young Botham it was more akin to a game of space invaders where the opposition was there to be blitzed. Where Brearley had planned with the scientific brain of a Montgomery, Botham simply ran straight into trouble like the reckless Custer. Temporarily robbed of his attacking powers, he found his side shorn of its most potent weapon in the field – himself. Without Botham pounding in and swinging the ball at will, England's shortcomings were exposed. Jackman was a willing workhorse but unlikely to prosper in the West Indies. Dilley had little experience and Emburey was tight, but rarely a threat on pitches that offered little turn. The fact was that if Botham played well, England might just be able to conjure a win from somewhere. If he didn't, they couldn't. Where Brearley could throw the ball to Botham to win him a game, Botham had no such luxury.

Since Botham's time as captain, England have regularly capitulated once behind – Gower's sides were particularly prone to that. Botham should receive praise for inspiring his side to fight back in the final two games, salvaging some pride with a couple of hard-fought draws. In Antigua he saved England from oblivion when, with the West Indies at 268 for 3 in response to England's 271, he suddenly plucked out three wickets in five balls, while it was left to Gooch and Gower to secure an honourable draw at Sabina Park in the final game. Thus ended Botham's first, and only, tour as England captain, having lost two Tests from four. The tour was treated as disastrous and Botham dismissed as a five-minute wonder. Certainly his batting was poor: he registered just seventy-three runs, coming seventh in the averages, and never threatened to come to terms with the West Indians. However, it was only by his own lofty standards that he failed with the ball. He was England's top wicket taker with fifteen topping the averages too; remember that Greig had a truly appalling series with both bat and ball in 1976 yet few questions were asked about his position in the side. With the bowling attack lacking penetration once Willis departed, Botham often had to operate as a stock, rather than strike, bowler, mounting a damage limitation exercise by blocking up one end; Botham later suggested that that compromised his effectiveness with the bat, the hot sun taking its toll, leaving him physically spent by the time he got to the crease. As Jack Bannister noted, it was a role for which he was unsuited, having 'neither the technique nor the temperament to bowl long spells of containment'. Had Willis been there to help from the other end, perhaps Botham might have been the attacking first change he had been in the past; coming on with the West Indies 18 for 2 would have offered him the luxury of bowling with his characteristic aggression and his figures might have been better yet. Viewed dispassionately, the tour might have been regarded as part of a longer rehabilitation from his back problems and an encouraging sign that he was returning to fitness and form. Instead, his failure in the series to take five wickets in an innings was seen as evidence that he wasn't the man he'd been built up to be.

That contention was inextricably linked with concern over his future role as England's captain. Subsequent events were to suggest that his days were already numbered and that the match by match trial he had to undergo was just so much window dressing. Assailed by adverse press comment, embarrassed by his innocent yet potentially damaging role in the Joe Neenan incident in Scunthorpe, and maddened by his responsibility with the bat in Trinidad, Lord's could withstand the pressure no longer. Botham was to be made the scapegoat for a damaging, though scarcely disastrous, defeat at the hands of a far better team. Had the selectors had any real desire to see Botham continue as England skipper, maturing and growing into the role, they would have appointed him for the whole summer of 1981. That seal of approval would have allowed him and the team to attack a comparatively weak Australian line-up knowing they had a full six Tests in which to secure victory. On the basis of a game by game appointment, Botham never had the time to reassert his authority over his shell-shocked players. Such a move was never even considered, for short termism rules all in England. The real problem was that had Botham been given that opportunity and had England lost the first couple of Tests, the criticism would have moved away from the skipper to be trained on the selectors and the TCCB instead. Fearful of losing their comfortable place in the scheme of things, administrators tend to look for a sacrificial lamb rather than try to identify the underlying reasons for failure. (The same propensity is obvious in football. When the crowd calls for the manager's head, he goes, because if he doesn't the next chant is 'Sack the board'.) Defeat against the West Indies was not Botham's fault. England were simply outclassed, and sacrificing him was a case of blaming the messenger for the message, complaining that a general armed with a peashooter had been defeated by one packing four nuclear warheads.

Almost inevitably, the changes in leadership did little long term good: Keith Fletcher, appointed eighteen months too late, led England to a one–nil defeat in India the following winter, in a sense a worse result than that experienced in the West Indies. If nothing else, it highlighted and drummed home the deficiencies in the English team and provided proof positive that Botham was not the root of all evil. Fletcher's appointment was yet another example of short termism. If Botham had to go, then a comparatively sedate tour away from the public eye in India would have been the ideal time to give the likes of Gower or Gatting a chance to prove themselves in the job, growing into it away from the pressure cooker atmosphere of a home series or a series against vastly superior opposition. With relatively low profile home series against India and Pakistan to come in 1982, the selection of Fletcher and then of Willis to replace him was a retrograde step.

Returning to the start of 1981, Botham now had ten Tests under his belt – England had achieved a solid draw in the Lord's Centenary Test against Australia the previous year. Surely this was the time to take advantage of that accumulated experience and look to the future. Give him another six Tests in charge against more manageable opposition and then look at his record as both captain and player to see if he was starting to come good, especially with less formidable opponents on the horizon for the forthcoming year. No one at Lord's or among the selection panel showed the necessary will in the face of media pressure to stand up and say, 'This is our man, we'll stand by him.' So it was that England lost a potentially impressive skipper. With hindsight, Botham would have been best advised to decline the invitation to lead the Ashes side from the outset, but the England captaincy is not a job anyone turns down or relinquishes lightly, especially when the incumbent concerned is a fervent patriot, the coming foe is the Australians, and the odds are so heavily weighted against victory; if nothing else, Botham proved that he was not one to hide when things got tough. David Frith argued in a *Wisden Cricket Monthly* editorial that 'England's enchantingly bull-headed leader, Ian Botham, cricket's hellraising Hemingway ... needs the support of the press and public though not necessarily in respect of the captaincy ... it came not only too early but in the wrong sequence. Had Mike Brearley been retained, even his previously successful record would have been shredded by Lloyd's lancers.'

It was an argument few others were willing to accept. Botham had been written off, the selectors had made their lack of faith in him very clear, and his confidence evaporated. By the end, at Lord's in the Second Test, he cut a lonely figure, shuffling around the field he had once commanded. Morose and remote, incapable of inspiring himself, he and his colleagues spilled chance after chance in the First Test in Nottingham, handing the game to Australia, while Botham seemed reluctant to bowl on a pitch seemingly made for him. Bagging a pair at Lord's when in search of quick runs following Boycott's stultifying sixty was the final straw. Custer's last stand ended in ignominious failure. The fallen idol returned to the Long Room to stunned silence, the members writhing in paralysed English embarrassment, unable even to offer him a consoling hand; ironically, a year earlier he'd written in *The Cricketer* that 'Lord's is my favourite [ground] ... something always seems to happen there ... my love affair with Lord's will always bring out the best in me.' It seems to bring out the worst in some of its members, and Botham, who can hold grudges as tightly as ever he held slip catches, has yet to forgive them for what he felt was a callous betrayal. Deciding to stand down as captain, he was then stripped of his final shred of dignity when chairman of selectors Alec Bedser told the press that if he hadn't jumped, he'd have been pushed anyway – a barbed and unnecessary remark which nevertheless seemed to provide a fitting conclusion to this most fraught and, at times, bitter affair.

What are we to make of Ian Botham, cricketing captain? The accusation that the captaincy ruined him as a cricketer is palpable nonsense, a myth which needs to be dispelled once and for all. It was the might of the West Indies that brought him to his knees. The comparative figures against the West Indies tell the story: as captain, he scored 242 runs at an average of fifteen, while in the ranks he managed 550 at twenty-six; with the ball, the skipper took twenty-eight wickets at thirty-one, the player thirty-three at nearly thirty-nine apiece. In essence, his performances against the West Indies were decidedly ordinary whether he was leading the side or not. In terms of his wider-raging responsibilities, however, there were many errors. As a member of the selection committee he has to take a share of the blame for poor selections and wrong-headed policy. There was a reliance on bits and pieces players at the expense of specialists, folly in the face of a West Indian onslaught. He often appeared unsure about how best to use himself as a bowler. He mistook leading from the front for taking too much upon himself, becoming stock and strike bowler and consequently doing neither well. He could be insensitive of the needs and intolerant of the idiosyncrasies of some of his players. He rarely had any net practice himself and saw little use for it; he wanted to motivate the side in the bar by relaxing, while some players needed to get in another hour at the crease, something he had trouble understanding. Off the field, he sometimes seemed unaware of the import- ance of his office and reacted to pressure with an unap- pealing belligerence, though he was not alone in that among England captains of the 1980s. Yet on the positive side, it's apparent that for the most part the players did do their utmost, working at least as hard for him as for any other contemporary leader. In England in 1980, following the disappointment of losing the first game of the series, his side fought back well with the aid of the weather to keep the margin of defeat down to one game. In the West Indies, his team withstood the Jackman affair and the death of Ken Barrington to regain lost pride during the last two Tests of the series. In that regard, he was able to keep a tighter rein on events than David Gower managed.

Leading Somerset in the 1983 NatWest semi-final against Middlesex at Lord's, Botham proved beyond all doubt to the arrayed MCC members that he had the tactical acumen to make a good captain. It was his cool, calculating brain that took the club into the final: he scored a brilliant ninety-six and showed a rare appreciation of the unfolding situation, stonewalling through the final over to see Somerset home on fewer wickets lost. He led them to the trophy in the final too, defending a low total of 193 with ease. Though his prolonged absences from Taunton on England duty hampered him when he captained Somerset in 1984 and 1985, he led the side astutely at times and even managed to average a hundred with the bat in Championship matches in 1985 – no sign of captaincy affecting his form there. Sadly it soon became obvious that no one in authority was watching and that the England captaincy would never come his way again; this was in part due to the blinkered attitude of the Establishment, but it was also a result of his penchant for attracting unsavoury headlines. His response was to devote himself instead to other goals, such as maximising his earning potential away from the game, at the expense of making any sustained bid to win the role once more.

Perhaps the fundamental mistake Botham made is one which still haunts English cricket. His leadership was dogged by internal dispute, a few of the old stagers becoming increasingly hostile to him as time went on. Botham was unable to assert sufficient authority to rid himself of these turbulent influences, so they eventually ground him down. It was a lesson Kim Hughes failed to take on board but one to which Allan Border paid assiduous attention. Like other successful captains such as Frank Worrell or Clive Lloyd, over a period of time Border constructed *his* team filled with *his* players. He removed any disruptive influence, dispensed with the need for the time-honoured senior pro, and created a team built solely in his image. Gritty, aggressive, strong, taking no prisoners, they were ready to follow the captain to the hilt wherever he took them. Border took risks, losing plenty of games early in his reign, but once he had established that side with players like David Boon, Geoff Marsh, Mark Taylor, Mark and Steve Waugh, Craig McDermott, Merv Hughes and Ian Healy, he reaped the benefits. Had Botham been able to do the same, the 1980s might have been a golden period. As it was, the opportunity slipped by, the recurrent story of English cricket.

CHAPTER THREE

Reconstruction of the Fables

The Summer of 1981

It was the strangest of times, the English summer of 1981. Two years into its term, the Thatcher government's hermetic monetarist squeeze was decimating Britain's manufacturing industry. Unemployment was shooting up at an exponential rate, racing beyond the previously intolerable level of two and a half million and showing no signs of slowing. There were riots all over inner-city Britain, the most serious in Liverpool's economically ravaged Toxteth district. Meanwhile, in London, the heir to the throne married the fairy-tale princess in St Paul's Cathedral attended by all the pomp and circumstance the nation could muster. And in the midst of all that was the cricket.

Sport has a central role to play in any developed nation, yet commentators are often very slow to recognise the fact. In South Africa, for example, the various sporting boycotts played a crucial role in forming both world and domestic opinion and were a vital tool in the final dismantling of the odious apartheid regime. The Warsaw Pact countries were only too well aware of the propaganda value of successful athletes, bringing prestige to political systems reviled by the rest of the world. Hitler had his showcase Olympic games in 1936, Mussolini left no stone unturned in his determined pursuit of football's World Cup in 1938, and the Argentinian junta recognised that a World Cup win in 1978 would divert the populace's attention from the country's appalling economic plight, if only for a short time (the Falklands invasion fulfilled that role four years later, just as it did here). A high profile and thoroughly successful national sporting side can paper over cracks in the social fabric more effectively than almost any political measure could ever hope to do. The people at large are far more interested in the fortunes of their football, cricket or basketball team than in any remote and convoluted political ideology.

The above rank among the more extreme examples, of course. Nonetheless, even in a country as inherently conservative as Britain, sport's role is an important, if altogether more subtle one. There is little which is as good for the collective morale as a national victory – reflect on the lessons of Euro '96 or Tim Henmania if you need to be convinced of that. Orwell's dictum that serious sport is 'war minus the shooting' still rings true, in this country as much as in any other. Indeed, there are few countries for whom sporting victory is as important as it is for England, few where the fate of the national teams is of such consequence, few where the press is so obnoxious in victory and so pitilessly vindictive in defeat. There are far fewer still which take winning and losing seriously without ever making any real effort to assist their athletes. Just as the communist bloc used sport as an image-building tool in the propaganda war they waged, England has looked on sporting success as confirmation that she is still a force in the world. East Germany and the Soviet Union had far greater success in that respect, for the communists at least had the good sense to channel resources properly to fund their performers, something which we, locked in our time-warped romance with the amateur ideal, remain extremely loath to do. With its role on the world stage ever declining, England is a nation with a perpetual identity crisis. Entering this century with an empire, we look set to leave it without influence, perhaps even without our economic sovereignty. The sporting stage acts as a palliative, providing us with the opportunity to prove our worth and, on rare occasions, to beat the world once again.

In the 1970s, our national sense of self worth was at its lowest ebb. Our manufacturing industry was thrown into turmoil by the global oil crisis and we were then humiliated by the bankers at the International Monetary Fund who ordered the decimation of the nation's infrastructure before they would provide financial assistance. The UK, the nation that had stood almost alone in the cause of freedom in the early years of the last war, was now forced to go cap in hand to anonymous financiers and was subsequently brought to its knees as a result of their strictures. By the end of the decade the country was in decay and, apparently, terminal decline. Ironically, of course, such conditions provide the perfect breeding ground for renewed nationalism: the Silver Jubilee in 1977 offered a brief respite from the grim realities, eliciting a huge popular response. On a more sinister level, the National Front reported significant growth at the time – economic deprivation breeds nothing as quickly as iso-lationism and xenophobia. Thankfully, the more intelligent majority sought their patriotic refuge on the sports field.

If ever a feelgood factor were needed, it was in 1981. The 1979 Conservative election promises of revitalising the nation were already ringing hollow in the ears of their victims, those thrown out of work and on to an ever-expanding dole queue. An unemployment figure of 2.5 million was regarded as a national disgrace and it prompted the People's March For Jobs, a huge outpouring of anger at the situation and a final 'legitimate' expression of the majority's frustration with Britain's apparently irreversible decline. Callaghan's Labour government had failed to manage the country in 1978/79 following its refusal to confront the IMF. Now Thatcher's golden vision of a future where wealth cascaded down from the top of society to the bottom was proving stubbornly elusive. In early July the disenfranchised took to the streets in the worst outbreaks of rioting seen in Britain in living memory, the rioters' fury fuelled further by the impending royal wedding, a display of wealth and privilege that could only breed resentment among those who were being so comprehensively turned aside. Yet even then, the wedding was marketed as a unifying force. Union Jacks were peaceably unfurled for just about the first time since the Silver Jubilee four years earlier.

Spurred on by Margaret Thatcher's instinctive national chauvinism, through the 1980s Britain in general and England in particular lived through its most fiercely patriotic, some might say jingoistic, decade since the end of the war. Newspaper editors jumped on to the bandwagon, pumping their readers with stories of 'Great Britain', of a country apparently still fighting World War Two, the rest of Europe and the iniquities of the Common Market, of a nation still among the most important and influential on the world stage. It was palpable nonsense, but so keen were people to escape from the realities that surrounded them, the nation bought into the dream in a big way. The

New Right were perfectly positioned to take full advantage of the situation, and the idea of Britain, and especially England, as a superpower and a nation of which we could still be proud was relentlessly promoted.

A figurehead was required to satisfy these circumstances, a hero who could rally the nation behind this new-found devotion to the flag. Charles and Diana were busily doing their bit, lending a warm, if brief, glow to the ideal of Queen and country, yet no one could ignore the obvious parallels with happenings in the real world. Labour MP Tony Benn, for instance, remembers that 'just before the wedding, there was a huge fireworks display in London, a reaffirmation of the position of the Establishment, the way it had become entrenched again with Margaret Thatcher in power. It was televised and I remember watching that and then turning over to another channel and there were pictures of riots in Liverpool. The contradiction was so powerful, so vivid. Here was a country that seemed as socially advanced as the French before the revolution!'

Sport remained the most effective force for social cohesion and Ian Botham was the ideal saviour, a working class hero who was getting on through his own efforts. The timing could scarcely have been more propitious for the arrival of a natural born hero. Demonstrably proud of playing for his country, Ian Botham was a latter-day St George come to slay the foreign dragons. When he had first begun to smite the Australians in 1977, the national football team was about to miss out on qualification for the 1978 World Cup, there were no signs of any new top class golfers ready to replace Tony Jacklin, and as the careers of Virginia Wade, Sue Barker and Mark Cox wound down we were soon to be without a tennis player who could survive the first two days of Wimbledon. In Botham's early years, the greater part of England's sporting hopes and fears rested squarely on the shoulders of the national cricket team.

Timing is a theme that crops up again and again in relation to Ian Botham. No sportsman better represented the spirit of the times, the decade's zeitgeist, than Botham. That was why he transcended his sport and became a national figure of real importance, a legend that would endure. Timing is all in the propagation of a legend. It was wholly appropriate that England should regain the Ashes in 1953, Coronation year, and that Denis Compton should be there at the death. England's World Cup win would have been less satisfactory had it come in any year other than 1966 and at any venue other than Wembley and under any other captain than Bobby Moore – London was the centre of the universe, the swinging sixties was our gift to the world, the suave Moore the embodiment of English cool. If we'd taken the Jules Rimet trophy in 1962 or 1970 instead, the story would have lost some of its magic. In the same way, it seemed right that England should revive the Dunkirk spirit and take victory from the jaws of defeat in the royal year of 1981 – the script could not have been more dramatic had it come from Hollywood.

As is described elsewhere, Botham had suffered his own crushing defeat earlier in the summer. Shorn of confidence and with support from Lord's that was faint-hearted at best, he was forced into retreat and resigned the captaincy with England one down after two Test matches, a comparatively weak Australian side looking increasingly comfortable and dominant. Having been appointed on a game by game basis, Botham rightly and bravely concluded that such indecision was anathema to a side in sore need of decisive and dynamic leadership. His resignation was the action of an honourable, if bewildered, man, one who could be forgiven for wondering where all his friends had gone.

With Botham removed from their deliberations, the selectors were free to recall Mike Brearley. They had long since come to regret replacing him in such haste a year earlier. Having lost the role as captain when he reaffirmed his refusal to tour again, bringing him back was scarcely the most logical of moves, yet it was probably the only avenue open to the panel. Certainly, there's nothing to suggest they looked too hard for alternatives. The competition was decidedly thin: Bob Willis seemed, yet again, to be coming to the end of his Test career; Boycott was never seriously considered; Gooch, Gower and Gatting were every bit as inexperienced as Botham had been when he took on the job a year before and Willey was viewed as a staunch sergeant-major type rather than a leader. Ignoring Brearley would almost inevitably mean the new captain would still have to come from outside the team, which in itself would be potentially disruptive and would, by definition, further weaken the playing strength. Perhaps if the next Test hadn't been at Headingley Keith Fletcher might have been given the job, one he was awarded for that winter's tour of India. Certainly Fletcher was a better bet with the bat than Brearley, an important consideration given England's fragile middle order. His captaincy record at county level was at least the equal of Brearley's, inspiring Essex to the trophies that had eluded them throughout a hundred years of history. Unfortunately, the Headingley crowd were renowned for giving him a hard time and since it was a game England just had to win, or at the very least not lose, it would hardly be fair to have Fletcher battling with both the Aussies who had tortured him in 1974/75 and a packed crowd of unimpressed Yorkshiremen. When to that equation was added the fact that he hadn't played for England in more than four years, the case against him became overwhelming.

So Brearley was charged with the rehabilitation of England's cricketing superstar. That was his task, for if Botham could be made to fire on all cylinders once more the Australians were clearly vulnerable. A revitalised Botham, picking up his customary five wickets in an innings with the odd fifty or hundred added for good measure, would surely be too much for a side who were not the strongest of visitors. Once it had been determined that Botham would be playing at Headingley – and whatever his disappointments, at this stage of his career there was no way he would voluntarily miss out on a Test cap – the nation was waiting for his rebirth, though perhaps more in hope than in expectation. Following his agonising fall from grace, many had been quick to suggest that he was not quite the colossus in which the country had been led to believe. His runs and wickets had come against weak opposition, the West Indians had exposed his flaws, he wasn't the new Messiah after all – so ran the general opinion. In part this was undeniably accurate. His awesome figures *had* been bolstered by powerful performances against tepid opponents, but then all the greats have helped themselves to cheap runs and wickets when the opportunity has presented itself. The West Indians had reduced him to the ranks of the mere mortals but, as the 1980s were to show, no one could consistently thrive against such a fierce attack. This new wisdom also conveniently disregarded such displays that few others could match: he'd savaged a strong Australian attack spearheaded by Dennis Lillee at Melbourne with a thrilling hundred in a losing cause; he'd dismantled the Indians in their own backyard in Bombay.

To be more realistic, Botham was going to Headingley on the back of two poor games against the Australians when he could be forgiven for having his eye on anything other than the ball. For the first time since his arrival on the scene he had something to prove, but his overall reputation still remained in good shape in the eyes of objective viewers. The question marks now were against his mental, rather than physical, strength.

The most telling observation about the 1981 series, the 'Incredible Tests' as Botham's book termed them, was that the two teams were very evenly matched and were enduring similar internal problems. In terms of captaincy, Australia's Kim Hughes was as bedevilled as Botham. Just as the latter had been thrust into the breach when Mike Brearley declined to tour, the former had been elevated to the captaincy once Greg Chappell refused to visit England for a fifth time. As Botham had clinched the job with a virtuoso performance in a celebration Test – the Golden Jubilee match in Bombay – Hughes had pushed his claims with a scintillating display in the Centenary game at Lord's the previous summer. It had been his graceful and spectacular strokeplay that had enlivened a disappointing game that was otherwise best forgotten. And where Botham was undermined by those in the dressing room and beyond who felt the crown should have passed to Boycott, Hughes was put on trial and ultimately undone by similar elements who believed that Rodney Marsh would have done a better job. To compound his difficulties, the absence of Chappell's technique and experience from the most brittle of batting orders was to prove crucial. In a sense, that was akin to the loss England endured in the Caribbean when Ken Barrington passed away, a loss that exposed all the side's mental and technical frailties.

Leading an average side to success on the field requires a talented captain. With due respect to Clive Lloyd's part in formulating tactics and creating a formidable team spirit in a previously volatile dressing room, most experienced Test players could have made a fist of leading the West Indies through the 1980s. With Holding, Croft, Roberts, Garner, Marshall, Richards, Haynes, Greenidge and Lloyd himself in the side, it was almost as difficult to lose a Test series as it was to win one. It's hard to judge Lloyd as a skipper because great captains are marked out not so much by the frequency and regularity of victories as by their ability to inspire a team match after match to play *above* its collective abilities. In recent years Dermot Reeve has shown himself to be such a leader at county level; Hansie Cronje promises to reveal similar qualities on a consistent basis on the international stage. Mike Brearley has been seen as one of England's foremost leaders simply because he turned a losing team into a winning one, while it has passed into folklore that Botham was an extremely lucky cricketer, picking up wickets with bad balls and mishooking sixes. Yet Brearley was as fortunate, getting the rub of the green when he needed it most. There was so little to choose between England and Australia in 1981 that any slight improvement in England's form or a little dip in that of the Aussies would be enough to turn the tables. Brearley was inheriting a team that was being attacked out of all proportion to its defects. Written off as losers, in the first game at Trent Bridge England had actually come within a couple of dropped catches of being one up rather than one down. If any of those had stuck, Botham might well have gone to Headingley as captain. England were not fighting superior forces but a side on a par with their own and with the added disadvantage of playing away from home.

Brearley wasn't taking charge of a team without hope; his job was to restore belief, not perform alchemy.

There were other aspects to this series in his favour too. Dennis Lillee, though still a potent threat, had been hit by viral pneumonia early on in the tour. Obliged to marshal his reserves of energy, he operated at a fraction of his customary pace, though he continued to bowl beautifully throughout the series. A fully fit Lillee might have proved an insurmountable obstacle. His pace bowling partners, Alderman excepted, also had their share of ill health: Rodney Hogg appeared in just two Tests, his performance at Trent Bridge as back-up to Lillee and Alderman proving vital, before his tour was ruined by injury, and Geoff Lawson missed the last three Tests. So low were their bowling reserves, Australia had to call up Mike Whitney from league cricket where he'd been playing with Fleetwood. Remember too that Botham had rarely had the luxury of a fighting fit Bob Willis with whom to attack the opposition. Brearley's miracle was carried out with Willis right in the vanguard. In retrospect, prospects could scarcely have looked more promising for an English fightback.

From the moment Mike Brearley lost the Headingley toss on Thursday morning through to the fall of Bob Taylor's wicket midway through the Monday afternoon, with England still ninety-two short of avoiding an innings defeat with just three wickets intact, the tide had flowed remorselessly in Australia's favour. The only crumb of comfort to be gained by English supporters was the fact that Botham had top scored with fifty in the first innings and, as he'd promised his captain, had taken six wickets for ninety-five runs in Australia's 401. At last, he was beginning to recapture some of the self belief that had deserted him in the previous couple of months. By the fourth day, though, not even Botham thought the game could be saved unless the weather intervened. When he was joined by Graham Dilley with the score on 135 for 7, the game was up. Australia were two ahead with three to play, the myth of Brearley's miraculous captaincy would finally be laid to rest, and Botham himself might have been facing a lay off from the Test team. Over the weekend, the cricket correspondents were outspoken in their condemnation of the team and stalwarts such as Willis, Boycott, Willey, Old and Taylor were apparently about to contest the final moments of their Test match careers while others such as Botham, Gatting and Gower might well have been heading back to their counties for an extended break. Had Botham still been leading the team, the burden of responsibility might have forced him to try to play out time, stonewalling *à la* Trevor Bailey in the forlorn hope that a cloudburst might offer a reprieve. The game would almost inevitably have been lost, but it would have been seen as 'doing the right thing', particularly in the aftermath of Trinidad. With the vultures of the press pack hovering, he would have been unwilling to provide another hostage to fortune by swinging irresponsibly even in a hopelessly lost cause. Finally allowed the freedom that had made him so dangerous in previous years, Botham was able to enjoy his cricket again, and he treated that Monday afternoon as an excuse to amuse himself. Even before Dilley came to the wicket, he had swung himself almost off his feet in abortive attempts to hit the Australian quicks out of the ground. Had any of those deliveries which shaved the stumps induced a snick to the slip cordon, Kim Hughes would have been the hero of the hour, a touring captain on the verge of recapturing the Ashes. As it was, Botham survived and prospered.

And how he prospered! Time and again he opened those massive shoulders to unleash another uncomplicated swing of the bat, striking the bowling to some of the most unlikely parts of the ground. So spectacular, so spontaneous and so unrepeatable were some of his shots, it was impossible to set a field for him, though Hughes clearly blundered in his refusal to use the spinner Ray Bright earlier. While historians thought back to the turn of the century and the destructiveness of Gilbert Jessop, Botham himself regarded the whole innings as something of a joke, a wild slog where everything came off. The spectators also realised that this was not the controlled play of a batsman utterly in charge of the bowling, but rather a cartoon, intended to lift the spirits, entertain briefly and perish gloriously. Yet as each boundary boosted the score, Botham seemed to grow in stature; it was as if at lunch Popeye had finally got his hands on the keys to the spinach cupboard and had tucked in to the heartiest of meals, gorging himself after a year-long famine. Biceps bulging, Botham chuckled away as he enjoyed some extravagant good fortune, playing and missing, mis-hitting wide of the fielders – more slices of good luck in that one afternoon than he had had in the previous dozen Tests put together. Imperceptibly at first, but then more and more obviously, he wrested the initiative from the beleaguered Hughes whose tactical uncertainty, along with the vulnerability of his position within the side, left him paralysed, incapable of acting. Persisting with the tiring Lillee and Alderman for far too long, he was seemingly oblivious to the fact that the faster they bowled, the harder the ball was hit. As the Aussies began to fall apart long before England had posted anything like a threatening score, so the smile grew wider on Botham's face.

Even then, with his hundred reached and with Chris Old

now at the other end with just Willis to come, Botham didn't envisage victory. It was Brearley who, signalling wildly from the balcony, urged him to stay at the crease after he'd posted three figures. The chancier moments were generally confined to the early part of his innings, and though he often dismisses the 149 he scored at Headingley as being as much luck as judgement, the longer he stayed in, the better he looked. Despite playing like a millionaire, he somehow had an air of Boycott-like invulnerability about his play, such that the Aussies might have bowled at him for another full day without getting him out. When the players trooped off at the close of that remarkable Monday, England were 124 runs in the lead with Bob Willis, the perennial number eleven, lunging forward bravely and keeping Botham company. Interviewed by Peter West for the BBC, Botham boldly suggested that another thirty or forty runs might make it an interesting finish, but sanity returned, albeit briefly, when Alderman had Willis caught with just five added on the final morning.

One hundred and thirty to get for a two–nil lead seemed like a formality, especially when Australia reached 56 for 1, accumulating the necessary runs steadily. Yet the game had already been won and lost. No other sport is played in the mind as much as cricket and each Englishman knew that just one breakthrough could open the door. Botham himself recalled that the previous evening the Australians had sat slumped in their dressing room, unable to believe this new course of events, staring emptily around them in stunned silence, beaten men. With a number of the team lacking confidence in him as a leader, Hughes could not raise their spirits, and the spectre of a humiliating defeat hung in the air. Studying a batting order that lacked the calming influence of men like Greg Chappell, Doug Walters and David Hookes, and instead featured the promising but rather inexperienced skills of Hughes, Wood, Dyson and Border and precious little else, it was clear that England were anything but out of it. Once Willis, labouring ineffectively, had changed ends to bowl with the wind behind him, he was transformed. A vicious lifter undid Trevor Chappell, a smart catch from Botham removed Hughes, and once Chris Old bowled Border with a delivery that went through the pitch, the game was over. Bob Willis, pounding in and blazing away at the shell-shocked Australian batsmen, conducted the last rites, seemingly unaware of the drama that was unfolding around him until, the last wicket taken, he finally whirled away in relief as much as delight.

In the 1982 edition of *Wisden*, Mike Brearley wrote:

Sometimes the need is to rediscover the expectation of winning. Last summer, England had gone twelve Tests without a win. They were dropping as many catches as they were holding; the bowlers were looking, at times, slightly half-hearted. Spirits sagged if a fielding session yielded no tangible successes. Not long after, virtually the same team was catching everything and fielding with a new vitality. This transformation, I hasten to add, was achieved almost entirely by inspiring individual performances.

As Brearley was generous enough to concede, it was Botham that proved the catalyst for this upturn in their fortunes, just as it was he who had been the fount of their collective self doubt in the first two matches of the summer. As good a captain as Brearley was, he was unable to turn the tide alone. Instead, Botham once again became England's talisman, a freak display of hitting blasting away the dark

clouds that had surrounded him and his team-mates. Had
those runs not come, the game would have been lost, and
much of Brearley's reputation with it. In turn, Willis,
pensioned off a day earlier, was possessed by the idea of a
famous victory, Graham Dilley, astonishingly sure of foot,
ran backwards and held a steepling catch on the boundary
to remove Australia's last real hope, Rodney Marsh, and
Mike Gatting, never the most lithe of men, sprinted yards
to take a vital, tumbling catch to dismiss Lillee. All of
these feats would have been almost inconceivable on the
Thursday when Dyson ground out a dour but important
hundred and England were continuing their aimless drift
towards the next defeat. Botham alone was the inspiration.
In the midst of riotous national celebration, he had eclipsed
the forthcoming wedding of the heir to the throne.

With that one innings, the series was turned. Though
England contrived to get themselves into trouble on numerous occasions, Australia were fresh out of self belief and
purpose and, Border apart, had no batsman consistently
capable of holding things together when under heavy fire.
Indeed, the impact of Headingley 1981 is something that
Australian cricket is trying to deal with even now, strong
as they are. On a number of recent occasions Mark Taylor
has refused to enforce the follow on, determined to shut
the game up instead by batting again, closing the opposition
out at the risk of turning victory into a draw. If Headingley
still has antipodean repercussions sixteen years on, just
imagine how hard it must have been to deal with as the
series unfolded.

The Fourth Test was held at Edgbaston, in the golden
afterglow of the royal wedding. The ground was festooned
with union flags, the crowd vocal in their support for the
home nation, just the kind of atmosphere designed to fuel

England and strike fear into the downbeat tourists. Hard though Kim Hughes had tried to play down Headingley as some kind of freak storm, he and his team must have feared that Botham might be back to his consistently destructive best. Australia struck the first blow, bowling well on a difficult track, and it was only some dogged defensive batting from Brearley that enabled England to post a moderate score of 189. Botham struggled with the ball in Australia's reply, the main thrust coming from Old and Emburey who bowled beautifully. Batting again in response to a deficit of sixty-nine England were just ninety-eight ahead with two wickets remaining before Old and Emburey again turned things around with a perky stand of fifty. Faced with 151 to get, the echoes of Headingley were sounding in the ears of even the most detached observer.

Sunday play in a Test match was a new feature of this 1981 summer, and here it came to England's aid. Under a baking sun Edgbaston was packed, that vast concrete bowl a seething cauldron as the fiercely partisan crowd backed their cricketers as if it were an international football match at Wembley stadium. The home crowd's favourite, Bob Willis, stormed in to bowl backed by raucous chants more reminiscent of the hill at Sydney – for Willis, Old and Taylor, survivors of the 1974/75 tour, it must have been rewarding to hear English crowds baying for blood as the Aussies had done in the days of Lillee and Thomson, even if the physical threat was not quite the same. There's little doubt that the participation of that packed house was vital in inspiring England and forcing the Australians back on the defensive and into a cocoon of introspective indecision. Had the fourth day – one which dawned with Australia needing 142 with only Wood out – been played out on a Monday before a couple of thousand spectators instead of this full house, no such emotion could have been generated and the result might have been in greater doubt. As it was, following the events of a fortnight earlier, Australian morale was fragile. The fervour of the English crowd was enough to make some of them look as if they wished they were back home in Melbourne, Adelaide or Perth.

Allan Border made it apparent that his was a very considerable talent, batting with resolution to post forty runs as Australia inched their way in single, agonised steps towards their goal. At 105 for 4 it was his dismissal that again signalled the end, just as it had in Leeds. It took another unplayable delivery to get him this time, the ball from Emburey fizzing from a good length, catching the glove and flying to Gatting who held the crucial catch. The door open, Brearley acted with the decision that had often eluded his predecessor, calling Botham into action from the City End. With Border gone, England were suddenly favourites despite the small target. With the psychological hold Botham had established over the tourists in Leeds, the sight of this gargantuan hero marking out his run-up must have seemed like the coming of Armageddon for poor Kim Hughes, now helpless in the pavilion. As part of his ongoing rehabilitation, Botham had returned to Lord's, the scene of his cricketing nadir, and picked up a winner's medal in the Benson & Hedges final a week before the Edgbaston game, but thus far he'd done comparatively little of note in this Test. Now, just as the script demanded, he swept through the Australian tail, capturing five wickets for just one run. Bursting through the crease with a vigour that hadn't been seen since the onset of his back trouble, Botham was the irresistible force once more, tempting Dennis Lillee into one of the most horrible strokes he could ever have played, and wrapping up the game by the reasonably comfortable margin of twenty-nine runs. This was Botham at his intimidating best, threatening opponents with his size, his aggression and the prodigiousness of his gifts. Daring them to compete with him, he brushed them away from his sight with the same contemptuous disinterest with which a man might flick an insect off his sleeve. Brearley remarked that 'Ian is bowling without complications now which is the main difference to the way he bowled last summer'. The real difference was one of pace, for Botham was bowling with a will and at the kind of velocity that had regularly embarrassed tail-enders in the past. Australia's stunned cricketers had no answer to the speed and movement he generated.

It was to nobody's surprise that Botham dominated the Fifth Test at Old Trafford, the game that clinched the series. This time England were in a healthier position, 205 ahead with five wickets in hand. Botham then proceeded to play one of the finest Test match innings of all time. His 118 came off 123 balls and was as forensic a display of calculated aggression as his Headingley knock had been an example of simple exuberance gone mad. In 1982's *Wisden*, John Thicknesse described the carnage: 'His innings included six 6s – a record for Anglo-Australian Tests – and thirteen 4s, all but one of which, an inside edge that narrowly missed the off stump on its way to fine leg, exploded off as near the middle of the bat as makes no odds. ... Alderman and Lillee took the second new ball and Botham erupted, smashing 66 off eight overs.' It was an innings that any of the great masters of the game – from Grace to Trumper, Hobbs to Hammond, Bradman to Compton – would have been proud to call their own. It had a tempo and a fury that only the likes of Jessop or, compliment of compliments for Botham, Viv Richards could have matched. Where other English batsmen had been tentative, Botham was decisive and confident, handing Dennis Lillee the greatest pasting of his long career, the great Australian magnanimous in defeat, admitting that 'you couldn't do anything to stop him'. Jim Laker, commentating, called it the most spectacular Test hundred he'd ever seen, *Wisden*'s editor John Woodcock echoing the assessment in print, saying 'no-one, I believe, can ever have played a finer Test innings *of its type* than Botham's'.

For once, Botham's mastery seemed to inspire the Australians too, for despite being set more than 500 to win they fought long and hard. In this summer of the inexplicable, they even seemed to be in with a chance of victory on occasion. Border and Yallop made differing but equally valuable centuries, and England seemed drained by the dramas of the series. Finally, Bob Willis had Mike Whitney caught to seal a 103-run victory and the retention of the Ashes, 'Botham's Ashes', as the series became known. When the Sixth Test at the Oval ended in comparative anti-climax – the resurgent England unable to motivate themselves fully in the wake of their strength-sapping and mentally draining efforts, the punch-drunk Australians putting up a creditable display before a defiant partnership between Brearley and Knott denied them victory – thoughts turned back to the incredible events of the series as a whole. Botham's thoughts turned to sleep: twenty-six of the next thirty-four hours were spent with his eyes tightly shut. In the wider, waking world, questions were asked as to how the Botham who bagged a pair at Lord's could demoralise the same foe with such ease just a few days later.

The answer was Botham's astonishing belief in himself and his own abilities. The captaincy had become a burden by nature of his temporary hold on the job. Always looking over his shoulder, trying to do the 'right' thing instead of what came naturally, he was shackled. Even then he never questioned his own ability; every set-back was the fault of some outside agency, be it a change in luck, press harassment, an injury – nothing was the fault of Ian Botham. Stated brutally, that implies he was a churlish, childish character; more accurately, it describes the armour-plated bubble of confidence in which the real greats live. One of cricket's glories is its allowance of a collective ethos, alongside the most highly self-absorbed of individual battles to be housed in the same team. To have consistent success of the order of a Richards, a Waugh, a Warne or a Botham, you have to be utterly self-reliant, willing to back yourself in every situation simply because you believe you are the best and that no one can beat you without the assistance of some outside agency such as extreme good fortune. Deep down such players may know that's not strictly true, but it is that very ego which denies the existence of a superior force which drives them on to their remarkable feats. If Viv Richards seemed arrogant and unconcerned as he strode to the crease, it was merely affirmation of the fact that he expected to give the fielders a hard time for a few hours. Some bowlers were beaten before they'd sent down a delivery – his complete demoralisation of Bob Willis in 1984 is a case in point. Botham possessed that same sense of certainty. Ultimately, as his physical powers began to wane, that bull-headedness became a failing. In 1981, it was a great strength.

In Patrick Eagar's 1985 photographic study of Botham, John Arlott wrote:

If he never scores another run, takes another wicket nor

makes another catch, he must stand at the peak of cricket history. In 1981 he did what no-one else has ever done or is ever likely to do. He took up a Test series his country was losing and, reshaping it in those mighty hands, decided it by his own efforts from at least one virtually impossible and another quite precarious position; performed outstandingly in a third, and took ten wickets in the drawn sixth of a six-match series.

To achieve that from the unpromising raw material of Lord's was every bit as incredible as Arlott suggested. The only parallel is Bradman's performance in 1936/37 when, leading Australia for the first time against England, his side fought back from two down to clinch the series 3–2. Bradman, without a hundred in the first four innings of the series, scored 690 runs in his final five efforts. Like Botham, Bradman had no understanding of failure, believed that he would come out on top if all other things were equal. Botham's series was a triumph of his own powerful imagination. Nobody at Headingley felt that the game could be turned around, less still by the ailing superstar. Nobody could see this giant recapturing his bowling form at the precise moment that the doors had to be kicked down at Edgbaston. Nobody but Botham could have envisaged the blitzkrieg that finished the Aussies at Old Trafford as England's second innings had slowed to a crawl. For Botham, it was just a question of making up for lost time, time when external worries – largely the press and the Establishment at Lord's – had reduced him to the level of mortals.

The closing weeks of that summer must have been a bittersweet period for Botham. He was thrilled by the reaction of the people at Headingley, Edgbaston and Old

Trafford, as well as the other grounds he visited with Somerset between Tests. The recapturing of their affection meant a lot to him, but surely he must have dwelt on the fickle nature of the general public. Those who lauded him now were the selfsame people who had reviled him, barracked him, inflicted such misery on his wife and family just months earlier. A more reflective individual might have taken the praise with a pinch of salt, preparing himself for the day when the wheel turned full circle again. With Botham that was never an option, for he simply believed that those days would not come again. It would have been difficult for anyone not to get swept along by the public mood, the more so if you were at the very centre of events. The sporting public took to Ian Botham in 1981 in a way that no one individual has emulated since. There was delight in his cricket, relief in his return to fitness and form, pleasure in his rebuttal of astronomical odds. Once more Botham was a lightning conductor, a barometer of the public mood. The previous year had been grey and depressing with unemployment a frightening prospect for one and all, inflation racing ahead, the government seemingly in tatters. Botham, accordingly, was in his grey period, defeated, depressed, lacking in his customary spirit. By 1981, the press had tired of such despair. We had a royal occasion in the offing, the word spread that it was good news year, and Botham responded, not simply by winning games, but by winning them in style, acting not just as a cricketer but as a force for the social good. Writing of Headingley, David Frith was moved to call it 'a symbol and reminder of the fighting spirit which not only won a famous Test match but which can win much larger social and economic battles'.

Once you've rescued an entire nation from the grip of

doom, gloom and despondency, what do you do for an encore? That was the question that now faced Ian Botham, one which he rarely looked able to answer. Once someone has achieved something incredible, the rest of his or her life is judged by that yardstick. Understandably, it was a challenge to which Botham could only occasionally rise, and never quite so spectacularly. The rest of his cricketing career was built largely upon myth, on fables. The events of 1981 were so remarkable because they were unrepeatable, unique. So many chance elements came together at the right time to create an environment in which a legend could thrive that it's highly unlikely the same thing could happen again. If Greg Chappell had toured, Australia would have batted better, would have been led better, would almost certainly have gone two up at Headingley. If Bob Willis had broken down again, the Australians would have sailed to their target. If Kim Hughes hadn't been under such internal pressure, his captaincy might have been more assured. If Botham had fancied a Test match off to clear his head after the events of Lord's, or if the selectors had deemed it wise for him to have a rest, he'd have missed Headingley altogether. If the country hadn't been living through such a patriotic year, the emotional crowd scenes which spurred England on might not have been possible, the results would not have had such resonance. If India had been touring, such fightbacks would have been shrugged off as impressive but irrelevant. If the weather had been as it was in 1980, none of the Tests would have finished. If Botham had had the same ill luck at Headingley as he'd had in Trinidad, the game would have been over in four days. If Australia had had a consistently fit pace attack, England would have had to fight harder for their runs. If Botham had made his

Headingley runs in the first innings, it would have been a spectacular knock in a drawn game, just like his innings on the same ground against India in 1979, enjoyable but insignificant. The list of imponderables goes on, but if any one of those listed above had been the case, everything could, surely would, have been different.

Yet Botham never seemed to doubt his ability to replicate such moments of genius. That, more than anything else, dogged the rest of his career. Every innings had to be as good as the one at Old Trafford, every spell as incisive as that at Edgbaston. Viv Richards, one of his closest friends, summed him up well in Trevor McDonald's authorised biography:

> The main point about his play is that he plays cricket the way people like to see the game played. Ian Botham is with the public's thinking about cricket and you better believe it. They need the spirit and the enthusiasm he brings to the game. On his day, playing well, he is magnificent. There is never a dull moment when he's batting ... Ian has the ability to be a class batsman, but he believes that there is probably something equally important or perhaps even more important. He is an entertainer.

McDonald himself has long held that view. In an interview in the *Daily Telegraph* in 1992, he noted: 'I support the West Indies but I love to see Ian Botham do well ... to my mind, Botham is flashily brilliant and the English don't like him because they prefer the honest tryer.' There is an element of truth in that assessment, for Botham's style of play is naturally Caribbean. By the same token, you don't achieve greatness just by being flashily brilliant. Sobers – 'head and shoulders above all the all-rounders' according to Tom Graveney – was consistently brilliant, in a variety of styles. His view on Botham, as expressed in *The Changing Face Of Cricket*, is instructive: 'A very good player, yes, who could have become a great one. But he didn't ... if Ian had applied his talents, he could perhaps have ranked with the all-time greats.' Had Botham applied himself more, his figures might have avoided the hammering they took in the latter part of his career, but then he would not have been quite the crowd pleaser he was, nor would he have achieved cult status.

Having done what no others have ever done in 1981, there was an inevitable sense of anti-climax about the remainder of his career. Although he relished pulling on his England sweater, even Botham found it hard to inspire himself for the fray on a regular basis. It was only the sight of a baggy green cap from 22 yards that could get the blood flowing as it once had at Old Trafford and much of his most memorable cricket came against Australia. Had Botham still had Mike Brearley, Brian Close or Ken Barrington around him on a day to day basis, his career might have been very different. As it was, there was no one who could stand up to him, none who could persuade him that his way wasn't always the best, none who could get the ball out of his hand when he was taking punishment, none who could make him take his batting more seriously.

From 1981 onwards, Botham behaved like a man who had sleepwalked through the bloodiest of battles, emerging on the other side completely unscathed, and who was thereafter possessed by a sense of his own immortality. His tale became one of a man who had seen it, done it, and would not be deflected from his chosen course.

CHAPTER FOUR

What Do I Do Now?

Mentors & Miscreants

For the sake of Botham's equanimity, it might have been better had the Australians sailed comfortably to their small target at Headingley in 1981 and gone two up in the series. Botham's 149 would then have been remembered for what it really was, a great, mischievous talent sticking two fingers up at the thought of defeat in a glorious, ultimately futile, blaze of rebellion. That it became such an epochal moment was unfair to the man, for he was expected to repeat the feat time and again, something beyond any cricketer who ever picked up a bat.

Despite his obvious self-absorption, Botham was a genuinely committed team man, a player who always wanted victory for his side even if the plaudits went elsewhere. He knew well enough that his efforts in the summer of 1981 had been underwritten by the team, notably by Brearley's captaincy, by Willis and by Emburey, surely the real man of the match at Edgbaston. Even so, according to the orgy of publicity that followed it was Botham who had won each game single handed, he who could have played the

Aussies on his own, he who needed no assistance from anyone. However much he knew in his heart of hearts that that was just so much hot air, rubbish used to fill newspapers and TV retrospectives, the more times the myth was repeated, the harder it became to discount. Such adulation almost certainly impaired Botham's future. For one who always thought he knew best, this was proof positive that he had been right all along. Here was a real superhero, Popeye, Batman and Superman rolled into one; had the Gang of Four installed him as the new leader of the SDP, the Alliance really could have prepared for government. When someone possesses such overwhelming self belief, the greater is the need for sensible advice. With no one on whom he felt he could lean once Brearley left the England scene at the end of 1981, there was little to temper the wilder flights of fancy to which he was prone. His wife Kath might have been able to do so but such was Botham's outlook of macho bravado that he rarely took her into his confidence.

In his formative years, Botham had given due warning that he was a child apart, one who knew his own mind and refused to apply himself to anything that held no interest for him. He wore down his local careers master with his utter determination to play sport for a living, while simultaneously deciding that he had no need to gather a crop of 'O' levels, since that didn't get you into a cricket team. Had he embraced a slightly more academic range of interests, perhaps he might have had less trouble dealing with the man management side of captaincy. Nevertheless, here was a bullish, headstrong individual, the sort of child who had to win, had to get his own way and never for a moment felt there might be a different path forward. Twenty-five years later as his first class career was winding down, there was little to suggest that he'd ever really changed. He was still just a big daft lad who ignored advice and was generally proved right. Talking to Pat Murphy, he confirmed that 'I just knew instinctively what to do. In my life, I think I've only had about six hours' coaching and the only ones I've listened to have been Tom Cartwright, Kenny Barrington and Viv Richards.'

A physically strong child, one who is bigger and tougher than the rest, can get away with a lack of subtlety, even a lack of quality, on the playing field. A superior frame will carry them through, pure brute force riding tackles, clobbering forwards, clubbing sixes or knocking down wickets. At professional level, well though Botham disguised the fact, a player needs to have a little more intelligence than that, needs to employ a wider variety of skills. By the age of twenty-something, size isn't everything. For Botham, the chance to join the Lord's groundstaff was a crucial part of his development as a cricketer; without that experience he might not have risen to prominence with quite such speed. Deputed to handle him at cricket's HQ were chief coach Len Muncer and his assistant Harry Sharp, seasoned coaches who had seen countless young boys pass through the Grace Gates full of dreams of cricketing glory. Muncer and Sharp were both highly professional individuals who knew the game inside out. However, like many coaches of the old school, they were reluctant to alter long formed opinions, with Muncer in particular slow to warm to Botham's unorthodox approach to the game. A child of his times, Botham had little interest in the age-old maxim that appearances counted, that the means were more important than the ends. Although he conformed to some text book teachings – his action was admirably side-on early in his career; he generally looked to hit the ball straight – he viewed the game as more than just a scientific discipline. Cricket was a source of fun, of entertainment. Having grown up in the Beatle years, having taken Chelsea as his favourite football team at a time when Osgood, Cooke and Hudson were in full flight, Botham knew the value of flair, of excitement, of the extraordinary. He'd seen how these people had romanced their very different crowds and he wanted to be a part of that. Dull conformity had no interest for him. Muncer, on the other hand, had no time for flights of fancy. He wanted players to wear the right clothes, play the right way, do the right thing. It was inevitable that he and the irrepressible young Botham would be on a collision course from the outset. The more Muncer tried to make him conform, the less Botham did, turning his training into a classic battle of wills.

Muncer and Sharp were in a tough position in many ways. Not only was cricket changing at that time with the introduction of the limited overs game and the gradual increase in media coverage, but society was transforming itself too. For years boys had been turning up at Lord's with a naturally deferential temperament instilled in them: know your place, do the right thing, wear the proper clothes, don't speak unless you're spoken to. The 1960s and the arrival of cocky 'working class' heroes such as the Beatles and the Rolling Stones, Michael Caine and Joe Orton, George Best and Jackie Stewart, meant that those social rules were breaking down. Botham was in the vanguard of youngsters turning up at Lord's knowing what they wanted to do and how they wanted to do it. Lads like him wanted some of the fame, some of the glamour they'd seen others grabbing; it no longer seemed such a pipe dream that ordinary kids could become extraordinary adults. Cricket was lagging behind a little in the glamour stakes, but Botham believed he could change all that and do himself some good into the bargain. Faced with such an attitude, one they'd rarely encountered before, it's not too surprising that coaches like Muncer were taken aback.

The position was made far worse since Muncer didn't rate Botham as a bowler, continuing the general opinion that the Schools selectors had formed of him in Liverpool. Muncer knew his trade and so his views held some weight, and in fairness to the staff at Lord's, they were in the majority, for many good judges failed to recognise that this was a great cricketer in the making, labelling him instead as potentially a useful county cricketer but no more. Like so many, they felt that if he were to make anything of himself, it would be as a batsman, a feeling that persisted among most of his colleagues until he forced his way into the Somerset side. In the long term that might have been a good call, for Botham could have been an even more successful batsman than he was had he applied himself more.

Botham, then just sixteen, ignored the opinions of his seniors and determined to play the game exactly as he wanted to. Most kids, turning up to learn about the game at the home of cricket, would have been cowed by this received wisdom handed down from on high. The reaction of most would have been to accept these exhortations as expressions of harsh reality, working on the basis that Lord's didn't employ coaches who didn't know the game inside out. If Muncer and Sharp reckoned you couldn't bowl, they must have a good reason for saying so.

However cocksure Botham might be, it is still amazing that away from the security of his home and at such a tender age he should have been able to ignore the advice of those who ruled his life, who had it within their power to make it a misery should they so choose. Such a lack of confidence was not a part of the Botham character. Nor was the idea of standing around in the field while others took the glory particularly appealing. Botham had to be part of the action, the centre of attention at all times. It didn't make things easy for him, for Muncer ruled the lives of the groundstaff boys. Many would have given in to him but Botham's spirit could not be broken. Making his point in the only way he could, he bowled tirelessly in the nets, an activity which did him a great deal of good, building up his stamina and tightening up his action. He was also a good listener if he felt it was worth his while, and for all his run-ins with the chief coach, Botham learned a lot about the basics from him and his staff. He left Lord's a much better player than when he'd arrived. Muncer gradually warmed to him, telling his parents that he felt Botham could have done well in the Somerset Second XI in that summer of 1972. If nothing else, his time there had reaffirmed the value of standing up for himself. Harry Sharp was something of an ally in this for while he disapproved of Botham's occasionally loose technique, he understood that if the method worked for him, he was best to stick with it rather than trying to change. Sharp recognised the gifts of a 'natural' and allowed them to flourish, admitting that if what looked like a terrible shot ended up with the ball sailing to the boundary, there might be something in it after all. That said, even Sharp had reservations as to Botham's ability to carve out a successful career for himself.

Again in fairness to the staff at Lord's and many of his contemporaries at Taunton, Botham never really looked the part with the ball until Tom Cartwright and Brian Close got hold of him. Cartwright was the archetypal niggardly English seam bowler, capable of bowling length and line for hour after hour, nagging away at the batsmen, always probing and asking questions, rarely bowling a four ball. Unlucky that he was one of a crop of excellent English seamers, he managed just a handful of Test caps, but that didn't diminish the quality of his play – 1536 first class wickets at a cost of just nineteen each pay eloquent testimony to his skill. If Cartwright was bowling on a good wicket, batsmen knew they'd have to graft for their runs. If there was a little moisture in the pitch, a hint of green on top, then he could be lethal, running through the best sides in short order. Playing out the latter stages of his career at Somerset, Cartwright was delighted to see such an extrovert character as Botham coming into the game. Though he had played in an age when the game was treated with a siege mentality, often grinding out results in dour struggles, he was quick to realise that the game had to move on in the 1970s if it were to survive. The pace of life had quickened and cricket had to mirror that. It also needed personalities, striking individuals who would give the public what they wanted to see, keeping the game in the public eye. He saw that Botham could be very good news for the game.

As the two were on the same wavelength, Botham warmed to Cartwright and was eager to listen to his opinions. Never one to respect stories of how the game was 'better in my day' – he had had his fill of that attitude at Lord's – what struck him about Cartwright was the older man's acceptance that cricket was changing, that good players were good players whether they conformed or not. He wasn't mired in past glories but looking to the future. Once the two became friends, it was easy for Botham to listen to what Cartwright had to say. He admired, even envied, Cartwright's remarkable control, recognising that that was a skill he could use. His legacy to Botham was a structured, economical run up, an ability to pitch the ball precisely where he wanted, and an action that maximised the value of his powerful upper body. Cartwright pointed out to Pat Murphy that 'Ian worked very hard indeed at the nets. He didn't show the dedication of a Boycott, but it was there.' The lesson from this alliance is simple. If Botham responded well to someone's personality and felt they had something worthwhile to impart, he would listen and take the advice – though not necessarily right away. To avoid giving ground and to protect his macho status, he would often go away and implement the latest recommendations in his own good time. He admitted as much in *Wisden* when discussing another great mentor, Ken Barrington: 'he would get me a cup of tea, suggest something which I'd reject probably because I was tired, but then I'd do it and usually it worked'. Similarly, his antipathy to nets has long been a badge of pride – the kid who can pass exams without revision. Practice was for swots and cissies in Botham's book.

Though Cartwright was of immeasurable value to Botham on the technical side, it was his Somerset captain Brian Close who can be credited with turning him into an international class performer by forcing him to increase his pace with the ball; he told David Frith after that famous Benson & Hedges game in 1974, 'I'm going to make this lad into a fast bowler.' If Cartwright had helped teach him how to move the ball through the air and off the pitch seemingly at will, Close's need for a quick bowler, a shock weapon to get him wickets quickly, meant that Botham had another role to fill. Close was also lucky to get Botham at the peak of his physical development; once that frame gained the maturity it had lacked at Lord's, Botham became an altogether different proposition. With all the aggression a fast bowler could ever need, Botham was ideally suited to the job. Most impressive of all, the increase in pace had no discernible impact on his ability to gain movement for he'd already mastered those subtle arts under Cartwright's tutelage. Opponents now had no time to check a shot once they'd spotted the deviation because the ball – and the bowler – was already on them. As a result, Botham reaped a mighty harvest of wickets almost from the outset.

Close and Botham were made for each other, the latter admitting that 'starting out with Closey was vital for me because he taught me so much about attitude ... Closey had taught me there was no point in going out on the field with any other attitude than that I was the best cricketer alive'. There have been few more curmudgeonly or committed cricketers than Brian Close in the recent history of the game. Seemingly constructed from bits of granite and scrap metal, Close was as disputatious a man as you could hope to find, a cricketer who would never willingly give way to any opponent, a man, in short, cast from the same mould as Ian Botham. Perhaps the enduring image of this gifted all-round sportsman came in 1976 when, recalled to England's colours at the age of forty-five, he and John Edrich were subjected to a remorseless diet of fast bowling from the West Indies. Repeatedly struck about the chest, Close would not give ground but stuck to the task for which he'd been recalled – attempting to dull the edge of Holding's fierce pace by dogged occupation of the crease.

Perhaps that's an unfair and inaccurate memory of him. Close was a better player than his oft-recalled status as a punchbag suggests. England's youngest Test player when he made his debut in 1949, he was very unfortunate not to play more than his twenty-two Tests, particularly since he managed to make a fine reputation for himself as a Test match captain. That honour was taken away from him amid a welter of controversy when flagrant time wasting by Yorkshire at Edgbaston helped them save a game they'd apparently lost, a further example of Close's belief that you play sport hard, you play to win, and if you can't win you make damned sure you don't lose. As he got older, Close surely must have regretted some of the disaccord that seemed to follow his every move and which cost him so many Test caps and even the captaincy of his country (it might well have been him rather than Ray Illingworth recapturing the Ashes in Australia in 1970/71 had he taken more time over his public image). Recognising much of himself in his new young charge, he made strenuous attempts to save Botham from himself, trying to ensure that he was fully focused on his cricket. When his engagement to Kathryn Waller was announced in September 1974, Close was horrified. Young cricketers didn't get married! On this Close's opinion was duly noted and ultimately ignored. Nevertheless, his characteristic aggression and attacking attitude to cricket became ingrained in Botham; more accurately, Botham saw a successful cricketer who had just the same attitude to the game as he did and drew from that further confidence to play things his way.

Attack was the one thing they agreed upon, defence used as a last resort when absolutely necessary, Botham saying, 'I loved his attitude that you were better off losing a good game than boring everyone to death with a dull draw.' Botham was lucky that Close was his captain early on for although he owed much to Tom Cartwright, his view of bowling as a war of attrition held little fascination; indeed, had Cartwright possessed Botham's attitude he might well have been a more successful international cricketer. To the new all-rounder, every ball should be a potential wicket taker, not just a dot ball on the long road towards frustrating a batsman into error, a tactic that might work at county level but which would be less successful on the Test match stage. He wanted to experiment, to try new ideas, to attack, attack and attack again. In his first season of first class cricket, Botham was still in the Cartwright mould, conceding 2.4 runs an over, picking up a wicket every sixty-two balls, taking just thirty over the course of the season. By 1977, his breakthrough year, he was giving away three runs an over but was now striking every forty-five balls, his tally of wickets rocketing to eighty-eight. Some less adventurous county skippers would have taken more note of the runs per over statistic, but Close was wise enough to recognise that the strike rate was the crucial factor. If one end could be bottled up by a stock bowler, Botham might rattle through twenty overs and pick up four wickets for sixty-five where Cartwright might have taken one for thirty. To win games, the opposition generally has to be bowled out twice – that's certainly the case at Test level. Bowlers who can get their wickets quickly are a rarity, and they are real match winners.

By allowing Botham his head, Close helped him become one of the most incisive seam and swing bowlers in the country. Free of the containing mentality that reduced many of his contemporaries such as Mike Hendrick to the status of accountants, fretting over singles pushed backward of point, Botham had licence to try anything and everything. Consequently he could look very ordinary if things weren't going his way, and yet that was all part of his menace. A juicy half volley would be despatched to the boundary only to be followed a few balls later by an almost identical delivery. This, though, would be a fraction quicker, might be pitched up a shade further, might swing just a little more, might even go the other way. Botham would have another wicket from a seemingly innocuous ball. That type of cricket contributed to his reputation as a 'golden arm', a man who could bowl a lot of rubbish and still pick up a hatful of victims. Certainly he did have luck on his side from time to time: his first Test wicket, Greg Chappell, came from a ball Bob Willis described as 'the worst ever bowled in Test cricket'! Later on in his career, though, Botham made his own luck. It wasn't just what he bowled, but the way he bowled it. Every ball was fired down with such venomous belligerence and with such expectation of success that many batsmen were out before they knew what had happened. Always looking to unsettle a batsman with an unorthodox delivery, a stream of observations about how well he was bowling or how lucky the batsman was, or an extremely optimistic appeal, no one had an easy time while Botham was in the field, precisely the kind of attitude Close appreciated. Peter Roebuck wrote in *The Cricketer* that 'Close used to rail against cricketers with lazy minds', and certainly Botham was a first class product of the Close academy – alert, intelligent, instinctive, always looking for an advantage to seize, and with a solid understanding of the game to fall back on.

After two full seasons in the Somerset side, Botham was coming to the attention of the England selectors, finally winning a Test place in 1977. This gave him his first chance to work alongside Mike Brearley, the captain who was to have such an enormous effect on his career. Brearley was a nice contrast to Close, though both were excellent readers of the game who spoke a great deal of sense in a way to which Botham could relate. Neither was interested in overblown theories but simply cut through the jargon, motivating his players in his own way. It was extremely important for his well-being that just as Brian Close was announcing his retirement from the county game, Botham got into the Test team and so had Mike Brearley on hand to replace Close as his central adviser.

None could dispute that the partnership between Brearley and Botham was highly productive for both parties. Where Close had given Botham the confidence, the framework and the encouragement simply to let rip against county opposition, Brearley's use of him was altogether more calculated, as indeed it had to be in the international arena. It's interesting to reflect that in their early days together, Brearley saw Chris Old as his main all-rounder once Greig had left for Packer's circus. Botham got little cricket on the tour of Pakistan in 1977/78, his first senior overseas tour, having gone down with a stomach bug early on. Perhaps this was a blessing in disguise for Botham would have derived little movement from the baked Pakistani wickets that ensured the tour comprised three extremely tedious drawn Test matches. The only moment of excitement came in unfortunate style when Brearley was injured on a poor pitch, breaking his arm and leaving the captaincy open for Geoffrey Boycott on the second leg of the tour in New Zealand. If Boycott was not an ideal captain, few could fault his judgement of players. His frank, often highly critical assessments and a marked reluctance to accept simple human error as an excuse for getting out have won him few friends over the years, but there are still few shrewder judges of cricketing ability. Boycott's erstwhile Yorkshire colleague Brian Close had said of Botham that he was such a good batsman he should never get out; it was the central tenet of the Boycott faith that no one should get themselves out. Botham's ability was one of the few matters on which Close and Boycott could agree and Boycott quickly installed Botham in the side, letting him bat at six and giving him the responsibility and prestige on which he thrived. Botham reciprocated by running him out on vice captain Bob Willis's instructions in Christchurch after Botham had registered his maiden Test hundred in the first innings. It was in these games that Brearley, watching as a journalist, first saw how valuable a player Botham could be to him.

Back in England for the 1978 summer, Brearley quickly resumed the captaincy. That was the beginning of a relationship which oversaw most of Botham's best Test cricket. Within a matter of weeks he came to be the player on whom Brearley leant most often, the England captain recognising his astonishing aptitude for raising his game to the necessary heights, seemingly at will. Time and again, when a wicket was required to break a threatening or stubborn partnership, Botham did the trick with a swinging half volley or a blinding slip catch. Similarly, if England were struggling at the crease as at Lord's against Pakistan in 1978 when they were 134 for 5, Botham could stride out and take the bowling to pieces; in that Lord's match he did just that, clubbing a hundred in 104 balls to wrest the initiative. He then pocketed eight wickets for just thirty-four runs to complete an innings victory.

Brearley has to take some credit for getting the very best out of Botham, something subsequent captains often failed to do. If he was struggling to get to the crease, Brearley would give the nod to Willis at mid-on. Willis would meet Botham on his way back to his mark and advise him that he was bowling like an old woman. Once the inevitable flurry of bouncers had been hurled down, a couple of overs later Botham would, likely as not, have two more scalps to his name. Brearley was also wise enough not to overtax the willing tyro. Many of his later captains have said how hard it could be to get the ball out of his hand for Botham was always sure that another wicket was just around the corner if only they'd let him bowl (the events of 1984 against the West Indies and Sri Lanka, both at Lord's, proved conclusively that that wasn't always so, Botham taking some fearful stick with Gower unable to prise the ball from his grasp). Brearley was strong enough to tell him when he'd had enough and was intelligent enough to use him in a shock bowling role, his strongest suit when he was in his pomp. Under Brearley's leadership, Botham was used almost exclusively as an attacking weapon, with bat and ball.

Although Botham was obviously a far better cricketer than Brearley, the captain was the first among these equals. Like Close before him, Brearley was happy to give Botham responsibility. He understood that Botham needed to be in the thick of the action as much as possible but he also saw that Botham was a great team man. By ensuring he had a specific job to do, a fully articulated goal for which to aim, and by relating that to the overall success of the England team, Brearley ensured that his all-rounder was fully focused on the job in hand. He made it clear that Botham should only bowl at the right moment and that that moment was not every minute of the day. Botham had complete respect for Brearley because the captain was too sensible to be authoritarian in his approach to the players. His actions were taken for a reason, and his strategy evolved in team meetings that gave everyone a chance to have his say before Brearley had the last word. Having been denied a voice by coaches in the past, Botham responded well to this quasi-democracy.

Just as Brearley was intrigued by Botham's talent, his natural aptitude for the game and his general enthusiasm for life, so Botham was fascinated by Brearley's intellectual take on cricket. Each had the greatest respect for the other, each had things they could learn from the other, and each was willing to listen. They became firm friends off the pitch but that was a relationship that did not harm their work on the field; there was no playing of favourites under Brearley. If Botham needed a rollicking, he got one, but he only got one when it was deserved. Praise came when it was merited, consolation when necessary. That was the key to their partnership and the reason Botham was willing to accede to Brearley's wishes, accepting that he 'could read me through and through'. Quite simply, he respected his judgement as a cricketer who could do something he could not yet do himself.

When Brearley left the scene in 1980, Botham was exposed to and beaten by West Indian might. Had Mike Brearley been captain, England would still have been second best for much of those two series, but even Botham would have to concede that he would probably have returned better individual figures. Where Brearley had employed his bowling gifts sympathetically, Botham flogged himself mercilessly or gave other less deserving and penetrative bowlers first use of a helpful pitch. Asked to make the decisions, Botham took all his side's considerable failings about his broad shoulders and tried to fight the good fight alone. Troubled by his back, he inflicted an excessive workload on himself and was never really effective. With Brearley in command, Botham might have bowled as many as overs, but he'd have bowled them in shorter spells and at times when wickets were likely to fall; as skipper he seemed to put himself on mainly when the likes of Lloyd and Richards were on top – brave, but ultimately foolish. Captain Botham was always looking to take on extra responsibility, an instinct Brearley had kept in check, recognising that he needed to stay fresh to be a threat.

Brearley had also provided a shoulder to cry on. Although Botham would never break down in that way, Brearley was always on hand to keep him going when things were going against him. Without him in the side, Botham had nowhere else to turn for advice on the field of play. In his early days, Botham seemed to have some kind of guardian angel looking over him, for he was lucky to be taken under the wings of some impressive men who could offer a steadying influence. It's probably no coincidence that, with both Close and Brearley off the scene in 1980, he first got himself into trouble with the Joe Neenan incident in Scunthorpe. Though Botham was acquitted of all charges when the jury could not provide a unanimous decision, it suggested that here was a man who might be lacking in judgement and who needed some authority figure to keep him in check. Like it or not, as England captain and sporting hero Botham was a sitting target for any local toughs who wanted to make a name for themselves. Able to turn the other cheek most times, it was inevitable that Botham would snap on occasion, just as any other man would do under intense provocation. The sensible course would have been to avoid nightclubs and pubs where things can always get out of hand, but the sensible course never appealed to him. Botham was his own man who did his own thing, but had he known he would have incurred the wrath of Close or the displeasure of Brearley for such an ill advised escapade, he might have stayed at home more.

Going to the Caribbean as captain in 1980/81, he was again fortunate in his advisers, accompanied this time by the TCCB's Alan Smith and, more importantly, Ken Barrington, who had not been included in the original touring party. That was a surprising omission since Barrington had become an integral part of England's management and coaching set up, especially abroad. Just as when he was playing, having Barrington aboard as a coach was a distinct plus for England; certainly he was one of the few people to whom Ian Botham ever listened. Graham Gooch felt the same way about him, noting that 'his influence on me was massive. An uncle, a friend, a wise counsellor.' For his part, Botham respected the fact that Barrington was as fierce a patriot as he himself was, that he would give every ounce of effort for his country and would never accept defeat until the stumps were drawn. Like Cartwright, Barrington was not one of the old school who felt the game was going downhill and that today's players couldn't hold a candle to those of yesteryear. He understood that the game had changed, that different demands were placed on players, and that good players now would have been good players in the past. He also accepted that the West Indian attack was more formidable than anything he'd had to face, endearing himself to Botham and his players in the process.

As a coach he was excellent. Having been forced to reconstruct his own game early on in his career when his profligacy with the bat had found him out, he had an encyclopaedic grasp of the game's technicalities coupled with an ability to put it across in the simplest of terms. A straightforward bloke who was extremely popular with everyone in the touring party, Barrington made a huge contribution to English cricket, Jim Laker averring that 'he upset no-one and did not make a single enemy on the way'. He was especially helpful on that tour to West Indies, advising Botham on practice facilities, giving him pointers on his own game, and so on. While England's hero was under fire from every quarter, he could always rely on Barrington to give him support as well as any of the unpalatable truths he would refuse to hear elsewhere. It was impossible to take offence at any criticism Barrington might make for he would offer it simply and genuinely while always trying to stress any positive moves that had been made. Most engaging of all, he regularly put the needs of others before himself.

The nervous energy this born worrier expended on behalf of others must surely have hurried his untimely demise. When he died during the Third Test in Barbados, the saddest outcome of the strains placed on everyone by the Jackman affair in Guyana, he left a void no manager or coach has subsequently filled. A partnership featuring Botham and Barrington might have gone on to great things through the 1980s. His premature death robbed the game of a great character and stripped Botham of perhaps his last great adviser. In a short space of time, Close, Brearley and Barrington had passed out of his day to day life, leaving him with nobody on whom he could, or would, rely. Had Brearley continued as captain, had Barrington lived, had Close been six or seven years younger, the remainder of Botham's story might have been very different. As it was he was left to sort things out for himself, not always in the best manner. In his tribute to Barrington in 1982's *Wisden*, Robin Marlar pointed out his worth to players such as Botham: 'To the generation that is coming to full maturity Ken Barrington had become as important as the maypole; something solid. He was the "Colonel" around whom a team of cricketers could revolve.' More importantly perhaps, given the respect in which Botham held him, was his attitude to practice:

[Barrington] was brought up in a generation which believed as an act of faith that once a cricketer had played at Test level he knew it all. How else could he have been selected? Furthermore, and this is still a more prevalent attitude than Barrington liked, a player who makes as much of a fetish about practising as Boycott is regarded as a freak. *As one who had to work out his technique, to subordinate under a layer of discipline the stroke-making ability he had acquired in his early days* ... he was ideally suited to the task of developing younger talent and skills.

The words in my italics are crucial, for if Botham ever wanted to come to terms with West Indian bowling, he would have had to make changes in his game. Viv Richards has suggested that since Botham was such a born entertainer it would have been quite impossible for him to do so. Perhaps Barrington might have persuaded him otherwise. At the very least, he might have managed to get him to net practice more often and to work more assiduously at his game. Barrington was ahead of his time in coaching terms, never decrying practice and always ready to point out the virtues of application and the study of technique, attributes that today's top coaches such as Bob Woolmer are utilising to the full with excellent results.

Barrington was a very down to earth man. Had he been around to enjoy Botham's successes of 1981 and then to work with him in India, he'd have been the first to congratulate him and the first to remind him that the hard work started all over again in this new series. Barrington had absolute conviction in the ability of Botham, Gooch and Gatting, but the other two had fewer conflicts in their lives, were better able to focus on their cricket. Someone who lived the chaotic, kinetic lifestyle of Ian Botham could not always keep his eye on every ball he was juggling. He needed regular reminders of the right path. Tellingly in Barrington's obituary in *Wisden Cricket Monthly*, David Frith wrote that 'all the fighters in Test cricket – Bailey, Edrich, Lawry, Burke et al – could belt away like one-day cricketers if they chose. Their exceptional common gift was self-denial. Certain other batsmen, touched with genius, could bat forever if endowed with this discipline.' Perhaps the art of self-denial must be inbuilt into a person's character, perhaps it cannot be taught like the forward defensive. Even Barrington might not have been able to tame Botham's wilder flights, though it should be recalled that one of Botham's most heroic efforts, his dogged innings of just six in ninety minutes at Sydney in 1978/79, came under the watchful eye of Barrington and Brearley. What must be certain is that Botham would not have wanted to do anything to disappoint the genial Barrington, for he had become family. That determination alone might have saved him from a lot of trouble in subsequent years. Of all the losses Botham had to endure, it was that of Ken Barrington that was the most grievous.

One of the problems inherent in replacing any of those figures was the generation factor. Close, Brearley, Barrington and Cartwright were elder statesmen as far as Botham was concerned; though they didn't automatically command his respect because of their seniority, it was easier to listen to them since they were not his exact contemporaries chasing the same goals. In 1982, the main players in the England set-up were all around the same age as Botham. Inevitably they were as competitive with one another as with the opposition, for the England captaincy would eventually pass to Gower, Gooch, Gatting or Botham again, though Gooch quickly ruled himself out of the running by going on the rebel South African tour. Keith Fletcher might have been helpful to him, but his role as England leader was over in a matter of months following a disappointing tour of India. Fletcher's case wasn't helped by a show of dissent, knocking over his stumps when given out – frustrated displays of temper were clearly not the sole preserve of young lions. Bob Willis stepped into the breach at England level and, as a close friend of Botham's, their relationship was a healthy one, Botham returning to the role of court jester within the dressing room, maintaining morale with his range of practical jokes. His respect for Willis kept his natural exuberance in check and his performances for the gangly fast bowler were generally solid. Notably, under Willis, he managed to maintain the consistent improvement that was being seen in his batting. Following on from his Ashes successes, Botham had been superb on Fletcher's tour of India, scoring 440 runs at fifty-five, with four fifties and a century. That was quickly followed by a couple more hundreds in the home series against the same opponents in 1982, including a superb 208 at the Oval which was as technically accomplished an innings as anyone could wish to see. Admittedly India were not a great bowling side, Kapil Dev apart, but Botham had often exhibited a degree of vulnerability against the spinners. This innings nailed those doubts.

Willis's tenure as England skipper was always destined to be a short one, age and injury catching up with him. Looking to the future, David Gower had been installed as vice captain, but Botham also skippered England on tour on occasion. He clearly had hopes of getting another crack at the job in less taxing circumstances, but recognised that Gower was the undoubted front runner. His lingering hopes of getting the job evaporated on the infamous sex 'n' drugs 'n' rock 'n' roll tour of New Zealand and Pakistan in 1983/84. As if the bad publicity engendered, inevitably and inaccurately centring on Botham's alleged bedroom exploits, were not enough, his return home with a knee injury left Gower to step into the breach when Willis also fell ill. With Gower leading the side well and batting superbly, his selection as captain for the forthcoming summer's Tests against the West Indies was a foregone conclusion. Meanwhile, back at home, Botham was inserting his foot in his mouth, as much out of frustration as anything else. In the course of a long radio interview he made a feeble stab at a very stupid joke, suggesting that Pakistan was the kind of place you'd send your mother-in-law on holiday for a month. The diplomatic gaffe merely hardened the Establishment's prejudices that the boy was a talented loudmouth, a latter-day Fred Trueman, who couldn't be trusted to use the right knife in company. His aptitude for leading a cricket side was irrelevant; the feeling was Botham would let the side down off the field, a grossly unfair attitude given his exemplary performance in the hothouse atmosphere of Guyana in 1981. All the same, it consigned him to a future with little hope of regaining the England captaincy.

Most colleagues agree that Botham was never a great one for taking criticism, however kindly or constructively it might be meant. Especially since the trials and tribulations of his captaincy, he has taken any rebuke as being personally, rather than professionally, directed. Given the nature of so much press comment he was entitled to be sensitive, but the cricketing evidence suggests that his unwillingness to take direction embraced those who captained him. By the time Bob Willis left the England scene in 1984, the dressing room had been stripped of its senior players – Boycott, Brearley, Taylor, Willis and Underwood had all gone. Botham himself was now the senior pro, but operating without any real responsibility. He undoubtedly found it hard to take orders from players who were his own age and who had played less Test cricket than he had himself. Where Willis had in the main been able to temper Botham's ego, Gower was the first to find it hard going, the results under his leadership pointing out his comparative failure to harness Botham's talents.

In Willis's reign, Botham's role in the side was developing, changing by degrees. From being an all-rounder whose predominant value was with the ball, circumstances rotated through almost 180 degrees. Although the opposition was not always the strongest, Botham enjoyed some of his most consistent batting form when Willis was in charge, the captain giving him extra responsibility to bat for long periods and to construct an innings. To his frustration, in the past Botham had often come in at number seven, by which time he might only have the tail left for company. Willis tended to use Botham as one of his front-line batsmen from whom he expected an average of around forty. Botham complied with those needs, passing fifty on nine occasions out of thirty-one, averaging forty-one over Willis's eighteen Tests in charge. In contrast, as a bowler he would often find himself deprived of the new ball, even coming on as second change. Though he managed three five-wicket hauls for Willis, it was apparent that he was not the force he'd once been. Indeed, when England had allowed New Zealand to score 307 in Christchurch on what *Wisden* described as a 'suspect pitch', Willis called the England bowling 'some of the worst' he had seen. With Willis taking four for fifty-one and Cowans three for fifty-two, *Wisden* saw Botham as the main culprit, bowling seventeen overs to take one wicket for eighty-eight, 'Hadlee [striking] 99 in 111 minutes (81 balls), taking heavy toll of a surfeit of long-hops from Botham'. It was not to be the last time Botham tried to bounce batsmen out with disastrous effects.

By that time it was becoming increasingly obvious that Botham had to play as a batting all-rounder, for his bowling was often little more threatening than Basil d'Oliveira's had been in the late sixties when he'd performed a similar role in the England side. From England's return from Australia in 1983 to the end of his career, Botham played forty-three Tests, taking 116 wickets at 37.4 each, striking every sixty-seven balls. That contrasts with his first fifty-nine Tests, studded with 267 wickets at 24.5 each, one every fifty-one balls. The decline is obvious, but the figures would have been acceptable had Botham been operating in a Steve Waugh type of role for England, picked for his batting but capable of bowling a few overs and picking up the odd wicket here and there, helping the balance of the side. It's a point many picked up on at the time. In his book *On Reflection* in 1984, Richie Benaud was already suggesting that Botham's back was in need of further treatment and that he should adapt his action to enhance the threat he posed and to protect his spine. Benaud, shrewd as ever, posed the vital question: 'Now ... does Botham have the dedication and the will to regain maximum fitness to hold off the challenge of [Kapil Dev, Richard Hadlee and Imran Khan]? Does he have the will to train hard and remain a bowling all-rounder, or will he become a batting all-rounder instead? This could be accomplished easily enough because there is no doubting his ability with the bat and his ability to win matches for a captain in that department.' Benaud was not alone in his regard for Botham's batting. In his book on the 1986/87 Australian tour *Ashes To Ashes*, Peter Roebuck wrote prior to the First Test, 'here in Brisbane, Ian Botham is steeling himself to score a century ... no man in cricket is more certain of scoring a hundred when his mind is set upon it, not even the great Richards. To Botham, these things are acts of will-power. He has an extraordinarily strong will which, if he uses it, rarely fails.'

There's little to suggest that Botham took the decline in his bowling as seriously as he should have. He remained convinced that he could roll over a side at will, yet the evidence was stacked against him. At Lord's in 1984, a pivotal Test in David Gower's career, England had the West Indians in trouble for once. Set 342 to win in five and a half hours, everyone imagined they'd be looking to bat out time. With only Bob Willis looking remotely Test match class, Gordon Greenidge took England to pieces. Botham bowled twenty overs for 117 runs where Willis bowled fifteen for forty-eight. Similar discipline from Botham might have saved the game but, recalling his prime, Botham felt he could win the match by virtue of his own aggression. As he ruefully recounted in his autobiography, his conviction that he could bounce batsmen out undid him: 'I overdid the delivery ... as far as I was concerned, the next one was bound to get him, but, of course, it never did.'

Benaud's argument that Botham needed either to get fit or to change his priorities made more sense with every passing day. Still capable of bowling well – his eight wickets for 103 in the first innings of that Lord's Test was a case in point – the good days were fewer and further between. Yet Botham's competitive instinct was so well honed that he could not stay out of the action, demanding the ball, always trying to get men out. There's no question that he continued to get wickets that no one else could. Returning to the England side against New Zealand in 1986 following his 'drugs' ban, he had Bruce Edgar caught at slip by Graham Gooch with his first ball. Eleven balls later he snapped up Jeff Crowe, leg before wicket, to move past Dennis Lillee and become the greatest wicket taker in Test match history. Nobody but Botham could conjure events like that into being, no other cricketer has ever had such a mastery of the art of the impossible, none has had such a vivid imagination. Yet at that time for every day like that when the fires burned bright there were days of humiliation, such as the beating he took from Sri Lankan captain Duleep Mendis at Lord's in the 1984 Test. In mitigation, Phil Neale, Botham's skipper at Worcestershire, points out:

> when he was getting older, the problem was that England always desperately needed an all-rounder and often he just had to bowl. We've still not properly replaced him in that role. And you could never rule out his knack of getting a wicket – on a flat pitch, nothing happening, he'd bowl a long hop and get somebody out for you. His past record always discouraged you from ruling him out of doing anything. While he was in the side, you'd always give him the ball to see what might happen. You'd have struggled to make the decision to play him just as a batsman and stop him from bowling.

Even in the light of Neale's assertions, that decision

needed to be taken for him. As much as at any other time in his professional career, in 1984 Botham needed someone to turn to, a mentor whose advice he respected. The laid-back David Gower was never likely to fit into that mould. The two were friends, rivals for the cricketing public's favour, too close in age and attitude to the game and to life in general to be able to give wise counsel to each other. Botham needed an ultimatum along the lines of Benaud's question: Do you want to bowl at your best again? If so, get fit. If you don't want to, or are physically incapable, take your batting more seriously and win your place in the side on that alone. There was never any reason why Botham should not have settled into the number four or five berth for England and made it his own for another decade. He had the ability to get close to England's run scoring record as well as being its leading wicket taker. For want of good advice, that chance went begging.

So far as Ian Botham was concerned, David Gower's captaincy was disastrous. Gower had far too much faith in Botham the bowler when such a belief was no longer warranted. Phil Edmonds, for example, noted that Gower remained convinced of the power of Botham's golden arm throughout the West Indies visit of 1984, letting him bowl when there was little prospect of him making a breakthrough. Admittedly, Gower was short of quality quick bowling with the demise of Bob Willis and was enduring the same misfortune Botham had lived through – facing the West Indies early in his captaincy. Accordingly he lost many games and his own figures suffered, as did Botham's. Even bearing all that in mind, under Gower Botham averaged twenty-six with the bat and thirty-six with the ball, both much poorer than his overall figures, and only ten of his twenty-one Tests under Gower came against the West Indies. There was ample time to repair the figures elsewhere, but Gower simply could not get the best out of him on a regular basis. Most telling of all, at no time under Gower's leadership did Botham produce a genuine match winning display, though he was an important figure in the team that reclaimed the Ashes in 1985.

Of the four men who skippered Botham in ten or more Tests, it's reasonable to suggest that Gower did less for his career than any of the others. Though his overall figures under Gatting were not vastly superior, the Middlesex man was at least able to coax two match winning performances from his waning all-rounder; indeed, it was Botham's electrifying presence on that glorious Australian adventure of 1986/87 that first stamped England's dominance on the entire series, before he finally sealed the retention of the Ashes with a superb spell of intelligent medium pace bowling at the Melbourne Cricket Ground. Gatting gave Botham the freedom he required but within a sensible disciplinary framework, and also managed to keep his superstar pretty much out of the limelight on that tour, allowing Botham to concentrate on his cricket. The fact that Botham took his wife Kath with him on the trip was also a tactical masterstroke, keeping the press hounds at bay.

In contrast, the laissez-faire Gower so lost control of England's Caribbean trip in 1985/86 that Botham was never in any frame of mind to tackle Viv Richards' men. Again, in fairness to Gower, it's hard to see how England could have done a lot about the five–nil result, but they should surely have made a better fight of it. Just as in 1984, once Gower's team was under attack from the opposition, the wheels fell off. The 'optional practice' idea, while trying to keep the pressure off players already under withering fire, was a move that backfired, in PR terms if nothing else. In addition, while natural touch players like Gower and Botham were not always helped by long net sessions, they did set a poor example to the rest of the party, giving the impression they were unconcerned by persistent failure. Allowing Botham to do his own thing while giving him the idea that he was fireproof was an approach doomed to failure. Less gifted players struggling with their form and technique against the fast bowlers would clearly have been helped by sustained practice, though again the facilities provided were generally awful. Seeing that Botham and Gower had such disdain for practice, younger players fell in with their habits. Botham seemed not to appreciate that not all players had his strength of character, some lacking the necessary fibre to go their own way. As in everyday life, some simply followed the herd and failed to do what was best for themselves, choosing instead to court easy popularity among these heroes of the game.

While almost everyone suffered statistically at the hands of the West Indies, one would have still hoped that Botham would be the best of a poor bunch. Instead, his bowling decline was dramatically underlined. Reporting in *The Cricketer*, Christopher Martin-Jenkins had this to say of his opening spell in the Second Test in Trinidad: 'Taking the new ball when it ought to have been given to Ellison, [he] bowled five wayward, powder-puff overs which cost England no fewer than 39 runs. It also cost Botham his pride and it was a little sad to see a bowler once so dangerous blaming everyone but himself for the fact that Greenidge was laying into him with such pleasure.' The series ended with Botham fifth of five in the bowling averages behind John Emburey, Neil Foster, Richard Ellison and Greg Thomas. The batting was little better: he rolled in sixth with 168 runs at 16.8. That statistic was quite appalling since it was painfully obvious his future must lie with his batting. At a time when Botham should have become nothing more than a useful change bowler, his ego wouldn't allow it, and he demanded that he be respected as an all-rounder when he did not deserve it. Meanwhile David Gower was either unable or unwilling to initiate the very necessary transformation of Botham into a batsman who could bowl a bit, something which Gatting tried to do.

The nadir of Botham's partnership with Gower came on that tour. In his autobiography, Gower noted that 'this trademark of [Botham's], that he is in his mind always doing, or about to do, great things, is a mixed blessing. When it is going right, everyone knows what remarkable things can happen. When it's going wrong, he doesn't always step back and look closely enough at himself from the outside. The rest of the team were looking closely at him all right, and all they could see was someone who hardly bowled in the nets, and was disappearing for five an over. No wonder they got disgruntled.' The problem was that Gower was the captain of the side whose job it was to impose some kind of discipline on Botham. If his presence was affecting other players as that final comment suggests, it was up to Gower to get him back into line. He failed to do so. *Wisden*'s John Thicknesse did not mince words in his summary of the trip: 'Much went wrong that with firmer captaincy and management might not have ... in cold fact, England never had a hope. That they could and should have done better, few who saw them would dispute. Their lack of commitment was reflected in their attitude to practice, a department in which West Indies showed them up to be amateurs.' Suggesting that while

Gower was an excellent leader in victory, he did not have the steel in his character necessary for such a taxing trip, Thicknesse noted that 'it was not only that he had no faith in practice – a weakness exacerbated by Ian Botham's presence – but sometimes he seemed even to lack interest'. For Botham the tour was a catastrophe. Thicknesse remarked that he 'had a dreadful tour in every imaginable way ... his aversion to net practice set a bad example and only once, when he was under threat of being dropped, did he produce a good performance with the ball'.

In fairness, the media had had a major effect on Botham's form once more. Perhaps if Gooch or Gatting had been made England's leader earlier on, he might have survived the slings and arrows of outrageous tabloid speculation. They would certainly have stood more chance of keeping him in check. Although he was never wild about Gooch's management methods, the dressing room atmosphere he encouraged might have made a difference. Speaking in 1992, John Emburey, admittedly a close friend of Gooch, told the *Daily Telegraph*'s Paul Weaver that on his return to Test cricket under Gower 'there was a lack of discipline, the atmosphere in the dressing room was unbelievable, noisy, loud and full of bravado. David Gower was the captain and Ian Botham and Allan Lamb were making their presence known ... Graham Gooch has done a fantastic job [as captain]. He is a disciplinarian and if players don't fit in, he won't have them.'

The vice captaincy situation in the West Indies is crucial in trying to understand the rest of Botham's career. Given the events of the 1983/84 tour, it was perfectly reasonable that Botham should have chosen not to winter in India in 1984/85, taking the opportunity to rest a body that had been pushed to the limits for ten years. Surprisingly selected as vice captain, Mike Gatting grasped the opportunity and had an excellent tour to leapfrog ahead of Botham in the pecking order. It was understandable that Gatting, now looking like an authentic Test cricketer at long last, was the automatic choice to understudy Gower in the West Indies. On Gatting's return home after having his face customised by a Malcolm Marshall bouncer, Graham Gooch was given the post, in spite of the fairly obvious mood of discontent – as captain of one of the rebel sides that had toured South Africa, he was the subject of fierce protest demonstrations and could be forgiven for having things other than cricket on his mind. To make him vice captain was as daft a decision in the circumstances as the appointment of Geoff Miller on the previous tour of the West Indies when the incapacitated Willis had jetted back to England. With Botham causing concern among some who suggested he abused the freedom Gower gave him, this was an obvious opportunity to get him back on side; it would have been a brave decision given the prevailing media attitude, but brave decisions are often the right ones. Paul Downton felt that something needed to be done, telling Rob Steen that '[Botham] was a bit of a divisive influence; he spent a lot of time in the West Indies' dressing room. I, for one, felt he was too much under Viv's sway. He wasn't a good loser or a good battler; he found it hard to believe he was doing anything wrong.'

The selection of Gooch as vice captain made it apparent once and for all that Ian Botham would never again get the call to lead his country. It had been an unlikely dream for some time, but this was the last nail in the coffin. Most damaging of all, it came at precisely the moment when Botham was less committed to his cricket than at any other time. Wearied by the sheer physical effort of bowling quick, troubled by back and knee injuries, beleaguered by the press, and carrying the weight of a faltering legal action against the *Mail on Sunday*, being England's premier sporting hero suddenly looked a less attractive job than ever before. Perhaps he realised, subconsciously at least, that he would never again scale the heights of 1981, that the rest of his career would be more humdrum than the great days he had already enjoyed. Botham was looking for new challenges, fresh fields to conquer in order to restore his vitality and appetite for the game. The England captaincy or vice captaincy might have been one such challenge, but no such offers were forthcoming. Nor were any sustained ultimatums as to his form, Gower merely pointing out to him that he'd come close to being dropped for the Fourth Test, which prompted his best game of the series. Indeed, the Establishment seemed to go out of its way to cut him off from the decision making process, making it clear that he was in the team on sufferance because it didn't dare ditch him. Refusing to accept that Botham, now in his cricketing maturity, might actually thrive on extra responsibility, the powers that be withheld the very thing that could have prolonged the usefulness of his career and kept him out of the tabloids; in the West Indies in 1985/86, he was not even co-opted onto the selection panel. Instead, he and pals like Allan Lamb were given licence to enjoy the social side of touring as much as, and perhaps to the detriment of, their cricket. Whether anyone in the party was guilty of anything untoward or not, the freedom given to Botham simply gave the sensation seekers in Wapping the chance to let their fevered imaginations run riot, this in spite of the fact that Botham spent a lot of the tour locked in his hotel room, the better to avoid the squadrons of news reporters. With more of the same to look forward to on each subsequent tour until the body finally wore out and he hung up his bat, there's little wonder that Botham was becoming disenchanted with it all.

Botham was looking for another mentor. He was desperate for someone to give him a sense of direction, but engaging Tim Hudson as his manager was a reckless cry for help. Hudson was the kind of chap that could talk the hind legs off a donkey and then persuade it to enter the Grand National. A self-confessed eccentric, Hudson made his million on the west coast of America as a DJ and property developer (whether the two jobs were intertwined is, like much else that surrounds Hudson, a mystery). Botham described him as a 'likeable nutter' and Hudson certainly had the sort of character and ego to match his own. A friendship of sorts was therefore inevitable, the more so once Hudson began to make Botham sound like an exotic combination of John Wayne, Harrison Ford and Errol Flynn. ITB was the greatest thing since sliced bread and, according to Hudson, the rest of the world would soon fall at his feet.

The continuous press carping had only hardened Botham's attitude to the outside world. Since he had to read so much rubbish about himself, he felt he could only trust his own opinions, and as a man who had been proved right against the odds throughout most of his life, Botham was not one to underestimate his own value. After 1981, he believed he had the Midas touch and that it would never leave him; Hudson's views simply coincided with his own. Therefore, once Hudson began to articulate his vision of an action-packed future filled with all the money he could dream of, there was an inexorable logic about it all as far as Botham was concerned. Tiring of the circuit, no longer relishing the inescapable grind of the international cricketer,

Botham wanted something else to do with the rest of his life. He began to alienate even those who were his supporters: in the course of his benefit year in 1984, he arrived very late for one game especially arranged for him at Sparkford. His couldn't care less attitude caused club captain Graham Reeve to make it clear that Botham would not be welcome there in future. Stories like these were a worrying development. One of Botham's strengths was that he had the common touch and could relate to the ordinary supporters of the game. Appearing arrogant and contemptuous of those who were helping him raise £90,000 in his benefit season did little for his image and merely helped create a climate in which people were willing to believe the worst about him. If nothing else, it fostered a growing feeling that Botham thought he was above everything. For a time, things seemed to spiral beyond Botham's control. Jaded, world weary, he seemed unable to draw a line under his problems. Cricket was no longer the seductive mistress it had been in his youth and he yearned for something to replace it in his affections. Also, approaching thirty, even he had to accept that he was nearing the latter stages of his active sporting career. While he was financially comfortable, he'd scarcely made a fortune out of the game, certainly when compared with contemporary international footballers or the rock stars with whom he was now mixing. If Hudson could provide a pot of gold, that was to be welcomed.

Hudson took charge of Botham's affairs in early 1985, just as Mike Gatting was placing himself next in line for the England captaincy and ruling Botham out of the running for good. Hudson's early tactic was to make cricket seem different, new and exciting, essential music to the ears of the haggard Botham. Inviting Botham to his rural retreat,

Birtles, in the Cheshire countryside, the talk was Packeresque and Pythonesque in its hyperbole, painting a picture of private teams captained by rock stars playing televised matches while Pink Floyd performed an evolving soundtrack from the boundary edge. There was also the range of clothing, garish concoctions that only a genuinely colourblind man such as Botham could have been persuaded to endorse. Bit by bit the schemes became increasingly grandiose, but somehow Hudson made it all seem reasonable. Botham was enthralled by the prospect of changing the staid old game into something new, fresh, vital. So persuasive was Hudson that even Brian Close was roped in as cricket manager at Birtles.

Even so, Botham must have been at a low ebb to fall for Hudson's next ludicrous suggestion. He was going to become a Hollywood superstar, a star of the silver screen. Sporting swashbuckler he may have been, but since cricket means nothing more than 'grasshopper' in the States, Botham was a completely unknown quantity to the movie producers in Los Angeles. An unknown non-actor is unlikely to become the new James Bond, yet Botham fell in with Hudson's plans, so keen was he to make a change in his way of life. This was the real legacy of 1981. Ever since then, once he had walked upon the waters, once he'd transformed the bitter tears of defeat into the sweet champagne of victory, no one had been able to say no to him. Botham knew best because he'd proved it. He'd done things that no mere mortal could ever repeat. The people knew it, his friends knew it, the opposition knew it. Most of all *he* knew it. Headingley had shown that no challenge was too great for this man. All things were possible as long as you believed. If Ian Botham thought he could become a movie star, it was just a matter of time before it came to pass – that was how he'd reached the pinnacle of the cricketing world after all. Yet Botham was a supremely gifted cricketer, an instinctive natural athlete; there was no evidence to suggest he was a natural Marlon Brando. Of course, these seemed to be just petty details that would be addressed in due course. Nothing to worry about. The proposal was thrilling, it was novel, it was a gauntlet thrown down at the feet of a man who had done everything in cricket. The macho Botham even had his hair highlighted, something which would have been unthinkable a few years earlier.

Ultimately, it was Hudson's dreams of Hollywood that proved to be his undoing. Botham came to see him as a Walter Mitty character, an inveterate dreamer whose schemes often had little to do with reality. More sinister as far as Botham's family were concerned was the way in which Hudson seemed to live within a magic circle of followers who hung on his every word. Slowly, insidiously, Botham was drawn into the centre of this world. He was besotted with Hudson's panache and daredevilry, refusing to hear any criticism of his latest saviour. Kath, stubborn and sensible, refused to fall under the spell. She was concerned about her husband but felt he was big enough to look after himself. Her real worry was the effect Hudson would have on the children. Since Botham wouldn't listen to her criticisms, she reacted in the only manner left to her by issuing an ultimatum: either Hudson had to go or she would. Pig-headed to the last, Botham allowed her to walk out on him, though her action was the wake-up call he needed. Given that she had been able to weather the sex and drugs storms whipped up by the media, her initial determination to leave underlined the seriousness of the situation. When she returned to the family home a few days later for the sake of the children, Botham's faith in Hudson had been irredeemably shaken.

A few days later, when Hudson confided in Brian Close that Kath and the family would have to go if Botham was going to become a smouldering sex symbol on the big screen, the game was up, even though it took a few more months before Botham finally sacked him as his business manager. Finally coming to his senses after a year-long interlude, Botham put his family life first and got his marriage back on an even keel. The final parting of the ways with Hudson came when, with the sex and drugs allegations flying through the air while England were in the West Indies, Hudson allegedly told the press that Botham smoked dope and didn't everybody? Given that Botham was still embroiled in legal proceedings having sued the *Mail on Sunday* over the New Zealand articles, this was not quite the sort of publicity he required. Hudson was finished, not before time as far as Botham's family were concerned. He left a legacy of eighteen months during which Botham had become more hooked on the idea of fame and fortune than at any stage, to the exclusion of his family and to the undoubted detriment of his cricket. He had failed in the Caribbean again, but once more his tour had been wrecked by external events beyond his control. When the record books show that Botham always had a terrible time against the West Indies, the other pressures that always seemed to accompany series against them need to be taken into consideration.

Free of Hudson, the remainder of Botham's career was comparatively sedate, once the 1986 drugs storm had been weathered. He seemed more willing to listen to the views of his family, notably his wife Kath, who had long been a voice of sanity amid the madness; as Botham was happy to confess later, she was the rock to which the entire family clung in the midst of the turbulence. While her husband could escape onto the pitch or into a huddle of confidants around the bar, she had nowhere to go. The kids still had to be taken to school, the visits to the supermarket had to be made. Without her, the whole family would surely have gone under. Tongue firmly placed in cheek, Bob Willis wondered aloud whether Botham might not have ended up in prison had he not married Kath so early. An exaggeration or not, the consequences for Botham in the absence of her counsel would have been desperate indeed.

On the field, too, there were people with his interests at heart. Moving to Worcestershire in 1987, he found Phil Neale to be an intelligent skipper who used him well and who allowed him to be himself, within reason. At county level, the years beneath the cathedral at Worcester were perhaps the best of his life. If nothing else, at that lower level he was still a consummate performer, a genuinely threatening all-rounder who could still make a decisive contribution with the ball. Neale was the ideal county captain for a player like Botham. Simply by getting Botham to the club he had gone out on a limb. Some members had voiced their disquiet over Botham's reputation and were worried that his arrival might disrupt the smooth running of the club. Botham was anxious to repay his new captain's confidence in him. Neale used him better than any captain since Mike Brearley, Botham stating in his autobiography that 'here was a man who knew how to handle his players and understood enough about their personalities to get the most out of them'. For his part, Neale makes the whole thing sound so easy:

Ian has a good cricket brain. I always tried to get his input wherever possible. He accepted that I was the captain and made the decisions but he was always ready and able to offer an opinion and I went out of my way to seek it. Even on the field, crossing between overs, I'd say, 'How do you think it's going, Beefy? What d'you reckon?' We only had one disagreement that I can remember which was about him wanting to carry on bowling when I wanted Graham Dilley to have a go! A lot was made of 'can you handle Ian Botham' but his commitment to the players he was working with was excellent. He's at his best when he's one of the boys in the dressing room with the team aiming for something in particular. His commitment to whatever side he's playing for means that he's not difficult to handle as long as you're sensible and you accept that he is different, that he's got a lot of other things going on in his life. You can't just treat him like any ordinary cricketer and that was our approach. I think by the time he came to Worcestershire the England captaincy ambitions had gone and at county level it would have been difficult for him to lead a side, going off to Tests and so on. He had a lot to contribute if you were prepared to ask and he was an invaluable senior professional and vice captain. If you involved him, he had a lot to contribute.

That assessment is an interesting contrast with Brian Lara as seen through the eyes of his county captain, Dermot Reeve. On his arrival at Warwickshire in 1994, Lara had just beaten Sobers' record for the highest individual Test score with his 375 in Antigua and was the biggest cricketing star since Botham. Despite the occasional problem, Lara had managed to sustain an enviable reputation as a nice young man coping well with stardom, quite the opposite to the perception of Ian Botham circa 1986. Yet in Reeve's book, *Winning Ways*, he devotes an entire chapter to the disruption that Lara caused at Edgbaston among the players and in the committee rooms. One thing that Lara understands far better than Botham ever did is the value of good public relations. If Botham had, just occasionally, done the 'right' thing, the 'expected' thing – a net session here and there, or a contrite, if insincere, apology from time to time, for example – he might have saved himself a lot of trouble. That was not the Botham way however, and he often found himself in trouble simply because of his honesty.

Though David Graveney skippered him for a couple of inconsequential seasons at Durham, the last captain of any note in Botham's career was Graham Gooch. Though the two had a great deal of respect for each other's abilities, neither was sold on the other's means for arriving at an end, nor were they always personally compatible. In the end, Gooch was proved right, at least in so far as cricketing longevity is concerned. Even now, at the age of forty-three, Gooch could still open the innings for England in a home series and give a good account of himself, while Botham had ceased to be fit enough to play convincingly at international level even before he played his swansong games under Gooch. Just as Boycott had turned net practice into a way of life, so Gooch and England manager Micky Stewart were fetishists where physical fitness was concerned. Though Botham and Gower had never needed to worry about that early on – Gower naturally fit, Botham incredibly strong – in the second half of his career Botham would have been helped by paying a little more attention to his diet and to his overall levels of fitness. Yet even after Gooch's revolution, referring to England's out cricket on the Ashes tour of 1994/95, Peter Roebuck pointed out in *The Cricketer* that 'England's cricket takes too little heed of fitness, not too much'. Mike Atherton concurred in the

December 1996 issue of *Wisden Cricket Monthly*: 'I am not a fitness fanatic and I don't enjoy it per se. But I have never known a fitter cricketer be a worse one and have known plenty who have benefited by it ... over the last two winters, my own performances have certainly suffered at the end of a long, arduous tour.' Few would suggest that Atherton's poor form with the bat in Zimbabwe was down to his being too fit, while the English team as a whole was not beset by the rash of injuries that had attended many previous tours.

In truth, Gooch and Botham were always a potentially combustible mixture because their attitudes to the game differed so much. Furthermore, circumstances conspired so that they must have viewed each other with some suspicion. Back in 1982, Graham Gooch had been the captain of the South African Breweries XI that made the rebel tour of South Africa, threatening Test cricket in its wake. Botham had been the prime target of the organisers but had turned down the opportunity. That decision was partly conscientious objection out of deference to friends like Richards and Garner and his own distaste for apartheid, partly a careful weighing up of the financial implications of such a move, and partly a refusal to betray his country by ducking out of Test cricket for a lengthy period. Having already been at odds with Gooch over fitness training in the West Indies, Botham must have felt let down by those younger players who sold out to the South Africans. Just as dispiriting for him must have been the way in which he took all the criticism for England's failure in the West Indies in 1985/86 when it was Gooch who had done as much as anyone to undermine team spirit, another legacy of that South African odyssey. Selected for the tour in the wake of his wonderful summer of 1985 against Australia, Gooch was England's great hope against the West Indian fast bowlers, but he spent much of the tour in bitter introspection as anti-apartheid demonstrators targeted him wherever he went. That was enough to wear anyone's resolve down and Gooch cut a morose, dejected figure for much of the tour, even threatening to fly home at one point after Antigua's deputy prime minister suggested, erroneously, that Gooch had apologised for going to South Africa. Just as one has to have some sympathy for Botham's outrageous treatment at the hands of the press, one must accept that Gooch was under immense pressure in the West Indies and could be forgiven for snapping. But Botham had never threatened to quit the tour as Gooch had, and yet England's poor team spirit was supposedly all his fault. His pronounced sense of injustice must have found that hard to bear.

Perhaps the final straw with Gooch came when Botham was controversially omitted from the 1989/90 tour of the West Indies, of which more later. Suffice to say at this point that Botham had turned down an extremely lucrative offer to go to South Africa that winter on the understanding that he would make the plane to the Caribbean, only to be let down at the final moment. Having made himself unavailable for just two England tours in his entire career – one to India when he was in desperate need of a rest, the other to Pakistan and the World Cup of 1987 when he was trying to avoid the press pack by wintering in Australia – he was now cast aside by a hierarchy which had apparently begged him not to go to South Africa. And the captain of that side who didn't need him? Graham Gooch, a man who had in Botham's opinion turned his back on his country in 1982. If Gooch and England manager Micky Stewart felt the presence of the 'champagne set' players like Botham and Gower undermined them, Botham must have been every bit as uneasy with their rise to the summit of English cricket.

As a reaction to these disappointments Botham had subsequently scoffed at Gooch's methods as captain, and perhaps they were too rigid, not allowing some players to be themselves. The slack that Phil Neale cut Botham at Worcester was essential for his psychological well-being, yet it has to be said that Gooch is living proof that there is some sense in the medicine he prescribed. England's up and down performances under his captaincy cannot be laid purely at his door – like many leaders before him, he was often let down by the material with which he had to work. Of course David Gower should have been selected far more regularly than he was, but it was Botham who ruled himself out of contention by reason of his own inadequacies, not Gooch or Stewart. The facts are that by 1989 Botham's bowling was not of international class and he rarely showed the application necessary to displace the likes of Allan Lamb and Robin Smith from England's top order, while it was also surely time to give up and coming players such as Alec Stewart and Mike Atherton a chance. If Gooch has some culpability in the premature end of Gower's career, his hands are clean when it comes to Botham. A healthier partnership between the two post-1989 would have been most welcome for English cricket, for potentially Botham still had a lot to offer as a batsman and even more to offer as an entertainer. Even when he was struggling, Botham had that charismatic magnetism that drew people into cricket grounds. Had he looked at his technique and health as rigorously as Gooch did, he might have been packing Test grounds for three or four years longer, enchanting his fans with pyrotechnic displays.

Like the rest of us, Botham made his good decisions and his bad, and he was unfortunate in losing those who could have made a difference at crucial times. He was not the only person who was badly advised though, for the men who run the game at Lord's all too rarely did the right thing by their hottest property.

CHAPTER FIVE

Whom Lord's Would Destroy
They First Drive Mad

The Establishment

One of the more tempestuous relationships in Ian Botham's career has been that with cricket's establishment, be that the England selectors, management, or the Test & County Cricket Board. To simplify matters, these can all be classified under the all-embracing umbrella of 'Lord's'. Botham is not the first player to feel that he has grievances against the powers that be and nor will he be the last. Any cricketer who threatens to transcend the game can expect to feel the wrath of the Establishment coming down upon his head. Anyone who whips up frenzied public support, intentionally or unintentionally, while behaving in an unconventional manner is looking for trouble. And anyone who can crack a century on a couple of hours' sleep after a good night out is just too damned clever for his own good in the eyes of some.

The irony of Botham's position was unconsciously made clear in Trevor Bailey's obituary to Bill Edrich. Published in *The Cricketer* in June 1986, just after England's squad had returned from the vilification heaped on them for their lackadaisical attitude in the West Indies and Botham's banning from the game, it was hard not to smile at Bailey's portrait of Edrich: 'Bill lived and played hard, firmly believing that life was for living, not for existing. Blessed with exceptional stamina, he considered it neither necessary, nor desirable to retire to bed early simply because he happened to be batting in a Test, an outlook which did not always appeal to the establishment who did not possess the same enthusiasm for the parties.' This is of course the same Bill Edrich now commemorated at Lord's by the Compton & Edrich stand. Let's not forget that Mr Compton also knew a thing or two about parties. From Bailey's sketch, it seems likely that Edrich and Botham would have enjoyed each other's company had they been contemporaries.

Other players from the past have upset the apple cart in differing ways. Fred Trueman was as popular with the cricketing hierarchy as an outbreak of cholera simply because he spoke his mind. Consequently, he made just four of the eight England tours conducted while he was an active Test player, despite being England's most explosive bowler. He dedicated his autobiography, *Ball Of Fire*, to 'all young cricketers of independent spirit, in the hope that they might learn from it some of the pitfalls into which their pride and self-respect will surely lead them'. Although Botham and Trueman have rarely seen eye to eye, *Ball Of Fire* could have been a set text for the young Somerset all-rounder; media intrusion aside, Trueman was assailed by all the same difficulties that were to besiege Botham.

Players from Yorkshire have seemed particularly prone to problems with Lord's, proof of the existence of the north/south divide, presumably. It was a tension exacerbated by the particular strain of bloody-mindedness that

made the county such a formidable outfit but which failed
to endear them to the old school tie types that ruled the
game. Brian Close lost the captaincy as a disciplinary
measure. Ray Illingworth's relations with Lord's were rarely
cordial, and even Geoffrey Boycott was heard to complain
that 'the establishment seems to want my ability but not
me'. In his aggressive attitude to the game, Botham's
mentality was similar to that of the great Yorkshire sides
of the 1950s and 1960s, though his sometimes extravagant
batting would rarely have gone down well in their dressing
room. It was no surprise that he was in regular conflict
with Lord's.

Ian Botham's problem was simple: he was the first
cricketing superstar of the media age and, as such, he
swamped the game. People who didn't want to know
anything about cricket wanted to know everything about
Botham. He was talented, exciting, charismatic. He pulled
people into the grounds wherever he went and the press
and TV responded warmly to him, at first. For a time, Ian
Botham was English cricket and English cricket was Ian
Botham. He appeared to wield enormous power and threatened the cosy hegemony of Lord's. Understandably wary
of the cult of personality which had inflated Tony Greig
and Ian Chappell to the point where they could front Kerry
Packer's circus, the Establishment did not wish to run the
risk of Botham being able to do likewise in the company
of another multi-millionaire mogul.

It's vital here to look at the priorities of the authorities.
The World Series circus which was rooted in the idea of
selling cricket for its true value, expanding the game's
popularity, making a few more dollars for Kerry Packer,
and putting a more reasonable salary in the pockets of the
players, was treated as a Judas-like betrayal. Decades-old

friendships were destroyed as the Establishment worried about the loss of players to this media tycoon, and yet the life of international cricket was never actually threatened, simply the position of Lord's and the MCC as the arbiters of the game. The players who plumped for Packer were reviled and Greig in particular has never been forgiven by some. All this over what is, after all, just a game. Yet when Gooch and then Gatting led rebel sides to South Africa, threatening to rip the very fabric of Test cricket on racial lines and, more importantly, giving succour, however unwittingly, to a repugnant form of government, the atmosphere was less vitriolic. The prodigal Gooch and Gatting along with others were welcomed back to the fold at the first opportunity, Gooch ascending to the England captaincy. At one stage, the MCC even tried to organise a touring side of their own for a visit to South Africa. That was perhaps its darkest hour, but then as cricket's greatest writer, C.L.R. James, points out in *Beyond A Boundary*, 'What do they know of cricket, who only cricket know?'

The governing instinct of any form of establishment is survival if only for survival's sake. It does not matter if there are no other objectives, no plans for the future. All that matters is the retention of power. Once a group's status is under threat, it is galvanised into action, taking up arms against those who would defeat it. It is the fate of any iconoclast therefore to be mistrusted and despised, to be attacked with the full might of that establishment. These authorities may appear genteel and gentlemanly but they are street fighters at heart for whom all is fair in time of war, willing to deploy all the weapons at their disposal. This is perhaps their greatest, most lethal advantage, for those who are considered their opponents are regularly taken aback by the vitriol of these city gents, their venom couched in terms of apparently sweet reason. That is not to say that rebels are always in the right. It is in the very nature of rebellion to swipe at targets indiscriminately, often behaving every bit as badly as the quarry. Perhaps this is just from a lack of thoughtful analysis, perhaps it's the natural excesses of the wayward, unconventional spirit, perhaps it's done deliberately to provoke and annoy. Whatever the case, one has to remember that the aspects of a rebel's character upon which society frowns are often the roots of their greatness. Botham's stubborn belief in himself and his refusal to 'play the game' could be exasperating at times, but without that determination to go his own way, he would not have been half the cricketer.

Truly arriving on the Test match scene in 1978, Botham was the proverbial breath of fresh air. With English cricket having lost some of its greatest personalities to Kerry Packer, most notably Tony Greig and Alan Knott, here was a man who could take the centre stage and fill the gaping void they'd left behind. In any era, Ian Botham would have been a giant; in 1978, he was the answer to cricket's prayers. To use the vernacular, he put bums on seats, more bums on a greater number of seats than any Englishman since Denis Compton. Even though the Tests against Pakistan and New Zealand were woefully one-sided affairs, spectators still came through the gates, most of them to see the latest Botham performance; Gower's arrival that year had a similar, if far less dramatic, impact.

For the next couple of years, Botham's star was relentlessly in the ascendant as he routinely picked up man of the match and series awards as England won Test after Test. He achieved the fastest Test double of 1000 runs and 100 wickets in history. Blasting the Indians into submission, he missed a Test hundred before lunch at Headingley by a single run. He regularly notched up centuries and bagged five wickets in an innings as though such an achievement were routine. So completely did Botham dominate the field of action that for a while it even looked as if he might become the first man to take 500 Test wickets and score 9,000 Test runs. He was irresistible, unbeatable, unstoppable. All the while, the cash registers were whirring and ticket office telephones ringing. Botham was doing well out of the game but the game was doing much, much better out of him. It's in the nature of life that such a run of unbridled good form and fortune cannot last for ever. Yet Botham was such a phenomenon, such a force of nature, that it seemed he might rewrite every rule and every record in the book. If he continued to take on all comers and to improve at such an exponential rate then there was no telling what he might achieve in a full career. By 1979, a paranoid hierarchy at Lord's was certainly starting to become more than a little apprehensive of his potential for he was winning broad popular appeal. To the frightened men in power, this was akin to a leader of the opposition having huge support among the electorate, support that might be utilised not at all benignly or, more worrying, in the pursuit of change. Having just resolved the Packer crisis, Lord's had no wish to see its power compromised by a member of the national side.

Human nature is deeply distrustful of the messianic, with good reason. However, before we go nailing every messiah to a tree just for the sake of it, we should ask if we are doing ourselves harm in the process. In a different sphere, for instance, the public crucifixion of such left-wing leaders as Tony Benn or Nye Bevan, both adherents of the kind of radical politics that might have done the country more good than certain policies we've had since the war, did democracy a great disservice and robbed the nation of the opportunity to choose a different set of ideas and ideals to those which prevailed. The systematic humbling of Ian Botham, a man with no wider agenda than to live his life in as enjoyable a manner as possible, was handled in the same way and did the game of cricket a great injury. The attitude percolating from Lord's may well have been at the root of the eventual public vilification that threatened to destroy him, but it was achieved with the active connivance of the media, particularly the tabloid press. It's fair to say it was also achieved with the assistance of Botham himself.

It is true that those with remarkable qualities are often seen as slightly unhinged, fairly or not. Often that is evidence of little more than indifference to what people may think of them and a determination to do things their way, to behave in a manner that is ahead of their time. Those that have sometimes been derided in life – Presley, Lennon, Dean, Cobain – are often granted iconic status in death, usually because they die early before they've had the chance to ruin their iconoclastic reputation. (Had Botham conveniently passed away at the Oval in 1981 – better still, had he been assassinated by a distraught Kim Hughes – we would now have shrines to Saint Ian up and down the land.) Botham *was* different, undeniably so, and he was attacked for it by many old-stagers. He had no time for the niceties of diplomacy. He had no need to observe the time honoured social graces of the game. He was not deferential to authority, offering his support only when it was deserved. He lived hard and yet was still able to play hard. He never thought defeat was possible, no matter what the situation. He made extravagant promises that seemed to be nonsense, but then he'd go out on the field and turn them into reality. He may not always have had the composed assurance of a Viv Richards or the grace and guile of a Dennis Lillee, yet he managed to perform feats that equalled the best of either of them. His huge frame was important, just as is currently the case with the dominant All Black Jonah Lomu (a confrontation between him and Liam Botham would be worth watching), but again we must accept that the crucial difference was his self confidence. To mere mortals, seeing someone so sure of himself can be an unnerving experience. To make us feel better, we label them eccentric. They're just different, that's all.

Botham was a little unfortunate in some ways. From the point of view of the authorities he was the wrong personality at the wrong time. When, in 1962, the forces held within Pandora's Box demanded their release and the distinction between amateur and professional was abolished, the men at the top of the tree must have suspected they were living on borrowed time. That distinction was one of the most stultifying aspects of the English game, one which had become quite ludicrous by the time of its repeal. Though we are still some way from the ideal classless society, that 'upstairs downstairs' mentality was utterly repugnant in the post-war world. The end of 'gentlemen' and 'players' was a simple acceptance of the new egalitarian realities that were shaping the world. Though no one could have guessed how things would unfold, in hindsight the emergence of someone like Ian Botham was the logical conclusion of this period of change involving one day Tests, Kerry Packer, television and money. Taking the country with him, not only was he post-amateur man, he was post-Packer man too. For those at Lord's, there must have been genuine concern that these lunatics might take over their asylum – Botham was the pop star as cricketer. In truth, he was more Elton John that Johnny Rotten, but Lord's had him marked as the establishment-shredding punk rather than the outrageous entertainer.

Lord's resented Botham because he was the irreverent embodiment of change in what to them were its most repellent aspects – dear God, he was even attracting football supporters! Totally unimpressed by social ranking, Botham was in the vanguard of a meritocracy. If you deserved his respect, you got it; if you didn't, he wouldn't lower himself to worry about your values or your opinions. That refusal to suffer fools at all may have been evidence of a character lacking in tolerance, but it caught the mood of the times. The 1980s were the years when you did what you wanted to do. Who cared about anyone else? Botham was the 'me' generation gone mad and it must be said that some of his more boorish behaviour was evidence of the general coarsening of England. But against that, he was good, bloody good, at his job and he deserved the loadsamoney rewards and the power it gave him. The crowds loved him not just for his unrestrained joy and his cavalier play but because he so clearly put the fear of God into the fuddy-duddies who ran the game. As part of the first wave of international cricketers who actually got paid rather well, the more so for their off the field endorsements, Botham was not beholden to Lord's. He didn't have to go cap in hand to them to apologise for any misdemeanours, real or imagined, just so that he could keep his meagre pay and his place in the side. Botham wasn't just a cricketer, he was that new phenomenon, a celebrity. He was newsworthy and therefore marketable, and with the nation on his side he didn't need to worry about his behaviour, within reason. The public demanded that he play for England and the authorities did not dare leave him out. His constituency was the country, not the committee rooms in St John's Wood.

If cricket were an American game, there's little doubt that Oliver Stone would already have turned Botham's life into an epic movie, fuelled by conspiracy theories; Botham's autobiography is sufficiently paranoid – justifiably at times – to warrant it. The estimable Mr Stone would have men in bacon and egg ties crouching behind grassy knolls at the Nursery End, concocting wildly inappropriate England teams while Alec Bedser, the poor patsy, was locked in the apparent safety of a book depository somewhere in the Long Room. Even now, bearing in mind the fact that the English cupboard was pretty bare at the time, it's hard to understand how Ian Botham came to be elevated to the captaincy of England in 1980. That our finest cricketer, the man on whom our batting and bowling rested, a man with no real experience of leading any side, should suddenly be made responsible for leading a team against the most powerful bowling arsenal that had been assembled in almost fifty years is incredible, even more unlikely than the events of Headingley a year later. It's noted elsewhere that this was a surprisingly bold move by a nation that usually insists players should be all but in their dotage before getting a whiff of the captaincy. That's probably an understatement. To have a twenty-four-year-old lad who hadn't even been to public school, let alone university, running the England side was simply bizarre. It flew in the face of English cricketing history. At the time it seemed thrilling, a break with the past and the chance to embrace a new age. Oliver Stone would suggest he was promoted above his ability in order to destroy him, particularly when looking at the itinerary he would have to face. That would be taking things a little too far, but few at Headquarters were broken-hearted when Botham fell to earth in such dramatic circumstances.

Botham had done himself little good with his innocent, if reckless, involvement in the Scunthorpe night club brawl at Christmas 1980, when as England captain that was the last sort of situation he should have been getting involved in. There were other offences to be taken into consideration too: an unwillingness to accept any blame or criticism for England's defeats; the Blofeld scuffle; and a verbal altercation with the police when stopped for speeding on the eve of the First Test in 1980, police evidence reporting that he had said, 'I am Ian Botham and I will fight this all the way.' These were unfortunate, unsavoury incidents, best learned from, forgiven and forgotten. They were hardly evidence of incipient megalomania but they were matters that anyone hostile to him could use when the time was right. Certainly they were used to keep the England captaincy away from him for good once his tenure had ended in defeat. His sad demise was cause for some relief in the corridors of power, though once he had demolished the Australians at Headingley and re-established himself in the public mind, perhaps they might have reflected briefly that having Botham around as a loose cannon was rather more dangerous than having him on the inside.

In a candid moment, Botham would have to admit that he is in the Olympic class when it comes to bearing what he feels is a legitimate grudge. In his dealings with the members at Lord's over the course of two Tests in 1980 and 1981, he had more than enough justification for concluding that some of the MCC members were not worth the time of day. A more famous episode came when he returned to the pavilion after registering his first pair in Test cricket, his miserable walk back up the steps accompanied by a stony silence. Perhaps the members didn't know how to react to him, maybe they were genuinely embarrassed on Botham's behalf, but ignoring him was no way to treat a man who had given several virtuoso performances on that hallowed turf in the preceding seasons. What of his eight wickets and a century against Pakistan? What of his eleven wickets for 140 in the game against New Zealand? What of his five wickets against India? These great deeds were soon forgotten. In retaliation, whenever Botham made runs or took wickets at Lord's subsequently, he refused to acknowledge the members. Some might feel that was petty, but it was no less petty than their treatment of him.

His first run-in with them had come the year before during the showpiece Centenary Test against Australia. That gala occasion was ruined by bad weather and woefully inadequate ground covering; one might have expected the world's premier ground to have had rather better facilities given that cricket was now back in profit. Despite bright sunshine, following earlier heavy rain, play did not get under way on the Saturday until 3.45 p.m. In their frustration, some MCC members struck Botham and jostled umpires Dickie Bird and David Constant as they returned to the pavilion from yet another fruitless pitch inspection. When reading the leader articles in the national press castigating him after his brief flare-up with Henry Blofeld, Botham might have wondered why he was so virulently attacked when the behaviour of the MCC members had received scarcely any condemnation, despite taking place under the nose of their guest, the visiting Australian captain. Outrage targeted against Botham was rationalised on the grounds that he was a 'public figure' and 'role model', always nebulous justification. Surely bad behaviour is bad behaviour? David Frith's editorial in *Wisden Cricket Monthly* noted that the disgraceful conduct of this self-appointed elite destroyed 'any concept that violence lurks only in the "outer" ', a telling point against those lamenting the loss of those far off days when cricket grounds were silent places ringing to occasional polite applause.

Not content with attacking the captain of England physically, many members of the Establishment were willing to assault him mentally too. The Centenary showpiece petered out into a dull draw, an 'honourable' one as John Arlott termed it, certainly more honourable than the members deserved. However, Botham was again seen as the villain of the piece for refusing to chase 370 to win in 350 minutes. With Boycott making a typically dour century, England were never likely to get on terms with the asking rate and Botham was blamed for turning the game into a damp squib. He should have forced his team to score more quickly to make a game of it, it wouldn't have mattered if England had lost, ran the argument. That conveniently ignores the roasting Botham would have got for losing a Test match, the more so following his unsuccessful series against the West Indies. If the result was so unimportant, why did Greg Chappell set such a stiff target? If he had wanted to make a game of it, maybe he should have set England, say, 320 in even time. Chappell certainly wasn't willing to risk defeat, though his hand was forced a little by his desire to allow Kim Hughes the chance of registering a second hundred in the game. There can be little doubt that sections of the hierarchy held against Botham this failure to give the game a glorious finale. If England had engineered a nail-biting finish, that would have been the abiding memory of the match. As it was, the Centenary Test is still remembered for the inadequacy of the covers and the unforgivable irascibility of the members. Since Botham failed, indeed refused to try, to get them off the hook, he made more enemies in high places.

From then on, whenever there was an opportunity to annoy or undermine him, the authorities took it. For instance, when Botham finally took his weight problem seriously at the end of the summer, he took to playing football for Scunthorpe United. It helped him shed a few pounds and stay in trim. An edict was immediately issued to the effect that he should stop, that he was risking injury – this just before he was to face Michael Holding hurling a leather ball at his head at 90 mph. But as Jim Laker wrote in *Wisden Cricket Monthly* in December 1980, 'I cannot recall anyone offering this sort of criticism when Denis Compton, Willie Watson, Arthur Milton and scores of others were concerned.' Nevertheless, the whispering campaign intensified as results went badly. In the West Indies, Botham was then made to look foolish among his own players when Lord's refused to allow him to appoint his own vice captain once Bob Willis was forced to fly home injured.

His departure from the captaincy was a blessed relief to his admirers, like seeing a suffering dog put out of its misery. There was the inevitable lull, a drawing back from confrontation, partly because Botham concentrated on repairing his reputation, and partly because so successful was he in that, that for a time he became fireproof. Botham would occasionally do something stupid to let himself down – his haranguing of some Indian batsmen in 1981/82 was unnecessary, and his attack on Australian umpires in 1982/83 was unsportsmanlike, even if his comments were meant to be off the record, a naive hope for a man of his stature – but a truce was called in his relations with the

Establishment. They had more than enough on their plate with the constantly developing situation in South Africa. Following the end of the 1981/82 tour to India, fifteen English cricketers chose to tour there with a rebel side, throwing the whole future of Test cricket into doubt. Among those who did not take the rand were Bob Willis, David Gower and Ian Botham. Botham had been offered £85,000 to make the trip but refused. In part that was a financial decision, but unlike some players who felt that politics had no place in sport, the more so since there was nothing preventing big business making money out of South Africa, Botham was a genuine opponent of the apartheid system and refused to betray his basic principles. No man could be such a close friend of Viv Richards and remain unaware of the importance of the fight for racial equality. However, even Richards understood the realities of life for a professional sportsman, and when the offer came again in 1989 Richards encouraged Botham at least to talk to the South African authorities, telling him that 'you can't play for ever'. Of course, by 1989 there was cause for optimism that the struggle in South Africa was coming to a head, and that ill timed rebel tour had far less political significance than its predecessor.

This second honeymoon between Botham and Lord's was destined to be short lived; you can't be as frank, outspoken and successful as Ian Botham without making enemies on the way up. Never a diplomat, Botham rarely cared whether he trod on sensitive toes. Not only that, had he chosen to go to South Africa, he might have been considerably more popular with the upper echelons in English cricket. Their obligatory ban aside, many of those who went to South Africa have been treated well by the authorities: Gooch was made England captain and is now a Test selector, as are David Graveney and Mike Gatting; John Emburey is involved in the coaching set-up; Gatting took England's 'A' side to Australia in 1996; and Peter Willey is on the panel of umpires. Gower and Botham, two men whom the South Africans would have loved to get on board and who refused to go on both occasions, have been treated very badly in comparison. Perhaps there are other reasons, but one has to wonder if this is the payback for putting loyalty to the England side before the legitimisation of apartheid South Africa.

Cricket is still a deeply conservative game; it was even more so in 1982. There is a feeling among some that the Establishment secretly welcomed that first rebel tour and the prospect of cricket splitting along racial lines. There was bitterness, an angry reaction to their having been forced into a corner by the 'left wing' anti-apartheid movement throughout the 1970s, and having been forced to expel the South Africans from the international arena. Many MCC members had extensive business interests in South Africa and felt that the sporting boycott was the thin end of the wedge, preparatory to economic sanctions being demanded. There was a real desire to see the South Africans back in the fold. Since there was such sympathy for them, one has to wonder whether those who conferred legitimacy on them are now being rewarded at the expense of others.

The next storm broke on the 1983/84 tour of New Zealand and Pakistan under the stewardship of Bob Willis. The details of this particular episode are dealt with later but the reports carried in the national newspapers had important ramifications for Botham and his dealings with Lord's. Prior to leaving, the TCCB had again criticised him for taking 'ridiculously unnecessary risks' by playing two league games for Scunthorpe United, the board inviting

England's new hero prepares to meet Australia. Perth, December 1979.
© *Adrian Murrell, Allsport.*

(left) In the master's footsteps: Botham follows Brearley off the field. 1978. © *Allsport.*

(below) Stripped for action, Botham prepares to play for Scunthorpe United. December 1980. © *Adrian Murrell, Allsport.*

England's captain receives advice from Ken Barrington. 1981.
© Adrian Murrell, Allsport.

The quiet before the storm: David Bairstow and Botham join Viv
Richards and Clive Lloyd in the West Indian dressing room. 1981.
© Adrian Murrell, Allsport.

(above) The Messiah
and the multitude.
Headingley, 1981.
© *Adrian Murrell,
Allsport.*

(left) Botham goes
hunting for journalist.
Indo/Pakistan border.
January 1982.
© *Adrian Murrell,
Allsport.*

(right) Captain Gower and bowler Botham on point duty. Lord's, 1985. © *Adrian Murrell, Allsport.*

(below) 'For God's sake, keep going.' The fruits of Botham's greatest miracle. August 2 1986. © *Adrian Murrell, Allsport.*

'Who writes your scripts?' Botham equals Lillee's record with his first ball back after the drugs ban. England vs. New Zealand, the Oval, 21 August 1986. From left to right: Athey, Botham, French, Gooch, Gatting, Edgar.
© Adrian Murrell, Allsport.

Hannibal Botham arrives in Turin with his wife, Kath. April 1988.
© Adrian Murrell, Allsport.

(above) The King of
Panto! Oh no he isn't.
Botham meets co-stars
George and Zippy.
Bournemouth,
December 1991.
© *Chris Cole, Allsport.*

(right) 'Send your
mother-in-law next
time!' Pakistan's
revenge. Botham
dismissed by Akram
for 0. World Cup
Final, March 1992.
© *Ben Radford,
Allsport.*

Ian Botham always respects the validity of tabloid criticism.
© *Andrew Cornaga, Allsport.*

'Come on, Both. We'll flippin' murder 'em!' Botham the motivational coach in thoughtful mood with David Lloyd in Bulawayo, December 1996.© *Clive Mason, Allsport.*

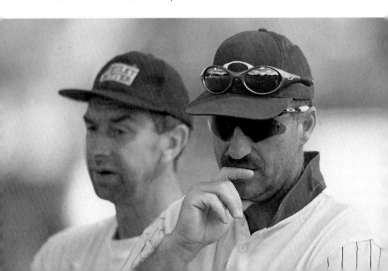

him to appear before its disciplinary panel on his return. While the suits may have had a point this time – his final game was just two days before the team flew out – it was poor motivational policy to threaten him in this manner. Given Botham's flagrant disregard for authority, the reaction provoked could only be an aggressive one which might impair his cricket. In addition, as Botham pointed out in his autobiography, at the same time Lamb and Gower were off skiing and Gatting was playing local league football. There were no reprimands for them.

For the first time, an English cricket team abroad was pricking the interest of the tabloid press, specifically their news reporters. The most serious allegation, carried in the *Mail on Sunday*, was that members of the team had been smoking 'pot' in New Zealand. It was a story given credence by England's abysmal showing at Christchurch when, on a poor wicket, they allowed New Zealand to rack up 307 before losing by an innings. Such amateurism could only be achieved amid the haze of funny cigarettes, according to the newspapers. A hastily organised TCCB inquiry quickly concluded that there was no case to answer and that the team had done nothing off the field that would adversely affect their performances on it. They stopped short of exonerating the players of the use of drugs and left the door open by saying that enquiries would be renewed in the event of significant new evidence coming to light. It was hardly a ringing endorsement of the party's behaviour. For the press, this verdict, of 'not proven' rather than 'not guilty' understandably smacked of a cover-up, Lord's brushing unsavoury accusations under the carpet. Our moral guardians were indignant. Given that Ian Botham was the most prominent member of the party and that he had acquired a reputation as a relentlessly enthusiastic socialiser and party-goer, most of the allegations adhered to him. The fact that he had to fly back home after the First Test in Pakistan for a knee operation was also seen as suspicious. Some tried to suggest that the TCCB had ordered him home to take the pressure off the rest of the squad (it's a little unlikely that Botham would have had his knee opened up by a surgeon purely to draw the hacks off the scent). One thing was clear, however: it was Botham who was the target of the press. He was great copy and he was also writing for the *Sun*, making him fair game for the rival publications. As one of the most celebrated figures in Britain, stories about him were the stuff of newspaper proprietors' dreams, and if no story existed, there were few problems in making one up. Once the TCCB had delivered their report, it was open season on Botham.

On tour each member of the party is an employee of the English cricketing Establishment. While that does not mean the TCCB owns them body and soul, it does mean they have a responsibility to them. Those found guilty of the charge of smoking dope could have been justifiably punished with heavy fines or a fixed term ban from the game, according to the gravity of the offence. (Given that the South African rebels were at this time still banned from Test cricket, maybe Lord's was frightened of what it might find, wary of outlawing, say, four or five more international class cricketers with a West Indian series looming.) Alternatively, the TCCB could have made a thorough investigation of the matter, rooting out the truth whatever the consequences. In the light of subsequent confessions (Ian Botham and Allan Lamb were candid in their respective autobiographies), the board must have been aware there was a certain amount of pot smoking going on in the privacy of hotel rooms. Intelligent men like A.C. Smith and Norman Gifford (manager and assistant on the New Zealand tour) were not easily hoodwinked; it is almost inconceivable that they were ignorant of the behaviour of their players. Once the facts had been established, a clearly worded statement could have been issued to the effect that, yes, certain players used pot in a social context but had absolutely not used any performance-enhancing drugs, that they had been fined a percentage of their tour fee, and warned that such conduct in future would not be tolerated under any circumstances. Instead, the authorities' desperate indecision sent out ambiguous, conflicting messages suggesting that players could continue to get away with anything. It's probable that had Botham been identified as the sole culprit in this sorry saga, such fudging would not have occurred: Lord's would have taken this chance to throw the book at him *à la* Ed Giddins. It was ironic that Botham should have behaved with such scant regard for the repercussions on a tour headed by A.C. Smith. After all, Smith was one of the very few members of the English hierarchy for whom Botham had any time. He had proved invaluable as manager of Botham's first trip to the West Indies in 1980/81, for Smith's skills as a cricketing diplomat cannot be underestimated. Later in his career, when he was marooned at Lord's, often having to defend the indefensible in his role as chief executive of the TCCB, Smith was mercilessly and unfairly lampooned by the press for his ability to speak on any subject at length and still say nothing. It would be fairer to say that by keeping his own counsel, Smith's behaviour might have been a good example that others could have followed. Without doubt, A.C. Smith has always had the good of the game of cricket at heart. The corollary to that is that he realises the players are the most important component of the game, infinitely more important than the Establishment and as such his brief, especially on tour, was to make life as comfortable as possible for his charges. For that reason alone, he was a man to whom Botham could relate, the latter noting in his autobiography that 'he saw the players' point of view and, when he could, he backed us to the hilt'. It was a shame, then, that Botham and Lamb should have let him down during the course of the 1983/84 tour. Although Botham enjoyed Smith's recognition of the players' pre-eminence in the game, he did not yet understand Smith's view that the game was more important than any player. Nevertheless, there remains a genuine warmth between the two men for Botham is quick to appreciate anyone who gives his all to the game of cricket, in whatever capacity. Where the TCCB was concerned, he failed to find any other such kindred spirits.

With these sex 'n' drugs 'n' rock 'n' roll stories surfacing on a more or less regular basis, Botham reacted in the only way he knew how: he took the fight back to the newspapers and instituted proceedings for libel against the *Mail on Sunday*. In retrospect, it turned out to be a catastrophic decision; though the specifics were wrong, the generalities about his use of dope were correct. Even so, it's easy to see how Botham fell into the trap. If he had done and said nothing, people would have assumed the stories to be true, the pernicious 'no smoke without fire' reaction to scandals. His reputation would be shattered, his commercial value reduced. As Botham pointed out in a later *Mail on Sunday* article, 'it seemed to me that everything I had fought for and worked so hard to achieve would be at risk'. The press had also challenged his virility, tempting him to put up or shut up. He couldn't resist that kind of challenge. In addition, his children were being hurt by the publicity, friends taunting Liam with the stories about his father. Botham might have been an idiot in some respects, but a six-year-old cannot be blamed for the inadequacies of his father, nor should he be put through the wringer on his account. Botham chose to clear his name for the sake of himself and his family.

If he'd been unpopular with the authorities before, he really put himself out on a limb this time. By taking on the Fourth Estate, Botham was threatening to blow everything wide open. The press never take a libel case lying down, especially if they feel there is some evidence to be found. In the absence of it, a little more mud slinging will make it impossible for the litigant, in this case Botham, to get a fair hearing. With that in mind, the situation facing cricket became more serious. Never mind what happened to Botham, this reflected on the integrity of the game.

As cricket's popularity had grown over the previous few years – thanks in no small measure to charismatic players like Botham, Imran, Richards and Gower – the game's place in the world had changed too. The treasured image of the quiet village game had gone for good. Cricket, like it or not, was now a part of the entertainment industry, no longer part of the Corinthian sporting world. Its profile had changed irrevocably and so had the position of its players. Cricketers like Botham were glamorous, comparatively wealthy, exciting people to be around. They were just like pop stars, a cricket tour running on almost exactly the same lines as a tour by a major rock band. Young men, often unencumbered by wives and girlfriends, rolled into town for a few days before heading out again. Cricket attracted more and more hangers on, even its own groupies, drawn by that romantic cowboy ideal. With attractive young women desperate to catch the eye of an international cricketer, it wasn't difficult for a resourceful journalist to put together a story or two along the lines of 'drug addled cricketer in three in a bed orgy shock horror' filled with lots of circumstantial evidence. A lot of those stories could have been avoided if wives and girlfriends had been allowed or even encouraged to travel with their men. There are practical and logistical difficulties, of course, but these could be overcome. Lord's, however, did not approve, though happily it seems as if that message has finally got home and the policy looks set to change in future. Mike Atherton's men touring Zimbabwe and New Zealand in 1996/97 were expected to endure the arduous three-month tour without seeing their families. Highly competitive, highly charged young men were expected to give their all for England on the field, come off the field and be tucked up in bed at nine o'clock. If we'd chosen a team of monks this would be fine. Otherwise, it is highly unrealistic and is simply inviting the press to write scandal stories, the more so if England are getting beaten.

That was essentially what went on in the West Indies in 1985/86 while the libel case was pending. The news reporters were sent out in droves to dig the dirt about Botham. The four-month tour became one long list of stories about Botham and drink, Botham and drugs, Botham and women. Had the tour gone on any longer, we'd probably have heard about Botham and a flock of sheep. Little wonder that the tour fell apart as a result, Botham living like a hermit, retreating to his hotel room, which became known as the Batcave. Rather fortuitously, Botham's father-in-law, Gerry Waller, flew out to join him in Barbados when he was at his lowest ebb. It was during this period that Mick Jagger invited Botham and some friends, Waller included, to a party at his island home. Lindy Field, a former Miss Barbados, was at the party too. A couple of weeks later, her version of events was splashed all over the tabloids, a story of cocaine and broken beds in the house of a Rolling Stone. The best alibi in the world in such circumstances is your father-in-law, and so Botham's marriage was preserved, Kath having long since realised that what you read in the tabloid press is not always the pure, unadulterated truth. Botham's reputation, however, was harder to salvage. By now, it was long gone.

Back in St John's Wood, stories such as these were just further proof of Botham's unsuitability to represent England. Yet the biggest blow was still to come. Recognising that the tabloid campaign of disinformation was unbeatable, Botham had to withdraw his libel suit. Making his peace with the *Mail on Sunday*, he was required to write a front page article that, when it appeared on 18 May 1986, confirmed he had used pot in the past. This time there was to be no reprieve for Botham. Disgusted of Tunbridge Wells would have preferred him to be strung up, but the TCCB had to act within its remit. Ironically, it had brought in a new set of guidelines the previous year dealing with the moot topic of bringing the game into disrepute. The motivation? Botham's conviction for possession of cannabis on 14 February 1985. Supporting him for once, the authorities had decided that no further action need be taken in what was, after all, a police matter utterly unconnected with the game of cricket. However, they made it clear that anyone caught in similar circumstances in future would be for the high jump. Since Botham was the first to come before the beak under these new rules, the results were inevitable.

Even so, the two-month ban he received, ruling him out

of almost all of the summer's cricket, and potentially the winter's Ashes tour, seemed draconian to many. In a strongly worded editorial in July 1986's *Wisden Cricket Monthly*, David Frith was staunch in his support for Botham:

> ... banished for indiscretions that would have remained known to him alone and a few intimates had not a "newspaper" posing as a moral guardian triggered off a tragic train of events by splattering sensation all over its newspulp two years ago. Botham's punishment, laughably administered for "bringing the game into disrepute" when all he had done was bring himself into it, would have been appropriate only if he had been found guilty of misbehaviour while "in uniform". Meanwhile, his 63-day ban seems to have been calculated on the basis of suspicion of far greater misdemeanours. For giving some kind of story to the newspaper in order to avert a costly and inevitably messy court case – that newspaper's "exposé" having driven the first shaft into the national hero's body – Botham has found himself roped down by Lilliputians.

That was the crucial point. Botham had done nothing wrong 'in uniform'. Unlike the days of yore, Lord's no longer owned the souls of its cricketers. They pay them for their performances on the field of play, and after stumps are drawn their lives are their own. Of course sporting personalities become role models, but that is not of their choosing. When Ian Botham was a young boy of thirteen playing cricket on the school field, his dream was 'one day I'll play for England', not 'one day I'll play for England, be a good role model and bring together all the peoples of the world in peace and harmony through the light of my shining example'. One would hope that all sportsmen could be articulate, clean cut, smooth examples of upright citizenship like David Gower or Gary Lineker, but it's an unrealistic expectation. Just because a fellow is able to wield a bat with distinction, this does not make him a nuclear scientist, a role model, or even a nice chap. To confuse the deeds with the doer and then to foist other responsibilities upon them is self defeating. It's also a little bizarre that the organisations that promote the likes of Botham as beacons of morality then attempt to destroy those very icons in order to boost their profits. No one will deny that Botham has a self-destructive streak, but he was surely helped along the road by the media. Botham has done things of which he should not be proud, but then so have we all. Fortunately, we don't end up on the front pages of the tabloids.

There is an argument that people like Botham have no right to a private life, that because they are well paid they are public property. This is plain nonsense. Everything they do on and in connection with the cricket field is under scrutiny. That is as it should be for they are representatives of the nation. Some, Botham included, would do well to recall that not all criticism of their playing performances is vindictive, that some of it is justified, is constructively meant, and is often written with a heavy heart. If a man puts in a bad performance, the public are entitled to know whether he had a long net session or not the previous day. They are equally entitled to know whether said cricketer was up until three o'clock that morning at a riotous party, though for the sake of balance it would be nice to hear about that side of things when a batsman has just scored a hundred as well as when he has registered a duck. At those times, they are on duty and have a responsibility to the side and the cricketing public who pay at the gate. Anything that does not impact on performance, however, has little relevance. That is why punishment would have been more appropriate after the New Zealand tour than when the *Mail on Sunday* article initiated it a couple of years later. In Botham's case, he did blur the lines somewhat by going public himself. Entering the public confessional only whets the appetite for more revelations. Nevertheless, that did not change the fact that his pot smoking was not connected with his cricket. His unusual contrition made it equally clear that he was not proud of what he had done, but also asked for understanding of the difficult lifestyle thrust upon celebrities. Essentially, Botham threw himself on the mercy of the court, the court being the British public, a public who, by and large, weren't bothered by his confession. Indeed, judging by the ovation he received on his return to Test cricket at the Oval in August, his popularity had increased. He knew which way the wind was blowing, and on this occasion he was bowling with his back to it.

Had the TCCB acted with more resolution back in 1984, perhaps the whole fiasco could have been avoided. Had it stood up to the press there and then, perhaps the message might have struck home. By abdicating its responsibility at that stage, it created a crisis far worse than that which had originally existed, letting the baying hounds know there was something to hide. It was inevitable the press would do everything they could to uncover it. At times like these, the instinct for self preservation takes hold; if sacrificial lambs are required, then so be it. In the modern age, self preservation effectively translates as doing whatever the media tells us to do. If the press can be appeased, if they can be bought off by some kind of remedial action, the crisis passes for another day. In another context, former Chancellor of the Exchequer Norman Lamont made the point quite eloquently: 'we give the impression of being in office but not in power'. That describes the cricketing authorities exactly: always reacting, never shaping.

The TCCB might have felt let down by Botham's actions, particularly in view of the events of the previous February. It had just cause for feeling disappointed. However, as Frith had pointed out, if anyone had been done harm, it was Botham himself. As a drug user and as someone who had broken the law – whatever his personal opinion of that law – his judgement was called into question. The notoriety would also harm his commercial profile. These were stiffer punishments than two months away from cricket, a break that did him little harm and a great deal of good if his performances in Australia that winter were anything to go by. It also ill behoves an organisation which gratefully receives large amounts of money from tobacco companies and breweries to deliver long sermons about the evils of drugs. Predictably, the hang 'em and flog 'em brigade felt that the punishment was far too lax. Botham was setting a poor example to our children and should be drummed out of the game. Surely if a famous cricketer has a greater influence on a child than his or her own parents, it was not Botham that needed to take a good look at himself but the parents concerned. In 1986 those children were as likely to have pictures of rock and pop bands plastered over their walls as pictures of Botham. It would be a pretty sheltered child indeed who hadn't heard of the seamier side of rock 'n' roll. Were we going to ban Bananarama or Eric Clapton for all eternity? A nice idea perhaps, but a shade unfair! And just how do those parents explain away the fact that then, they felt a cricketer should get a life ban for smoking dope, while now, just a few years later, the Oval Office in Washington DC is occupied by someone who has also admitted to smoking pot?

The drugs case out of the way, Botham and the authorities co-existed in a mood of mutual suspicion. Intelligently, when selected for touring duties in Australia that winter, Botham took the family. With his wife Kath on hand at all times, unearthing another sex scandal taxed even the most zealous reporters and he enjoyed his most successful and trouble-free tour. This was meant to be Botham's swansong overseas. Signing a three-year deal with Queensland from 1987/88, he had decided to set up camp in Australia for part of the year, an arrangement that failed to last the course. Even so, things remained on an almost even keel, the more so since 1988 was written off when Botham spent the year on the sidelines nursing his back; that 1980 injury had finally deteriorated so badly that surgery became essential.

Coming back to the game in 1989, Botham was bursting with life. With things to prove to himself and the world, he had a goal once more, vital if he was to concentrate fully on his cricket. He managed to reclaim his Test place while being simultaneously courted by the South African Cricket Board to go on Gatting's rebel tour. (Gatting had been another victim of the insensitivity at the top of the game and had lost out on the English captaincy in controversial circumstances. Disenchanted with his employers, he was off to make some money and also perhaps to gain a measure of vengeance.) According to Botham, sums approaching £500,000 had been mentioned, enough to give anyone pause for thought. Viv Richards had given Botham his blessing to go to South Africa and, with just a few cricketing years left in him, the opportunity to make that kind of money was sorely tempting. That the decision to go would have ended his Test career there could be no doubt: a four- or five-year ban for the rebels was a racing certainty. According to his autobiography, Micky Stewart 'on behalf of the England management was doing his best to persuade me not to go. They wanted me in the West Indies [that winter] he said and he pleaded with me to make myself available. They made it clear that if I did so, I was more or less guaranteed a place on the plane.' Though he hadn't been in great form in the three Tests he managed against Australia, Botham was desperately keen to go to the Caribbean one last time to exorcise the demons of his previous visits. The West Indians were the one blot on his escutcheon, the one team against which he'd never played well. Freed of his obligations to Queensland, this seemed like the ideal time to make amends. He told Ali Bacher of the South African board that he would not be making the trip.

Once the team for the West Indies was selected, all hell broke loose. Botham was not on the list. He received a call from Ted Dexter, who at least had the nerve to tell him personally of his omission. Dexter's part in events seems honourable; according to Alan Lee's biography, Dexter had always doubted whether Botham should make the trip. Gooch confirmed to Lee that 'before we even began the discussions, I was instructed to exclude both [Botham and Gower]. I think Ted and Micky wanted a new influence. They wanted to get away from the champagne-set image which had been around for a few years.' The record of the conversation between Stewart and Botham comes from Botham's autobiography. It may be that Botham wished to put a rosier tint on his omission from that tour, refusing to accept that he just hadn't done enough to be worthy of a place on the plane. It may be that there was a genuine misunderstanding between himself and Stewart or between Stewart and Dexter over the likelihood of his making it to the West Indies. Or it may be that his recollections are one hundred per cent accurate, in which case this was yet another in the ever expanding catalogue of appalling player–board relations, the result of crossed wires between Stewart and Dexter or a more malign attempt to ensure that cricket's biggest name did not go to South Africa with all the implications attendant upon that. Given that Gower was removed from the captaincy and dropped from the team at one and the same time, it's not hard to conclude that one way or another the men in charge were at fault once more. If that is the case, Botham's bitterness towards Lord's is eminently understandable. Given that they also had the power to make his life easier by offering a greater degree of support when it was needed, we the cricketing public might also feel bitter that they shortened the useful life of the most exciting player of his generation.

CHAPTER SIX

I Read the News Today. Oh Boy.

Life with the Fourth Estate

More than any sporting life since that of George Best, Ian Botham's career was one which unfolded in the pages of the newspapers. All manner of deeds, some true, some false, some exaggerated, some physically impossible, were ascribed to him over his cricketing times. Much though he protests at press intrusion and the exercising of the tabloids' collective imagination, it's hard to avoid the conclusion that, materially at least, it did him more good than harm. At a time when cricketers were anything but prosperous – his Somerset salary for 1986 when Botham was perhaps the most famous man in the country was just £15,000 – his regular appearances in the media helped make him one of the most marketable commodities in sport. Against that must be measured the psychological strain that was placed upon him and, more importantly, upon his wife and family who were frequently innocent bystanders, caught up in the storms of controversy that raged about him. Kath learned to cope with the outrageous stories, discounting the newspapers and getting all her information from the source, but it was everyday life that was difficult, having to put up with comments from friends or even complete strangers about her husband's latest apparent indiscretion. For the children, prey to playground taunts about their dad, that was a worse problem still. Perhaps if the scandalmongers were exposed to the havoc wreaked by their thoughtless use of innuendo and invention, we might finally get a responsible press. It's a forlorn hope.

Unlike contemporaries such as Gower who was always highly regarded by the public thanks to his essentially inoffensive nature, Botham had left numerous hostages to fortune over the years. His belligerence and occasional disregard for his fans did not endear him to everyone. Failing always to be nice on the way up, there were plenty ready to remember that when he was on one of his periodic trips down. He admitted in his recent autobiography that over the course of his career he had been 'aggressive, tyrannical, chauvinistic and hot-tempered'; to that might be added terms such as boorish, thoughtless, and selfish, not all qualities that sat well with significant sections of the population. *Times* journalist Simon Barnes made the important point that 'fame' should not be confused with 'uncritical love', a failing which he termed the 'Botham Error'. In truth, people were not promising to support him for ever more but were simply responding to the cavalier nature of his deeds, the successes he had earned, the brief flurries of excitement that he brought into their workaday lives. They were also responding to the nature and wider expectations of fame and celebrity in the 1980s, a period in which you were expected to flaunt power and influence and not feel that doing so was vulgar. Woe betide those who lost the Midas touch for they were destined for the scrapheap faster than ever before. Once the great deeds had dried up and Botham ceased to be the loveable big kid let loose to wreak havoc on the sporting world, the cliché that any player is only as good as their last performance took effect. However, where some are allowed to fail and fade from view, perhaps to regroup and return later, Botham had raised expectations to such a level that he could not retreat into the calm waters of obscurity. Britain, especially England, had pinned their hopes of glory on him and a disappointed public turned on him once those expectations had been dashed. A summer can last a very long time if you are constantly losing Test matches.

The demands were far too stringent for any man to bear. Within a year of his Test match debut, Botham was no longer a mere cricketer but a symbol of the nation, a man who would make Britain great once again. Media-fuelled jingoism is discussed elsewhere in reference to the 1981 Australian series when Botham revelled in the orgy of flag waving that attended the Royal Wedding, but he was a figurehead of a resurgent nationalism much earlier than that. Perhaps the origins of this new patriotism can be traced to the Silver Jubilee celebrations of 1977 when the dull greyness of British life was forgotten for a few weeks amid street parties, fireworks and bunting. While the 1979 election was finally decided by the winter of discontent, the Conservatives would probably have won without it as Margaret Thatcher deftly tapped into and then encouraged the Little Englander mood that still prevails to this day in some sections of her party. It was a message that the Conservative press had long since pandered to in their general disaffection with all things foreign. Yet to make any lasting impact, ideas need to be fleshed out by personalities. Principles need faces, willing or not.

Countless media figures looked back to the days of

Empire with misty-eyed nostalgia and while it was obvious that those days could never come again, they felt no need to apologise for them either. Political correctness in the 1960s and 1970s had put the very strong case that the United Kingdom should be ashamed of its imperial past, that our colonisation of vast parts of the world was not some great adventure but an act of territorial piracy. The heroes of yesteryear were held up as thieves, robbing the indigenous populations of their birthright. We should be proud of the way we gave India back to the Indians, not of the way we took it in the first place. The New Right, wrapped in the union flag and stung into action following our entry into the Common Market, dismissed these claims as heresy and tried to resuscitate the great dreams of Empire. As our international influence diminished, so their rhetoric grew louder and more strident.

In Jubilee year, comparisons with Queen Victoria were inevitable; where her court had been full of Empire-builders, explorers and adventurers par excellence, Queen Elizabeth was surrounded by dull conformity. When he burst on to the scene in 1977, Botham was a breath of fresh air, a burst of unrestrained energy whose obvious joy in his cricketing successes caught the public's imagination. He quickly filled the gap, satisfied the public need for a soldier of fortune in whom we could revel, whose deeds we could glorify. We might not run Australia any longer, but by God, we could give them a damn good thrashing on the cricket field. As the next few years unfolded and his feats became increasingly prodigious, Botham was represented as a latter-day W.G. Grace, the embodiment of the pioneering entrepreneurial spirit that had made Britain great.

The point about Ian Botham, particularly as seen through the eyes of the tabloids, is that if he hadn't existed, they'd have been forced to invent him. That was the problem. The Ian Botham who filled the pages of the *Sun* and the *Daily Mirror* didn't exist. That swashbuckling Errol Flynn of a cricketer was only one part of his personality. The caricature that took hold in the public mind belied the realities of the doting father, loyal friend or concerned fundraiser for leukaemia research. In the brash mood of the times, that was not the image the press wanted to sell. They wanted a larger than life superman who could fight the foes, win the wars, right the wrongs. In the face of a changing world, they wanted reassuring images of simplistic certainty. The press fed off Botham and Botham fed off the press image of himself. Throughout his story, it is his astonishing self belief that is the greatest cause for comment. Never short of confidence, probably the last thing he needed as a man was to be told that he was invincible. That inevitably led to the misplaced belief that he was fireproof and that whatever he said and did would be fine. Had his notices been a little more balanced, perhaps he might have been better prepared for the pitfalls that came his way.

Off the field, Botham had his problems. When the guardians of morality advise men like Botham to turn the other cheek to provocation, they are scarcely talking from a personal acquaintance with the burden of celebrity. Equally, the public was never told of the times that Botham might have followed that code and simply walked away from trouble – 'Botham not involved in a pub brawl' is not news. Botham's confrontational style and combustible temperament was the very thing that made him so effective on the field; it's hypocritical to suggest that he should be Batman on the field and then live like a village grocer off it, a point eloquently made by Peter Tinniswood in the classic book *More Tales From A Long Room*. Where

Botham did fail was in exposing himself to such threats, particularly when he was the England captain. It might be unfair to expect that a young man should turn himself into a monk upon the conferral of that title, but Botham was all too often guilty of not fully accepting his responsibilities off the field. The captaincy of England is still an honour rather than a right, and with that honour goes a duty. Ian Wooldridge summed up the problem in the *Daily Mail*, pointing out that 'Botham's electrifying deeds on the cricket field have made him an incandescent figure whose influence on impressionable youth is probably greater than that of any other British sportsman. This carries a responsibility which all too often he has not acknowledged.' It is rough justice to saddle a rumbustious young man with the position of role model for a generation, but that now goes with the territory. Today's players are perhaps happier with that since they've grown up with those expectations. As one of the first stars of the media age, when flaws were exposed with relish, Botham was exploring uncharted waters, the rules evolving around him.

The first perceptible downturn in Bothamania came in 1980 when he was reduced to the status of the mere mortal by a lethal combination of a bad back and Clive Lloyd's West Indians. The level of criticism this drew was perhaps out of proportion to England's real defects, but then this is always the case nowadays. Very few people take criticism of any kind well, but Botham and his team were remarkably thin skinned. Attacks on the side's perceived deficiencies were fair game. The press were there to write about the cricket as they saw it. If Henry Blofeld felt Botham's captaincy was childish, he must be at liberty to say so, just as Botham should be free to say that he felt Blofeld's comments were uninformed, irrelevant, or plain wrong. If a cricket correspondent watches the game, he must be given his say and players must respect that right – after all, many only get in the team once a pressman has destroyed a predecessor or written up an innings of his in glowing terms. By 1981, though, relations between the England side and the bona fide cricketing press were at a low ebb. Mike Brearley remarked that on his return to the England side in 1981, he found his players 'more embittered by the press than I'd ever known . . . I myself felt that rows were planted, cultivated and encouraged . . . by the modern craving for excitement and sensation'. Some cricket writers go beyond the confines of their job in order to get exclusives on the line-up for the next game and so on, but generally speaking they continue to do a good job; it is often their sub-editors who add lurid headlines to pieces that are comparatively mild. But anyone who puts themselves in the public eye should be ready for attack if it's warranted; you have only to listen to the trenchant commentaries of Bob Willis to realise that it's a very different game on the other side of the boundary. Willis' comments are often accurate and well informed, but I wonder how he'd have taken to them had they been directed at him in 1980? Botham was equally upset when the press questioned his abilities but his angry reactions only gave the press more reason to taunt him on and off the field. By offering plenty of provocation, they could guarantee themselves a juicy story.

With their man weakened by poor play on the field, it only needed one moment of stupidity by the England leader to make himself front page news for all the wrong reasons. In order to keep his weight down, Botham chose to train with Scunthorpe United prior to leaving for the 1980/81 tour of the Caribbean. Immersing himself in the affairs of the club, he quickly became a vibrant part of the dressing room and consequently he joined the team on a Christmas night out at Tiffany's night club. During the course of the evening one of his colleagues, goalkeeper Joe Neenan, was given a very rough time by a few locals who blamed him for the club's FA Cup exit a few weeks earlier. As night club arguments often do, the banter soon degenerated into a fight. Botham was on hand when Neenan struck one of his tormentors, the two having chased them for 600 yards. Inevitably, the story got into the papers and was portrayed as Botham attacking some innocent bystander. Once the story had worked its way through the courts, it became apparent that Botham had not been involved in the fight. He was found not guilty.

The die was cast, however. The great thing about smears is that, unwarranted or not, they are pernicious. They corrupt because they stick in the memory – David Mellor will forever seem faintly ridiculous not because he had an extra-marital affair but because he was supposed to have made love in a Chelsea shirt, later revealed as a press invention. Although Botham was not guilty – a decision not confirmed in the Crown Court until 23 September 1981 – he was a condemned man, a front page exposé waiting to happen. That was unfair, imposing an additional pressure to conform that did not suit him. However, he was reckless in failing to respond to the warning shot he'd received. Botham being Botham, he confirmed that he would do the same thing again. His loyalty to his friends was such that had Neenan been set upon by a gang the following day, he would almost certainly have become embroiled out of a sense of obligation. That is an admirable characteristic in many ways, but it could easily have led him into even more trouble: he might have been injured or he might have inflicted an injury on someone else merely by trying to separate the fighting factions. That Scunthorpe incident could have turned out much worse than it did and as such it should have opened his eyes to the difficult position he was in. From then on, he should have had the wit to avoid similar confrontations, or at least to try to avoid situations that could get out of hand. His failure to do so was manna for the press pack that followed his every deed.

While the runs were flowing and the wickets were tumbling in the patriotic summer of 1981, all was sweetness and light. He was providing the head of Kim Hughes on a plate as a royal wedding present. It was as if he were colonising Australia all over again, such was his bullishness in keeping with the times of celebration. A great self publicist, Botham was in the headlines all the time, perpetuating the image of the superman in whose glory we all basked. Sadly, from a newspaper angle good news becomes dull if repeated day after day. It's not upsetting or startling. It doesn't sell newspapers. Rupert Murdoch's stable, which included the *Sun* and the *News Of The World*, had been leading a gradual decline in the standards employed by the tabloid press, a decline which accelerated once Robert Maxwell arrived on the scene with his rescue of the *Daily Mirror*. The intense competition for circulation between the two led to newspapers desperately trying to trump one another with increasingly bizarre stories.

On the 1982/83 tour to Australia Botham had a pretty lean time with both bat and ball as England surrendered the Ashes he had protected so successfully in 1981. In what he felt was an off the record chat to a journalist, Botham complained at some length about the poor standard of Australian umpiring. This was something of a mantra in the England camp, the more so as the series went on.

Approaching the final Test two–one down, a win would save the Ashes. On the first morning and without a run on the board, Australian opener John Dyson was given not out to a confident run out appeal. Television pictures showed that he was out of his ground by a good eighteen inches. Dyson went on to score seventy-nine, anchoring an Australian innings of 314 that left them all but safe. Tired and frustrated after nearly three months away from home and with another two months of the tour to go, Botham boiled over and the result found its way into the *Sun*. The Australian Cricket Board was inevitably furious and Botham picked up a £200 fine. More importantly, it was another nail in the coffin in terms of his relations with the newspapers, coming as it did just a month after the same paper had invented a story which stated in vivid detail that he and Rodney Hogg had had a brawl in a Sydney night club. After we had had Botham built up into the world-dominating Victorian hero, the call went out for a return to Victorian values, Victorian morality. Just as putting the 'Great' back into Great Britain had needed a figurehead, so stories illustrating the dangers of immorality needed a victim. Who better than Botham to remind the ordinary man and woman of the dangers of rising above your station in life? Who more likely to offer the kind of stories they needed? Anti-Botham propaganda had as much potential as articles in his favour – the dramas attending his weight problems of 1980 had proved that. Those stories from Australia in 1982/83 were just the start of a hellish period for Botham with fact and fiction blurring until they became indistinguishable to all but those actually caught in the crossfire.

The walls really came tumbling down on the winter tour of 1983/84 when England visited New Zealand. They went there never having lost a series to the Kiwis, surrendering just two Tests out of the fifty-seven played between the countries. In their typically patronising, paternalistic fashion, the English press simply dismissed New Zealand as cannon fodder, opposition which the English giants should overcome without working up a sweat. This conveniently ignored the fact that in Richard Hadlee they had a genuine all-rounder who was in the same class as Botham, and in Martin Crowe an accomplished batsman who was beginning to fulfil his golden promise. These two great players were backed up by a very useful side of supporting actors such as John Wright, Geoff Howarth, Lance Cairns and Ewen Chatfield. Having won their first Test on English soil in the summer of 1983, they were a real threat on their own surfaces. This type of caution did not wash with a nationalistic press still unable to come to terms with the fact that countries other than England might actually be able to play a bit of sport themselves. They demanded triumph after triumph.

The first game ended with honours even, centuries from Botham, Randall, Coney and Martin Crowe leading to a high scoring draw in Wellington. The Second Test was played at Christchurch's Lancaster Park. The England side were down to twelve fit men including Tony Pigott who had been wintering in New Zealand and was called up to play for his country at a moment's notice (he was forced to postpone his wedding which was due to take place on the fourth day). He needn't have bothered because England lost in three. Playing on a pitch that resembled crazy paving, England contrived to bowl so badly that the home team reached 307 having been 137 for 5. Richard Hadlee plundered a Bothamesque ninety-nine off eighty-one balls to push the score at least 130 runs higher than should have been possible. England were inept in the field, captain Bob Willis recording in his diary that 'Ian was unbelievably bad – right back to his worst days'. England were shot out for eighty-two and ninety-three, the first time this century that both completed innings had totalled less than a hundred. Hadlee took eight wickets in the match to reinforce his claims to Botham's throne, for as Willis pointed out, 'the batting may have lacked heart but it was not the main cause of the humiliation – that came on the first day'.

Such results look like damnable capitulation from the other side of the world, and this particular reverse came before we had all become so used to seeing England taking beatings overseas. The players had let England down. Surely they weren't so bad that they could lose to little New Zealand? There must be more to it than mere cricket. Stories needed to be found, and they came back from Christchurch in abundance: England's players went out on to the playing field befuddled by an alarming collective intake of cannabis; they locked the dressing room door to outsiders and spent their time smoking it. Firstly, it's ridiculous to believe that a tour party of fourteen or fifteen players would all want to smoke, or would all condone it; secondly, as Bob Willis pointed out – and this is what really undermines the story – 'anyone with the slightest knowledge of cricket grounds would know that people wander in and out of dressing rooms all the time, rendering the thought of surreptitious pot-smoking laughable, even if anyone was that way inclined'. Sadly, since England were playing badly, people were only too happy to go along with the reports. Had England won, the allegations would not have been printed. If they had been, the average reader would have laughed them off along the lines of 'if the cricketers are winning, maybe we can get the footballers to smoke it as well'. The story would have been absurd and ineffectual; look at how similar allegations made against Phil Tufnell in the winter of 1996/97 were ignored after England had taken the series 2–0.

If you're losing, then whatever you do you will get criticised for it. If you practice for six hours a day then tuck yourself up in bed at 9.30 with a cup of cocoa and an improving volume, then you are too reserved to give free rein to your gifts; if you're out all night burning a box of candles at both ends and in the middle too, you're wearing yourself to a frazzle and wasting your talents. In today's world, where success is essential rather than a nice bonus, there is no hiding place if you lose. Botham suffered from that truism, though ironically it was the very competitiveness and refusal to accept defeat displayed by great sportsmen like him that created that kind of climate. We in England – or certainly our tabloid newspapers – don't appreciate well enough the concept of sporting competition. In any contest there will be winners and there will be losers, that is the point of competition. But just because you lose a series heavily, it doesn't mean you are dissolute or dilettante in your approach to the game. It could simply be that you have come up against a better side. That's sport, but we cannot seem to accept that. We're England. We should always win. Unfortunately, it's not that easy any more. This is one of the biggest stumbling blocks in our attempts to gain sporting supremacy once again, for it puts players under intolerable pressure and forces selectors to chop and change a side unwisely just to escape censure. If Pakistan bowl us out in a day, the headlines scream of an 'afternoon of shame'; if Shane Warne rattles through the side we're 'Warne out'; if Brian Lara hammers the

English attack for 150, our bowlers should be put out to grass and the captain thrown out on his ear. But why? Test cricket is full of fine players, even great players. If they play well, better than we are playing, should we not enjoy the spectacle? As long as the best possible English team is selected and then gives of its very best, we should accept the results, win, lose or draw, not glorify or crucify the captain. Any other response is childish.

It seems that the press had gone to New Zealand in 1983/84 looking for such sensationalist stories and were only encouraged by England's defeat. Accusations of conduct unbecoming were trumped up from the outset. In the first, a businessman told the *Daily Express* that a drunken and surly rabble comprising Botham, Willis and Lamb had been in their hotel bar at one in the morning. This was shown to be a case of mistaken identity, and the bar had closed at eleven anyway, but it set the pattern for the tour. It was only a matter of time before the big stories began to appear. As noted in the previous chapter, cricket tours were starting to resemble rock 'n' roll tours; as Willis pointed out, 'ever since I have been in the game, tours have involved a certain amount of drinking and a certain amount of female hangers-on'. It was drugs that the tabloids were really after, though. The attitude to pot in New Zealand is considerably more liberal than over here. As Allan Lamb pointed out in his autobiography, 'it was so much the normal and accepted thing there, that I did get mildly involved'. The media clearly felt that here was a chance to get a compelling front page story and bring down the great adventurer Botham, reinforcing the themes of their ongoing morality play. They were out to get him as part of the wider agenda and were waiting for the first cracks to form in his legendary armour. England's defeat at Christchurch provided the opportunity. There was no documentary evidence of his use of dope, just a hopeful suspicion among the press pack. To add spice to it all, they gilded the lily and added a couple of young girls to the scenario too. 'England cricketers in sex and drugs scandal' was splashed all over the front pages. It was these unfounded allegations that caused Botham to sue so ill advisedly, when he'd have done better to follow Lamb's dismissively flippant, yet more believable, approach: 'as I pointed out at the time, if I'd got a girl in my room for a bit of the naughties, I wasn't likely to leave the door open for anyone to walk in as [the girl who sold the story and later withdrew it had] admitted she'd been able to'. Again, Botham helped get himself into this fine mess. The stories were written by the press on a separate agenda. Botham was just another victim. The point was that his general demeanour meant that the pressmen could write salacious stories about him and be believed by a lot of people. They could never have written the same stories about David Gower because he had always been perceived differently. Since Botham played up to his yobbish image at times with his over-aggressive farewells to opposing players when he had taken their wicket, his theatrical appealing, those unsavoury comments about Aussie umpires a year earlier, few seemed to doubt his capability to perpetrate further crimes and misdemeanours.

By this stage, Botham had a real dilemma. He was always one of the lads, a 'new lad' before the term meant anything. He loved a few beers and a yarn in the pub. He loved to hunt, shoot, fish, play football and go out with the boys. That was the root of much of his popularity for it struck a chord with the general public. He also enjoyed that particular image, yet it made him more of a target. City boys and beer boys alike greeted Botham with a 'nudge,

nudge, wink, wink, say no more!' attitude. They envied him these fictitious nights of passion with exotic New Zealand beauties, all believing that the stories were true. The macho bravura of Botham must have been tempted to play up to the audience, while the devoted father must have despaired at the mess he found himself in. If he was to preserve his position, perhaps even his marriage, he needed to improve his image. He had to update it, make himself look the mature family man.

To the press, it was part of their ongoing game, the sport they simultaneously enjoyed with the royal family or with Boy George. Here was a mighty hero brought down to earth by his all too human failings. The destruction of the House of Botham might even be seen as a dry run for the destruction of the House of Windsor. He was certainly the bridge between the factual but relatively deferential treatment of George Best and the relentless, highly focused campaign waged against Paul Gascoigne. They pushed Botham as far as they could, continually testing the waters of public morality to see how much they could get away with. It's an ongoing process even today. If Botham had 'taken his medicine' in New Zealand, no more would have been said. Indeed, the press would have organised some great pictures of the tearful reunion with the devoted wife who was standing by her man – happy endings all round in hypocrisy land. Instead, he chose to take on the press. Honest, courageous, but ultimately daft. However hard you fight, they have the typewriters and the ear of the man in the street. They can make your life a misery without ever straying from the truth, by angling it, distorting it, putting it through the wringer, adding a little spin to your every word and deed.

Without hard evidence to back up their claims about

Botham's exploits in New Zealand, it was still possible he might inflict an expensive defeat on them in the courts, the more so since the public were still generally sympathetic towards him. The press, therefore, needed to discredit him. The first piece of good fortune dropped into their laps, though if Botham is right in his autobiography it was all part of an elaborate set-up, his solicitor Alan Herd having warned him of the possibility some weeks in advance. Having chosen not to tour India in 1984/85, he was looking forward to a break from the game. He wanted to spend time with the family, let the aching muscles take a rest, and recharge his batteries for the visit of the Australians in 1985. On New Year's Eve, the police arrived at the family home in Epworth with a search warrant; a pair of Botham's trousers sent to a local dry cleaner's had been found to contain a small packet of drugs in the pocket. Once the police searched his home they found dope in a drawer which Botham freely admitted he left there, having been given it by a supporter some years earlier, then forgetting all about it. The whole story is bizarre, another example of Botham's naive belief that he was fireproof. The find in the local dry cleaner's sounds questionable to say the least, but then if Botham had not held drugs at his home there would have been nothing for the police to find, there would have been no charges, and there would have been no story for the press to ram down his throat. Intriguingly, it was precisely the kind of story they needed at precisely the time they needed it. The whole campaign was redolent of the orchestrated attempts to attack the Beatles and the rock fraternity in general in the late 1960s once the whole hippie ethic started to frighten the Establishment. The Beatles were no longer lovable mop-tops but supposedly a threat to society. In his exhaustive biography of John Lennon, Ray Coleman says this of the 1968 raid on Lennon and Yoko Ono:

> He was always convinced that the bust was a 'set-up'. Don Short of the *Daily Mirror* had warned him three weeks previously that the police were on the way, so John said he had 'cleaned the place up, especially as I knew Jimi Hendrix [renowned for his chemical intake] had had this flat before Ringo and me'. He maintained that the dope had been planted in the trunk, a spot in which he would never have tried to hide it. 'It was a frame-up. I guess they didn't like the way the image was looking. The Beatles thing was over. No reason to protect us for being soft and cuddly any more – so bust us!'

The parallels with Botham are striking. Just as the Beatles had been at the forefront of the swinging sixties, so Botham had been representative of a resurgent Englishness; just as the Beatles threatened to take on the Establishment – 'we're more popular than Jesus now' said Lennon with good reason in 1966 – Botham's popularity was equally frightening. Both represented the rise of the working and middle classes to a position of power in society, threatening the age old supremacy of the ruling aristocracy. The Beatles supposedly controlled the minds of teenagers; Botham's legal attack on the press promised to expose their duplicity. Both needed to be put firmly in their places. The difference is that Botham didn't clear up the house. Had he done so, he would have been in the clear since there's no reason to believe that the police were involved in any conspiracy against him. What is likely is that the original find in the dry cleaner's was planted; by whom and why is a matter for speculation. Of course those who were to stand against him in the libel court gained from his public exposure as one who kept cannabis in the house. Following these dramas, according to Peter Roebuck, 'Friends told him that he had been betrayed by someone in the village, the village where he believed he was understood. He concluded that he could not stay in Epworth, though the vast majority of people there were still his friends. He decided to sell his house and move to a still more remote part of Yorkshire.'

It became public knowledge that Botham had kept drugs in the house. Whether he had intended to use them or not, it was a damaging revelation for his case against the *Mail on Sunday*. It gave added credence to one plank of their story and it would be hard for anyone to find in Botham's favour where drugs were concerned. The other side of the case, that he was a womaniser, would also need to be reinforced by the media. He knew he was comparatively safe during the English summer of 1985 and he spent that season winning over public opinion with some of the most incendiary batting ever seen. Eighty sixes in the season was a new record and his belligerent attack on the Australians helped pummel them into submission, creating the environment in which Gooch, Gatting and Gower could reap a mighty harvest of runs and recapture the Ashes. All summer, as soon as Botham got to the wicket the country stopped, just as it had in 1981. His innings were usually brief but they were always explosive – 250 runs in 289 balls in the six Tests including a spectacular eighteen off seven balls at Edgbaston.

By this stage, Botham was a wiser man. He knew full well that the tour to the West Indies in 1985/86 would be fraught with dangers for him. Having attacked him on the drugs front, it was always likely that the tabloids would try to find him *in flagrante* with another woman. They were so desperate to catch the players in the act that they even thought they might be able to use Lindsay Lamb and Ally Downton in their schemes, Allan's wife explaining in his autobiography that 'the players had gone off to Jamaica while we stayed on in Antigua, and the day they were due back, we moved from our flat into the team hotel. As we were booking in, a journalist heard the two of us asking when the players would be coming and told us that we'd be all right, as they were all keen to meet new girls!' Unfortunately, Botham was not yet wise enough to take Kath on tour with him, the single most effective safeguard against stories of this nature. Though he cut an isolated figure on this tour, restricting himself to his hotel room for the most part, he did venture out on occasion. He went, for instance, to that party thrown by Mick Jagger. The fabricated stories that came out of that evening of Botham and the former Miss Barbados Lindy Field snorting cocaine as the preamble to a night of passion destroyed any lingering hope of his libel case meeting with success. From there followed the drugs admission to the *Mail on Sunday*, the final acceptance that this was one battle that Ian Botham could not win.

Once Botham had taken his beating, draped himself in sackcloth and ashes, and prostrated himself at the feet of the Fourth Estate, normal service was resumed. While the war was being waged, the agenda had moved on yet again. Morality had gone out of the window. This was 1986, Nigel Lawson's boom was in full swing, the cry of this age was Loadsamoney! Lager louts were in, Gordon Gecko wannabes were all the rage. Now was the time for red braces, fast cars, enjoying yourself, flaunting your wealth, and who was the best example of the ordinary lad done good? Botham. The papers loved him again, championing him as England's great saviour at a time when those messianic powers had long since deserted him. They recognised that having him in the side was exciting, certainly better copy than the athletic clones Micky Stewart and Graham Gooch were soon to be accused of fashioning. They indulged him his boorish off days once more, as was demonstrated once Allan Border had taken him off to play for Queensland. He signed a three-year deal to play for them from the winter of 1987/88 in the hope of securing their first ever Sheffield Shield title.

Initially, the new scenario appealed. He had his family with him, the pressure was all on the field rather than off it, he was back to playing cricket for the thrill of it and being handsomely rewarded into the bargain. The family situation was absolutely crucial. Botham had been trying to relaunch himself, putting the past firmly behind him. His move to Worcestershire had been a successful one and now he was hoping to mend fences within the family. Although Kath had stood by him through all the press speculation, the events of the last few years had taken their toll. Though it had been the arrival of Tim Hudson which had put their relationship under the greatest strain, life hadn't been that much fun for several years now. For the sake of her and the children, it was time Botham spent more time with the family, something which his connection with Queensland seemed to offer. In addition, it would be nice to enjoy the quiet life for a change away from the tabloid journalists who would be following England's every move in Pakistan. In one sense that worked, for following the Shakoor Rana affair when Mike Gatting had a full scale argument with the Pakistani umpire, it was the England captain who would take up the front pages for the foreseeable future. Winters in Australia had other attractions too. In spite of his pugnacious attitude to their cricketers on the field, Botham enjoyed the country and the people. He was firm friends with similar spirits such as Rodney Hogg and Dennis Lillee, and had many good memories of previous tours there. Allan Border was another good friend, and though Botham liked to include regular references to Australia's history as a penal colony whenever he discussed the country, he had a genuine affection for the place. This was hardly surprising since his approach to the game was typically Australian, brash, tough, uncompromising. If those characteristics didn't always win him favour in his homeland, they were appreciated by those Down Under. Just as Tony Greig had made a name for himself there, so too did Ian Botham.

Botham had long since been an anti-hero in Australia. Ever since he'd had that now legendary fight with Ian Chappell during his stay on the Whitbread scholarship back in 1976/77, the Aussie public had enjoyed hearing stories about this highly unconventional Englishman. On that occasion, Botham, unsurprisingly, found himself in a bar during the course of the Centenary Test. At one stage, England looked likely to be overwhelmed before a brilliant innings from Derek Randall almost snatched victory for the visitors. With England apparently out of it, Botham heard Chappell holding forth on their deficiencies, leaving no one in any doubt that the Australians were their masters. Though Botham wasn't involved in the conversation, he told Chappell to watch what he was saying about his country or there'd be trouble. Since Chappell was a former captain of Australia and was on home turf, he paid scant attention to this upstart and carried on with the attack. Botham's self control snapped after issuing a third public warning, and he belted Chappell with enough force to knock him over a table. According to Botham, Chappell then made to leave but, at the door, he turned and hurled another insult at Botham. Botham then chased him into the street, backing off only when he saw a police car come into view. Given that that argument had arisen from Botham's fierce patriotism, it was ironic that a decade or so later he should choose to forgo further Test caps for three winters in Australia.

On the field with Queensland he was an all-round success, spearheading the side and playing some of his finest cricket in years. They topped the Shield table for a time and cruised towards the final. All had been quiet on the media front, but as the season was drawing to its climax the side was rocked by reports in the Australian press that, following a game between Queensland and Tasmania, Botham and Dennis Lillee had wrecked a club. Botham denies that charge but does admit to breaking a few glasses, still pretty unimpressive and rather stupid behaviour. Only too well aware of Botham's highly developed nose for controversy, officials at the Queensland Cricket Association started to get a little twitchy. Their carefully planned assault on the title was in danger of being undermined. In his defence, Botham might not have been aware of just how much success meant to Queensland, though given their position was similar to that of Somerset back in 1978 he of all people should have been in an ideal position to understand it. The sensible course would have been to fall in with the team's plans and keep religiously to the party line. Keep your head down, turn up at the nets, if only to offer moral support to the other lads, win the Shield, and then you could party like there was no tomorrow. That would have been indulged by one and all as a fitting response to a much sought after triumph.

Botham had to go his own way. As the tensions rose, he fell out with Allan Border, refusing to accept his team order of no drinking prior to the games. In losing to Victoria in their final match, Queensland lost the chance of home advantage in the final, which in turn meant that a draw against Western Australia would not be enough to secure the Sheffield Shield. They had to win that last match.

On the flight out to Perth for that game, the Queensland players began bickering among themselves. With so much riding on just one match, it was inevitable that tensions would run high. While an intelligent and personable individual, it's not for nothing that Allan Border is sometimes referred to as Captain Grumpy. Although the national side realised the value of following him to the hilt, an experienced campaigner like Botham was always going to have his own opinions, some of which were valid, others less so. With Border used to getting his own way, there was always the chance the two might fall out at some stage. On the flight they got into a heated argument, the two exchanging fairly robust language. A man sitting in front turned round to remonstrate whereupon Botham, ever the diplomat, put his hands on the man's shoulders and, according to his autobiography, 'redirected his gaze so he was facing the front again and told him to mind his own business'. Allan Border later suggested that what Botham actually said was 'it's fuck all to do with you'. Cooling down later on, Botham apologised to the man as he disembarked, and hoped that that was the end of the matter. In a matter of moments, however, Botham was charged with assault and found himself stuck in jail on the eve of the most important game of the season. He was only released once Dennis Lillee turned up to stand bail. Queensland duly lost the final and the cricket association took that opportunity to sever its ties with Botham, the members' minds made up by the field day the Australian press had with his discomfort. Revenge for Headingley 1981 tasted very sweet in some quarters.

Again, Botham has complained that this episode was blown up out of proportion, but was it really? Sticking him in a prison cell was obviously an over-reaction on the part of the authorities – with the Shield final about to take place, he was hardly likely to leave the country – but did Botham really have to 'redirect' the man's gaze in the first place? Could he not have thought twice about it, looked at the behaviour of himself and his colleagues, and accepted they were in the wrong? Could he not have apologised for the volume at which they were arguing and then moderate his own language? It is not always the world against Ian Botham. A simple disagreement shouldn't end up in a charge of assault. His confusion on these matters is justifiable to a degree since he was on the receiving end of so many conflicting opinions. The press had hung him out to dry over his use of dope, attacked him for fictitious flings with other women, but every time he was involved in a brawl, it made him more popular. He'd come to prominence for clouting Ian Chappell and had won a lot of friends in the press for that, presumably because Chappell was one of the hated Aussies. The Queensland plane incident was also sympathetically received in many quarters. One can only conclude that again, this was because he'd been giving as good as he got with another loudmouthed descendant of a convict – the press are still allowed to be overtly racist where white nations are concerned. The yob culture louts loved it. Botham, they wrongly surmised, was one of their own. That was good for newspaper circulation, but it wasn't good for Botham.

With his Australian dreams dashed, Botham returned to a solely domestic agenda, though his next visit to their shores was again fraught with controversy. Arriving there in time for the 1992 World Cup after a season in pantomime, he viewed the forthcoming jamboree thus: 'What could be better than to beat the Aussies in Melbourne playing in front of 100,000 convicts?' Had Botham been nursing a grievance against Australians since the Queensland fiasco four years ago? Had he forgotten just where the convicts had come from in the first place? If that wasn't enough, on the eve of the final itself he and Gooch stormed out of the official dinner when an Australian comedian, Gerry Connolly, began to make jokes about the Queen. Botham reportedly made the ludicrous statement that 'I did it for the Queen. I love my country and I can't put up with that sort of crap.' Christopher Martin-Jenkins summed up the rather pathetic affair in the *Daily Telegraph*, commenting that

to walk out was both pompous and rude. Lampooning the Royal Family, whether one likes it or not, is hardly unknown on British television ... in the case of Botham, who, sensitive Australians might think, had already insulted his hosts by referring [to them as convicts], his hypocrisy is transparent. No two people's sense of humour is quite the same, as Gooch and Botham may well have already discovered from the increasing number of after-dinner speeches which both now make for considerable rewards ... they have set themselves a dangerous precedent. The danger with celebrity is that those who achieve it take themselves too seriously.

Botham was soon to find that such actions were unpopular with his hosts. Blunt banners calling him a 'Queen Lover' appeared at the final while his dismissal for a duck got the loudest cheer of the day. A few days later, a £43-a-head dinner at which he was the main attraction pulled in fifty-seven people rather than the 500 anticipated. One of the organisers noted that the billing 'Ian Botham & Friends' was sadly inappropriate, and that the turn-out would have been better had they invited his enemies.

Botham's life, his actions and reactions, were constantly dictated by the media in the 1980s. For those who have never suffered media intrusion, the question must be why did he not simply ignore it all and lead his own life? Part of the problem is geographic and cultural. England is not a big enough country to accommodate legends. They cannot disappear and nor will our pathologically curious nature allow them to. The tabloids do on a national scale what the old woman down the street used to do on a local one; they are the source of the gossip, the scandal, the rumour and the innuendo that oil the wheels of everyday conversation. How much more exciting it is to have revealed the veritable *Satyricon* that was supposedly the private life of Ian Botham than the details of the new settee arriving at Mrs Dawkins' home.

Trial by tabloid is an insidious punishment that seeps into every aspect of the victim's life. Most disturbing of all, it affects the family who are often put under awful pressures by journalists trying to find another quotation to take out of context. Botham had no idea where it would all end. The 1980s were the tabloid years, the years when they were constantly pushing back the boundaries of taste and decency, searching for the limits. Just where would their quest for a story end? Any seasoned journalist could see that given enough rope, he'd hang himself. Why hit Chappell? Why not lose weight in 1980 to protect his back?

Why not hang around the nets a little more, if only as a good PR exercise? Why keep dope in the house? Why take such delight in rubbing people up the wrong way? Why make so many enemies? Why leave yourself open to charges of assault on an aeroplane? Botham would say that his attitude of no surrender was crucial to his success on the field, yet surely, once the press had taken their first pot shots at him, it would have been possible to exercise a little more self discipline if only for the sake of his family. He was obviously not the monster of media invention, so why did he keep stoking the fires with such silly indiscretions? Writing in *The Times* in March 1995, Simon Barnes explained the Botham quandary: 'Botham never got the hang of fame. He was convinced he was always loved by the people and brought low by the press. Handy villains! ... the part played by the newspapers in all this was hardly edifying but they could not have done it without Botham. Uncritical public support drained away, became equivocal and for Botham, for all his million comebacks, life was never quite the same, quite as easy ever again.'

Probably the greatest lesson to be learned from 'Botham – The Tabloid Years' is that we should not be foolish enough to confuse the mighty deeds with the doer. It would be so much easier to admire and enjoy the skills of Paul Gascoigne if it were possible to erase pictures of the leering oaf with the obsession with comedy breasts, a grown man whose idea of rapier wit is to belch as frequently and loudly as possible. It's not easy to do, the more so since personalities such as Gascoigne seem to believe that such behaviour is charming and lucrative. On the latter point, they may have a case. Is Gascoigne that much more gifted than, say, Alan Shearer? Probably not, but in terms of extra-curricular activities he is a far more attractive proposition. Ignorance and boorishness have become a substitute for charisma in the relentless downmarket drive of popular culture, and for a time that suited Botham well. But when a man wants to rehabilitate his reputation and be taken seriously, the loutish moments come back to haunt him. Lord's and the media did much to make sure that Botham was never England captain again after his first fling at the job, but they didn't do as much as Botham himself.

CHAPTER SEVEN

Grace and Danger

The People's Champion

It's little wonder that Ian Botham has held the attention of the nation for twenty years and more. No cricketer has better embodied all the classic ingredients of great drama: meteoric rise, swashbuckling performances, an iconoclastic turn of mind, accusations of betrayal by those he called his friends, attacks by those he knew to be his enemies, and all the while he kept on coming back for more. Even then, in the moments of his greatness, he was often to be found sowing the seeds of his own demise.

Let's talk cricket and not controversy. Grasping his chance on the Test match stage, for the better part of three years Botham launched his career with a ferocity of intent and a consistency of purpose and of results not matched since the days of Bradman. In his first twenty-five Test matches he picked up 139 wickets at eighteen each, averaging one victim every forty-five balls. Fourteen times he took five wickets or more in an innings, getting ten in a match three times. He made, or rather blasted, 1336 runs at an average of forty. He clocked up six hundreds, three times accompanying that by grabbing five wickets in an innings, a staggering feat of virtuosity and of stamina which is unparalleled in the annals of the game. *Wisden* tells us in its 1996 almanac that of the other great all-rounders Sobers managed that particular feat just twice, Miller, Imran, Wasim Akram and Benaud once each, and Hadlee and Kapil Dev not at all. Yet Botham then went on to do it twice more in his career. He completed the Test double of 1000 runs and 100 wickets in just twenty-one matches, two faster than his closest rival. When he wasn't batting, he was taking slip catches with ease, hurling himself to left or right to clutch edges, displaying reflexes that many a top class goalkeeper might have envied, grabbing the ball with a nonchalant yet intuitive anticipation reminiscent of a great bird clamping its jaws shut around a leaping salmon. To see Botham at work in the slips was a rare privilege, his catching like some elemental force of nature, the more so since he stood with hands resting on his thighs against the advice of all the text books. In those twenty-five Tests, England won fifteen, tasting defeat just five times, three of those coming in the final four games of that triumphant period.

With those statistics to back him up, Botham's place among the greats was already assured. And yet of all the great players, Botham's place in the affection of cricket lovers has the least to do with statistics and the most to do with personality, with the manner and timing of his deeds. We don't relish memories of Botham in the physical act of reaching a hundred as we do with Boycott or Atherton, men who have chiselled their way deliberately to a milestone. It's the shots that he played on the way that endear him to us, whether it be in a two-hour century or a twenty-minute knockabout for twenty or thirty. In those early years, Botham transformed Test cricket from the dour legacy of the 1960s where matches were ground out in interminable wars of attrition into a game of glorious entertainment, transported back to its roots on the village green. Botham was the local blacksmith hurling the ball down or striking it out of the ground to the amusement of all those who looked on. As David Frith recalls, 'I'll never forget how the crowds responded to his deeds. Even fairly staid people forgot themselves in their eagerness to show their delight at his performances.'

In those glorious early years, Botham seemed never to contemplate failure. Whether he came to the wicket at 276 for 5 with England in command or 134 for 5 with England struggling, the position in the first two Pakistan Tests of 1978, his attitude was the same. If the ball was there to be hit, he hit it. Very often he hit it even if it wasn't there for that purpose. And once he did hit it, that ball stayed hit. Such aggression was unheard of; even his predecessor Tony Greig had played with some caution when deemed necessary. Botham never felt there was such a need because he never felt there was an adversary worth worrying about. Perhaps in those early Tests he was right. Just as England suffered a nightmarish itinerary from the winter of 1979/80 into the winter of 1981/82, they were lucky in their opponents from the end of the West Indian series in 1976 until they flew out to Australia in 1979/80 to heal the Packer rift. There were comparatively cheap runs and wickets to be had. The remarkable thing is that Botham claimed so many of them himself when other Englishmen returned moderate figures over the period; Gower scored quite heavily but good players like Gooch and Gatting just could not fully establish themselves, neither registering a Test century between those dates. With the ball, a great bowler like Bob Willis couldn't match Botham, while good performers like Old and Hendrick scarcely got a look in. It's easy to construct a thesis that suggests Botham was too much for his contemporaries, that some of them found his escapades too daunting to compete with and retreated into their shell. Botham bridles at the suggestion, seeing it as a slight, intimating that he was not a team man. That is not the case at all, it's merely that others were caught in his shadow, unable to shine. Such was his all-encompassing brilliance, their efforts were lost in the shuffle or ignored by a press and public who couldn't get enough of Botham, whatever he was doing. Ultimately the confidence of some players was dented. Even though Botham made all the right noises about it being a team effort, they were not granted the same public spotlight. This must have had an effect on the self esteem of some.

Back in 1976, Botham and Mike Gatting were seen as the future of English cricket, more so than Gooch and Gower. It was nip and tuck as to who would make the biggest impact the quickest, who would go on to be the dominant personality in the English game for the next decade. Both flew out to Australia on the Whitbread scholarship scheme in 1976/77. On the field of play Gatting outshone Botham who displayed relatively unimpressive form. Nevertheless, it was Botham who caught the attention courtesy of his much reported contretemps with Ian Chappell. He also used the playing experience to good effect, rounding out his game, adding a little more Australian-style aggression to his manner, improving his fitness, and he started the 1977 season in the best form of his career thus far. In addition to his sense of physical well-being, he had a great incentive: the Packer-bound Tony Greig had to be replaced in the England side. For Gatting there was no such glaring opportunity. Some suggest that the relish with which Botham seized his day set Gatting back some years. It was the first major upset in his career and he was unsure how to deal with it. He captured a place on the tour to Pakistan and New Zealand – just ahead of David Gower, perhaps because he could offer a few overs of useful medium pace – but failed to shine. He played a Test in Pakistan while Botham was ill on the sidelines but could not grasp his opportunity, scoring just five and six before falling to the spinners. In New Zealand he managed one match too, failing to score as Botham plundered fifty-three and took five wickets. This established a pattern for the first half of Gatting's career and one which Graeme Hick is in real danger of repeating. A bully of county attacks, he was initially diffident, sometimes too cautious in Test matches; the image that endures is of him padding up to a ball on off stump only to be out lbw time and time again.

It's interesting that while Botham was struggling for form and fitness at home in 1980 and 1981, Gatting seemed more at home on the international stage, making a greater impression on the team. When Botham returned to the ranks and began to flay all and sundry once more, Gatting seemed browbeaten again. Perhaps this was the work of coincidence, but by 1984, with a poor summer against the West Indies behind him, it looked as though Gatting would never make the transition to Test cricketer. He finally made the step up once David Gower chose to take him to India as vice captain on a tour that Botham missed. Batting with renewed vigour, Gatting scored 136 in the First Test, 207 in the Fourth, and totalled 575 runs at almost ninety-six for the series. From that time on he was established as one of England's leading players. Not only did Botham's aura of invincibility inhibit the opposition, it seems to have troubled less robust team-mates, though one might argue that Gower was the first England captain to display the requisite faith in Gatting's talents.

Botham's innate self confidence meant that he was never overawed by the Test atmosphere. This was crucial to his success. But even in his early career, his sense of certainty could be overbearing. He made enemies in the press and in the England set-up because he overshadowed the efforts of everyone else. Some, such as Willis and Brearley, were delighted to have this breath of fresh air on the scene, but others were less positive. The annoying thing about Botham from their point of view was that he made it all look so bloody easy. Once he had made his mark, nets were there for him to loosen up, not to hone technique; while Boycott was grinding out his third hour with the club bowlers, Botham would have been long gone. If he was about to bat, he might have five minutes blasting the ball into the far distance and then walk out and bat in exactly the same manner, tearing Test match sides apart. If he had to bowl, he'd send down a couple of looseners in the nets, take the field, bowl another wild delivery and find the ball nestling in the hands of the man at cover point. That golden arm reputation has been overdone over the years, David Frith asking us to 'forget the fabled long-hops that took wickets and remember instead the late-swerving outswinger (from an inswing action)'. Even so, it does reinforce the point that here was a cricketer who made things happen. Life was never dull when he was around; in the dressing room that was equally true as his practical jokes maintained the morale of those with like minds, but irritated others.

One skill he never learned was that of diplomacy. His attitude on the pitch made it clear he had little respect for some of his opponents. He delighted in their humiliation, their utter defeat, a vital part of his combative approach. Botham's game wasn't simply built on his quality with the bat or ball, much of his menace came from his psychological impact. He wanted, indeed *had*, to intimidate opponents, make them feel they had no place on the same field as him, that they were there simply to be brushed aside. When he was running through the Pakistanis at Lord's in 1978, it was obvious they didn't want to face him. There was nothing physically threatening about his pace especially when Willis might be pounding in from the other end; it was his bristling aggression that had so completely overwhelmed them. Some of those batsmen were dismissed even before they'd reached the crease. It's an attitude that Dominic Cork has tried to adopt with mixed results, but the man who learned most from Botham's tactics was big Merv Hughes. His sheer size and appearance were enough to put the fear of God into any opponent. When he added a lengthy follow through after delivery so he could eyeball the batsman who had just played and missed outside off stump, here was a bowler who could walk over the faint hearted. Botham was the same. That's why both were able to take wickets with seemingly innocuous deliveries. It was the cumulative effect of their hostile actions that got so many scalps. Botham understood this only too well and always looked to dominate Hughes in their meetings. In the First Test of 1986/87 when Merv was still a relatively new Test match cricketer, Botham laid into him to the tune of twenty-two off one over on his way to 138, before bowling him for a duck. Thereafter Hughes was no real threat in that series, Botham having categorically established his authority. Things had changed by 1989 when Hughes was a crucial component in Border's triumphant team that recaptured the Ashes.

Fiery at play, Botham was a Jekyll and Hyde character. He was a genuinely relaxed and friendly individual off the field in those early days before his cynicism grew in response to the tabloid maulings, driving him back into his shell. Get him down the pavilion steps and a whole new character emerged. Much of it was bravado, macho pride that insisted no challenge was too great for him. That was perhaps at the root of his disdain for nets. Real men – great men – don't need to practice, they just do the job. Since he took little advice from anyone, there was no need for coaching either. It was this fault that led him into his first trough of form. As suggested, stamping his authority on a series was a matter of pride for Botham. He had to assert his dominance in order to weave his magic. If he could cow the opposition into believing he was a superman, then he could perform like one. However, it was always likely that the West Indians would be the side to finish his golden run. His technical and temperamental weaknesses against express pace have been outlined elsewhere. He had to fight fire with fire to assert his masculinity. This character that he and the press had created could not back down in the face of enemy assault. That veneer of confidence was crucial, but of course he wasn't as good as he pretended to be; nobody in the history of the game has ever been *that* good. Consequently, he could bully bowlers with his power, implying a great eye but not necessarily a watertight game. The very best bowlers soon realised that this was a facade that could be crushed if they aimed their fire at the fault lines.

The West Indies targeted his flaws ruthlessly. Though it is always the over that Holding bowled to Boycott in Jamaica in 1980/81 that is discussed in hushed tones of reverence, he bowled one that was every bit as quick to

Botham later in the game. Botham was left looking like the worst number eleven, all at sea against the onslaught, scratching his head in response to bowling that was almost inhuman. Some commentators suggest that this was psychological warfare aimed at Boycott, but it's just as likely that Holding was simply underlining his mastery and his majesty for Botham's benefit since he recognised that he would be around for a lot longer than the Yorkshireman would. It was a lesson that stayed long in his psyche; it may never have been fully erased.

That West Indian side was fearsome, brimming with exciting natural talent. That in itself is enough to explain Botham's failing form against them, but was there more to it than that? His need to hold the psychological upper hand has been demonstrated. Against every side in the country, then every side in the world, there was no man who could strike fear into Botham's heart. There was seemingly only one contemporary cricketer whom he held in awe, his Somerset team-mate Vivian Richards. Watching Richards bat when in full flow was a remarkable thing to behold. Be it in a Test or a one dayer, at the top of his game Viv was the master. Just as Botham loved to dominate, so too did Richards. That lazy, unconcerned stroll out to the wicket, the nonchalant fiddling with a sweat band, the cold stare down the pitch at the bowler, these were all calculated movements that said 'I'm here, I'll stay as long as I feel like it and you can't stop me'. For seven or eight years, that was no idle boast. Phenomenally powerful, Richards had the finest eye in cricket. Apparently able to see the ball so much quicker than anyone else, he could whip a ball from outside off stump into the crowd at midwicket, a shot he performed again and again at Lord's in the 1979 World Cup Final. That knock took the trophy away from

England and underlined the fact that here was a batsman who could rank with the very greatest from any era. Botham saw innings like that day in, day out with Somerset. He admitted that, Ken Barrington aside, Viv Richards was the only man from whom he sought advice. They were great friends, but on the field Richards was the first among these equals.

Inevitably, then, Botham must have gone out to face the West Indies with confidence dimmed. No longer was he leaving the pavilion expecting to win, sure that he would steamroller his opponents. Richards must have loomed large in all his thoughts; the world's greatest batsman was on the other side, a batsman whom Botham rated as at least the equal of Bradman. Botham the bowler, injured and ailing, must have wondered about his own capacity to dismiss him. Looking around the side, he must have questioned just who else could get Richards out. It was that psychological blow as much as the genuine quality of the West Indian cricket that finally beat him. How else to explain his consistent failures against them, whether burdened by the captaincy or not? Why else would he have failed to impose himself on them once his back injury had eased and was causing fewer problems; once it had improved by the following year, the Aussies still felt his presence. The common denominator in all these failures was Viv Richards, the only man consistently to psych Botham out of the game and therefore the only man to overcome him, though it could be argued that Imran Khan was to have a similar effect on him later in the decade.

Defeat can have different effects on different personalities. Some are wrecked by it, nerve and confidence shattered for ever. Some accept it as just the inevitable turning of the wheel, certain that their turn will come again in the fullness of time. Others simply ignore it, incapable of dealing with it and its consequences. Botham seems to fall into the latter category. It enabled him to dismiss the previous twelve months against the West Indians as an aberration caused largely by his back injury, those who had meddled with his captaincy back at the TCCB, and the influences in his side that had not been wholly benign. None of the problems revolved around Botham, his occasionally naive tactics, his inability to get the best out of the side, the fact that the West Indies were too good for him, the step up in quality of opposition exposing failings in his game. That kind of talk was defeatist nonsense. Just give him another go and he'd show everybody. All he needed was a fair chance. Headingley 1981 provided it. Without that psychological armour and selective memory, Botham could not have created the miracle at Leeds. Instead of fretting about his position in the side, he approached that Test like any other, knowing that he could win the game and that the selectors would have to be mad to leave him out.

Yet just as defeat can be damaging, so too can victory. Those three Tests which he won 'single-handed', according to popular legend, established him as an icon but ruined his never too reliable sense of perspective. Thereafter he was Indiana Jones, the lone adventurer who firmly believed he was the man for all eventualities, that he could turn any game however dire the situation, a mistaken belief that continued into his cricketing dotage. Failing to accept that the events of 1981 were built around a set of circumstances unlikely to be replicated, he apparently believed that he alone had fashioned the results, rather than being the beneficiary of wild circumstances. He couldn't have done it without being hugely gifted, but great deeds are often the result of being in the right place at the right time. There are times when getting down to some hard graft is essential, when pulling out a dull but worthy performance is more valuable than the swashbuckling approach which goes wrong as often as it goes right. Ironically, where most players are remembered for their failures as much as their successes, so overwhelming was Botham, so exciting his style of play, that his many failures do not linger in the mind. The images of Botham on the field are, Lord's 1981 apart, completely positive ones, a blur of runs, wickets and catches.

Initially, all the signs were that Botham had been a little chastened by his poor form against the West Indies in 1980 and 1981. Reminded that his gifts could be recalled by a capricious fate, he knuckled down to the job of Test cricket, accepting it as a rather harder grind than had hitherto been the case. In India he was exemplary. He accepted the dead nature of the surfaces England encountered once India had won the First Test. There were occasional bursts of hostility with the ball but he quickly realised that was futile, exhausting work. Helping captain Keith Fletcher by operating in a stock bowling role for much of the series, it was as a batsman that he shone. Unveiling a technique that was solid in all departments, he proved that he could build an innings and be depended upon as a front line batsman. Keith Fletcher must take credit here for promoting him to number five in the order, giving him responsibility for the side in the wake of the loss of the captaincy. That was psychologically vital. Accumulating 440 runs at fifty-five, the most notable facet of his play was his discipline. It seemed he was ready to use his gifts to the full, nurturing them accordingly. That impression continued into the English season of 1982 when he batted beautifully against the Indians, having bowled superbly in the first innings of the first game at Lord's. Building on that, he went to the Oval for the third and final Test match with England one up and batted the tourists into oblivion. Rather than the blood and thunder of Headingley in 1981, Botham now played with controlled aggression. Admittedly the Indians weren't the strongest bowling side, but Botham went about his job with such concentrated determination that it seemed he had achieved cricketing maturity. Without the customary blazing away, he still achieved Test cricket's fastest double century in terms of balls received, just 220.

Yet even in this hour of glory, Botham was about to hit another decline in his form. A puzzle over the years has been his stubborn refusal to concentrate on his batting once it became clear that his general level of fitness meant he was becoming less of a threat with the ball. Keen-eyed judges such as Ted Dexter felt he was such a naturally good technician that he was potentially the best of England's four premier batsmen of the mid-eighties. It was his firm belief that Botham could bat at four and hold together the order with Gooch, Gower and Gatting slotting in around him. That's a big claim given that Gooch and Gower both managed more than 8,000 Test runs, but it's a shrewd one. Botham played pretty straight, hit the ball cleanly, had a good eye and a basically secure game. His weakness against the fastest bowling could have been worked on and perhaps eradicated or at least alleviated since in part it was a temperamental as much as a technical shortcoming. In 1982 it seemed increasingly clear that his future lay with the bat.

In that 1982 season, despite a fine performance against India in the First Test, all was not well with Botham the bowler. In the second innings of that game he managed just one wicket for 103, one for eighty-six in the second game and two for eighty-five in the final match. The decline continued against Pakistan in the second half of the summer. He picked up nine wickets for 334 in the first two games, with his bowling at Lord's particularly inconsequential. He ended the season on a high, snapping up nine wickets on a helpful track at Headingley, but that did not disguise the long-term decline in his powers since that back injury had robbed him of his zip. He was still taking wickets, but they were taking longer to fall and costing him far more than previously: since April 1980, he'd taken 110 wickets in twenty-nine Tests at a rate of one every fifty-nine balls, a 33 per cent increase in his strike rate compared with those first twenty-five games. They now cost twenty-nine each too, a rise of 59 per cent per wicket.

Statistics can be misleading, of course. Even in that 'decline', those returns look good against the records of many Test bowlers. It's a similar record to that of John Snow's entire career, for instance, and Snow was a very fine player; if England could unearth another Snow tomorrow, many of Mike Atherton's problems would be over. Nevertheless, Botham's early success rate ensured he would be judged by the very highest standards. He'd performed as remarkably as Sydney Barnes, the choice of many historians as the game's greatest bowler. If he couldn't be expected to maintain such dizzy heights indefinitely, then the trend and the steepness of the downward curve gave cause for concern as did the physical reasons for it. It was a trend that was never reversed: in his final forty-eight Tests, he took just six hauls of five wickets in an innings; his first fifty-four Tests had seen twenty-one such feats. When people criticise Botham's lack of application at the nets or his lifestyle, his constant retort is 'look in the record books'. A powerful argument in total terms, but one wonders whether Botham took a look at his bowling figures beyond the first third of his career. His failure to do so meant that mentally he saw himself as still living in some golden age, while in reality the golden arm had become base metal.

He continued to pound in and unleash bouncer after bouncer, willing himself to take wickets. Somewhere along the way, he lost the plot and changed from an intelligent swing bowler into a man who apparently thought he was Bob Willis. He did not have the pace to blast good players out on decent pitches any longer and the results show that. Peter Roebuck pointed out that he seemed to mislay his complete control of devilish swing in both directions: 'In his early years [he] was a master of swing. He was strong, fit and very, very good. Easy to forget that he could also bat superbly giving himself licence with the ball ... the late inswinger with the old ball, turning nought for seventy into four for ninety, the transformation at which Botham was the greatest of all.' That nip off the pitch, that little zip through the air, had gone, taken by that back complaint and the way in which his body had filled out, distorting that once beautiful action. No longer could he be relied upon to roll over the opposition tail, wrapping up the last five wickets for thirty or forty.

A lot is made of Botham boosting his figures by insisting on bowling at tail-enders, arguing that his reputation was cheaply made. Certainly he did a lot of that but then he was very good at it; so is Waqar Younis. It's a much maligned skill but Mike Atherton knows only too well how useful it can be, having seen New Zealand's last pair put on more than a hundred to save the First Test in Auckland on the 1996/97 tour. In his prime, they'd have put on a dozen before Botham would have grabbed the ball, said 'bugger this for a game', and finished the match in an over or two. In these days when the lower order batsmen are increasingly well organised, such ability can mean the difference between winning and losing a game. Yet time took that talent away too.

Roebuck is especially accurate in his assertion that Botham gave himself licence with the ball with his excellent batting. The reverse is equally true. If he'd already got five wickets in a game, he'd go to the crease knowing he'd done his job and that any runs were a bonus. Once the wickets dried up, it had a detrimental effect on his batting. Botham was unsuited to being anything other than an all-rounder. In his head, he was always taking wickets and scoring hundreds. It was not an either/or situation. A crisis in one department heralded a crisis in the other. For a man whose whole reputation and career was built upon the enormous foundations of his self belief, it seems that that was quite a fragile base. Post-1982, there were 134 more wickets at thirty-eight each, a strike rate of sixty-eight balls. That's pretty mundane – of the England bowlers with more than those 134 wickets in a career, only Emburey has a similarly high average. Yet at the very time you'd expect him to be making more runs in order to compensate, he scored just 2204 more at twenty-nine, disappointing when so many batsmen improve with age and experience. As a combination, these are very useful figures indeed and better than the career figures of any other English all-rounder in history apart from Tony Greig, but again, Botham's greatness early on demands that we judge him by the very highest standards. He failed to live up to them, in spite of propaganda to the contrary.

It was in 1982/83 that the balance in his game seemed to be terminally upset. In Australia his bowling lost all its penetration. Significantly, his batting was woeful too. Robbed of the central plank of his bowling strategy, captain Bob Willis could do nothing but surrender the Ashes. Botham bowled without rhythm, and in his book on the series the first notes of doubt crept in: 'I believe I have two years left in me as a strike bowler in Test cricket.' Bearing that comment in mind, there is a counter argument as to why Botham did not give his full attention to his batting. Perhaps all the blame for his all-round decline should not be laid at his door. As he noted in the same passage of that book, who would replace him as a bowler, especially as Willis was nearing the end of the road? In that 1982/83 series, it was his wickets rather than runs that were sadly missed. From an English point of view, Botham was needed primarily as a bowler; with Gower, Gatting, Randall and Lamb to pack the middle order, runs were often less crucial. Botham was overworked in the field, particularly in the light of his suspect back, but his captains often had little choice. In his diary of the subsequent 1983/84 tour, Willis noted that during that disastrous defeat in New Zealand 'I was criticised for allowing him too long a spell. But we only had four bowlers in the side – two had to bowl into the wind for long periods and one of these, Tony Piggott, was a Test rookie. Botham simply had to bowl.' Just as Alec Stewart has been sacrificed in recent years, forced to bat at six and keep wicket in order to balance the side, Botham was the victim of equally insensitive handling.

As one who always liked to be involved, Botham was never going to hold up his hands and say he was finished as a Test bowler, capable only of a filling-in role, a handful of overs as and when required. It's in his nature to take on all comers at all times. The selectors and management had to make that decision for him. That, though, might have meant leaving him out – was he a reliable enough batsman to replace any one of Gatting, Gower, Lamb and Randall in the top order, assuming they were in good form? In 1982 the answer would have been yes; a year later, things were nothing like as clear cut. Perhaps that was one challenge Botham didn't relish. If he had been forced into that position, consider how the team might have improved. In the West Indies in 1985/86, for example, the team in the final Test was Gooch, Slack, Robinson, Gower, Lamb, Gatting, Botham, Downton, Ellison, Emburey, Foster. The bowling was to be done by Foster, Ellison, Botham and Emburey, yet it was obvious that Botham was struggling to take wickets. Gower was trying to bowl out the West Indies with three bowlers, with Emburey tight but lacking in penetration, Ellison relatively inexperienced, and Foster a perennial injury worry. How much better to have gone into the game with six front line batsmen, leaving out Slack, promoting Robinson to open and Gatting to bat at three. With Botham at six and made fully aware of his responsibilities to get around a hundred runs in the two innings, that would have left a berth free for another front line bowler. Botham could then have filled in with the ball as and when necessary – again we come back to him playing the Steve Waugh role. That would have better suited his changing abilities and would surely have prolonged his career at the top, protecting his back from further punishment. Allowing him only to bowl when fresh, he might have recaptured the form that made him so dangerous. If you bat at seven as Botham often did, you have to be considered a bowler first, yet English selectors have long been so concerned about batting frailties that they try to pack the tail. Surely it's time to take a tip from the Australians, something we seem to be learning at last.

Specialists win Test matches. If you have six good specialist batsmen, you shouldn't need runs from the tail. If they come, they're a bonus. And surely, if the top six have gone for 100, the last five aren't likely to muster many. Players have to be judged on results, and on those results Botham was no longer a genuine all-rounder, i.e. a player who would get in the side as batsman and bowler. However, he did maintain his place in the side with ease. That was down to a potent combination of reputation and the paucity of talent in English cricket. With a wicketkeeper who usually batted in the lower half – French, Downton, Richards – England were crying out for an all-rounder. When they went to India without Botham in 1984/85 they took Chris Cowdrey and Richard Ellison, neither of whom were remotely in the same class with bat or ball. That tour underlined the fact that Botham had to play, had to bowl, and any runs were viewed as a pleasing extra bonus.

With the strain placed upon him on and off the field, it's little wonder he was inconsistent. Even so, he had a good year in 1985. Walking straight back into the team and faced with the Australians, his confidence was fully restored, the sight of the old enemy summoning up the blood and stiffening the sinew. His absence had made it clear that he was England's number one – probably England's only – all-rounder. In a microcosm of his whole career, that season he blasted the Aussies with bouncer upon bouncer, smashed their bowlers all around the grounds, had a war of words with umpire Alan Whitehead, and generally behaved as though he owned every ground he played upon. Hammering sixes like they were going out of fashion, this was vintage Botham. There was a faint hope that the winter he'd had off had recharged his batteries, renewed his enthusiasm and set him up for a second coming. These were vain hopes, for that Australian visit of 1985 was Botham's final great series, at least on these shores.

Time had taken its toll on him. For eight years he'd held England together with bat and, especially, with ball. He'd been worked into the ground but, a willing workhorse, he had always come back for more. That willingness to bowl was his undoing. The body had taken a pounding; besides the back, he'd had a knee operation and was continually pestered by minor but significant ailments. Worse than that, he'd become a circus freak show, his life, or something vaguely like it, unfolding in the press each day. That distracted him from his cricket, reduced his mental preparation for matches, and his game did suffer as a consequence. His cricket became less and less important as other matters became central to his daily existence. It's equally true to say that he was losing his interest in the game. The captaincy of Somerset had turned sour, the England captaincy would clearly never come again. By the time of his return from the West Indies in April 1986, he'd done everything there was to do in the game several times over. The ill-starred Tim Hudson interlude had shown one thing: he needed more than cricket in his life. There was nothing left to achieve on the field though a little necessary prompting came his way with his drugs ban. When he returned from that, he was fully fired up with something to prove once again; the fact that he came into the last Test with New Zealand fresh after the enforced hiatus from the game showed what he could still achieve granted the right sort of handling.

Botham clearly felt victimised by the Establishment's handling of him; given the sympathetic and far more intelligent treatment meted out to the likes of Paul Merson in recent years, a man who used harder drugs far more widely, he must still wonder why he was dealt with so summarily. Yet this jolt provided new impetus. It was self-righteous wrath that propelled him into a powerful response. At the Oval against New Zealand he promptly broke Dennis Lillee's record to become the greatest wicket taker in Test history. For good measure, he then hit the joint second fastest fifty in Test cricket too, his half century coming in only thirty-two balls. Clearly the old magic was still there when the blood was up. That happened less frequently as he seemed to care less and less about results, more and more about making an impact. Perhaps after the media battering he'd taken, he wanted the public to love him again as they'd done in 1981. Any man who could be so destructive with the bat as he was in 1985 and 1986 was clearly still a considerable player. This was not wild slogging but strong, selective hitting of the ball, slamming bowlers into submission. Yet if he could score so rapidly, why did he not score more heavily? Simply put, he no longer had the appetite for it all. The game and all its attendant controversies seemed to bore him. Why else would such a rampant patriot opt out of the England scene by signing a contract to winter in Australia from 1987/88 to 1989/90?

The Hudson escapades suggested that Botham had become an adrenalin junkie, needed the impetus of new challenges to invigorate him. Why try to revisit past glories on the field? Even if he achieved them, they would lack the sweetness of the first time and there'd be plenty of experts on hand to point out that this was not as good an innings as Old Trafford in 1981, or that he'd bowled better in 1978 at Lord's. Perhaps cricket might have lost his services earlier had it not been for his move to Worcestershire in 1987, his subsequent period with Queensland, and then the back surgery of 1988. Between them they offered him a chance to prove himself as a player once again, gave him some time away from the game to think about how much it all meant to him, allowed the body some respite and gave him the ultimate challenge of reclaiming his spot in the Test side. Having back surgery is just about as serious as it gets for a quick bowler. A few have come back from it, like Dennis Lillee and Ian Bishop, but they were struck down as young men with still excellent physiques. For them there was always a light at the end of the tunnel for they had time to play with. When Botham returned from his surgery at the start of 1989 his new sylph-like figure stunned many, but it was an indication of the seriousness of his intent. Looking fitter than he had done in years, that still did not disguise the fact that he had passed his thirty-third birthday the winter before and that Father Time was catching up with him.

The 1989 season was make or break for Botham. However hard he had prepared for the season, it was only when he got out on the field that he'd know whether his back operation had been an unqualified success or not. All the requisite rewards were on offer: a visit from the Australians in the summer, and a final trip to the West Indies in the winter, the two foes he most wanted to face. Coming on as second change for Worcestershire, bowling well within himself at a pace he would have been well advised to adopt three years earlier, he made a promising start with the ball, though his batting form was scratchy. Nevertheless, he got into the England party for the Texaco trophy, his first representative duties in twenty-one months. There the pattern continued, economical with the ball, loose with the bat. Even so, Botham was named in the side for the First Test but was then struck by a ball from Steve

Barwick of Glamorgan, the result a depressed fracture of
the right cheekbone. The muddle-headedness of England's
selectors was then exposed when Robin Smith was called
up as his replacement. After all the years of persisting with
Botham as all-rounder, apparently he had now been chosen
primarily as a batsman at the time when he was in awful
form with 128 runs from eight completed innings – that
was the only conclusion to be drawn from the elevation of
Smith.

Back within three weeks, Botham walked into the
England side for the Third Test at Edgbaston with Gower's
England already two down and starting to panic in the
wake of massive defeats. To make way for Botham, Paul
Jarvis, the opening bowler, was dropped; selection policy
was still hard to fathom. Nevertheless, Botham performed
creditably with the bat: his two and a half hour vigil for
forty-six helped carry the team from 75 for 5 to 171 for 6
in reply to Australia's 424. England avoided the follow on
and with the help of the weather salvaged a draw. If
anything, this game should have been the pointer for
Botham's next four years in the game – batting sensibly,
holding the side together in adversity, and bowling within
himself (in the Australian second innings, he did not bowl
at all). Things started to go wrong in the next game at Old
Trafford where he failed both times with the bat when a
decent performance in either innings would have saved a
game lost by nine wickets. Admittedly, like most of the
team, Botham's thoughts were elsewhere, for on the final
day the rebel tour party for South Africa was announced.

Injury hampered the rest of his season – he dislocated a
finger in the Fifth Test when trying to hold a hard chance
at slip and that effectively ended his international season.
He left the ground looking set for a winter in the West

Indies following the assurances he felt he'd received from Micky Stewart. When, on 8 September, the touring party was announced, Botham's name was conspicuous only by its absence. It was a volte-face Botham has never forgiven, one that left him forever suspicious of the motives of Stewart, the newly appointed England captain Graham Gooch, and chairman of the selectors, Ted Dexter, all of whom he belittled in his autobiography. Dexter explained the decision on the grounds that his form had 'not even nearly approximated to Test standard this year'. The furore that Botham might have expected to follow was lost amid the sympathy for David Gower, stripped of the captaincy and then dropped from the touring party, apparently on the grounds of fitness since he needed a shoulder operation two months before the party flew out. Had Gower retained the Ashes, would his shoulder have been an issue?

In fact, it was Gower's omission that gave the strongest clue as to why Botham had been left at home too. Looking through the Test series, Botham was one of England's better players at Edgbaston in the Third Test, played poorly in the Fourth, and was injured and so was unable to contribute in the Fifth. This was hardly enough to condemn a man coming back from serious surgery. If anyone should have been questioned, it was the selectors for bringing him back into Test cricket too early. Perhaps choosing him at all was the greatest error. Rather than giving him hope for the future, England might have been better served pensioning him off there and then. His selection in 1989 was surely borderline, yet in selecting him then, it made no sense to leave him out of the winter touring party. Certainly his form in the domestic game had been less than inspired with the bat – 276 Championship runs at sixteen – but the back injury would not harm his batting. The niggling injuries which disrupted the flow of his season were at the root of that lack of runs and Dexter and company had had enough confidence in him as a batsman to pick him for the First Test when he'd scarcely scored a run to that point. Having adhered to the 'form is temporary, class is permanent' argument at the start of the summer, it was cast aside in September. The decision was all the more peculiar since, on the plus side, his bowling was much more reliable for having the pace taken out of it. Fifty-one wickets at twenty-two suggested that he might be able to turn his arm over quite usefully on occasion. He was closer to being considered a genuine all-rounder than he had been in several years. Look at the squad England took to the West Indies and those that replaced him. The batsmen were Gooch, Lamb, Rob Bailey (one Test), Nasser Hussain (no Tests), Wayne Larkins (six Tests), Robin Smith (eight Tests) and Alec Stewart (no Tests, reserve wicketkeeper). The two all-rounders were David Capel and Phil DeFreitas. At that stage of their careers, it's hard to see how Stewart, Hussain or Capel got the nod ahead of Botham on cricketing ability alone if Botham had been considered a good enough player to make the side in 1989. There had to be another agenda to explain the selection policy.

The Australian series of 1989 had degenerated into disaster by its close. Gower's leadership was again ineffectual, but he was also beset by problems. Every side England selected had to be changed before it took the field because of a spate of injuries. At the tail end of the season, half the side made it clear they had no interest in playing for England by signing up to go to South Africa – since those negotiations had gone on for much of the summer, they must have undermined team spirit. To blame Gower alone for the heavy defeat against Border's highly focused troops would be unfair. Nevertheless, as Ted Dexter pointed out, a change of direction was necessary. England could not go on simply surrendering to every half decent side they met. Better leadership was required while the team as a whole needed to be fitter, sharper, more dedicated to their game. This must have dawned on them earlier in the season when things began to accelerate downhill. Of course Stewart and Dexter knew of the South African tour that was coming up. Botham insists that Stewart talked him out of going by promising him a place in the side going to the West Indies, a decision that cost him £500,000, enough to make anyone bitter. With Gower's days as captain obviously numbered and Mike Gatting off on the rebel trip, what better time to make wholesale changes?

Graham Gooch had been England's captain for the final West Indian Test in 1988 and the game against Sri Lanka, doing a reasonable job at a difficult time. He had been chosen to lead the side to India that winter in a tour aborted because of the South African connections of some in the party, Gooch included. With that in mind, it might have been sensible to assume that he would have been England captain for the start of 1989. However, with Peter May resigning as chairman of the selectors a change was always possible, and Gower it was who took charge of the side through that troublesome summer. Gooch, unluckily, returned to the ranks and had an awful year with the bat, tormented by Terry Alderman and Geoff Lawson, even standing down from the England side at one point. With all these things in mind and a South African rebel tour in the offing, Gooch might have been thought of as the prime candidate to lead the side. He'd planned to winter with Western Province in 1988/89 before his elevation to the England job and still had strong links with the country. This time, however, Gooch was against going, knowing only too well the trouble that went with the money. With Gatting definitely going on the trip, though, a window of opportunity was opening once again for Gooch; with Gower gone as well, he was the only real choice left to the selectors.

Gooch and Stewart were always likely to make a united team at the top of English cricket. Gooch's devotion to physical fitness was already well known in the game and the punishing schedule which he set himself was surely instrumental in his long stay at the top. He was unimpressed by Gower's captaincy against Australia, noting in his autobiography that 'more and more, [he] seemed to let the game drift ... one thing which was plain to see during the English depression of that series was how fast disillusion can set in for a badly beaten side'. These sorts of sentiments chimed in perfectly with those of Stewart, who had never wanted Gower as captain anyway, preferring the more pugnacious figure of Gatting. With Gatting gone, Gooch stepped into a similar role with ease.

Before selecting the touring party, Dexter and Stewart had settled on the policy they would follow. On arrival at the selection meeting, Gooch was told that Gower and Botham would not be considered. This fell in with his own feelings for, as he wrote, 'I had set my heart on changing losing attitudes and needed concentrated single-mindedness without any non-cricketing distractions'. This was at the heart of Botham's omission. It was not so much a question of form, more one of attitude. If Botham went to the Caribbean, would he become a media sideshow yet again to the detriment of everyone? Quite simply it came down to a question of trust. Would Ian Botham stick to the party line, keep his head down and basically do as he was told, or might he instead be the liability he'd been in 1985/86?

Ironically, now that he had resolved to take Kath with him on future tours, he might well have been the more sober tourist Stewart and Gooch were looking for, but his past reputation, on and off the field in the West Indies, let him down. In that sense, one can hardly blame them for leaving him to kick his heels at home. They deliberately went for a young side that would fall in behind Gooch, mimicking the Australian line Allan Border had so successfully taken. Essentially, Botham and Gower were seen as a malign influence at the heart of the English team, bon viveurs who cared more about the recreational rather than the net facilities. They were seen as likely to lead the younger players into bad habits at a stage when Stewart and Gooch wanted to school them in the old-fashioned virtues of Test cricket – hard work, good technique, physical fitness. This is a moot point of course, for under Stewart and Gatting in Australia in 1986/87 Botham had been lauded as an excellent team man and a key figure in the Ashes series victory. Nevertheless, the die was cast and the England hierarchy had acted finally to break up the trio of Botham, Gower and Lamb whose apparently flippant attitude to their work troubled them.

Little has been made of Lamb's part in this for in the public eye he was a distant third among these musketeers. While his profile was lower, his form was also much better and throughout the second half of the 1980s he was the mainstay of England's fragile batting, notably so against the fast bowlers. But Lamb was no slouch when it came to having a good time. He and Botham were great friends because they shared a similar outlook on life, the classic live hard, play hard mentality – the two once put firecrackers on Bob Willis's run up inducing another panic attack for umpire Dickie Bird who thought the ground had been infiltrated by gunmen. The two were inveterate practical jokers and could generally be found in each other's company after stumps had been drawn. Lamb was often on hand when Botham ended in the mire – New Zealand 1983/84, West Indies 1985/86 – and it was to prevent just this sort of clique forming that the selectors acted. With Botham out of the way, Lamb was elevated to a position of responsibility, becoming Gooch's vice captain and actually leading the side in a Test when his captain was injured. Lamb was able to respond to that greatest need when you are upsetting the powers that be by being yourself; to preserve your skin, you have to play better than everyone else. For Botham scaling such heights was a distant memory, and so he was vulnerable to the great purge.

For all Botham's protestations that he should have made the plane – and if Stewart had made a promise to him, it should either have been honoured or Stewart should have resigned if he had made such a statement without the authority to do so – England did pretty well without him, much better than they had in many years against the West Indies. They won the First Test, and were denied the chance of going two up by rain and time-wasting tactics in Trinidad before losing the final two games of the series. Moreover, *Wisden* remarked, 'Gooch rapidly commanded an unfailing respect among his players and earned it by his quiet, individual counselling, his caring touch and his thoughtful tactics. In his own way, he was the most impressive England captain since Brearley.' Equally, Lamb was 'gregarious and positive ... just what was required as a support for the more complex ways of Gooch'. If the ends justify the means, the dropping of Gower and Botham was revealed as a masterstroke.

England were entering a new era and Botham would

have been well advised to accept that. Things were changing and he was no longer viewed as an integral part of the England set-up. He continued to perform well for Worcestershire and managed the occasional comeback when the resources of the national team were stretched, but his England days were long gone. Well into his thirties, surely this was no surprise, for not even a Botham can go on for ever, especially after the pounding he'd given his body throughout his career. But, like the Princess of Wales, he was not disposed to go quietly. Perhaps Graham Gooch and Micky Stewart did start to overdo the physical fitness side of things to the detriment of the side's sharpness, but to carp on continually about how this was costing England Test matches rang hollow. The more Botham attacked the Establishment, the easier it was for them to label him a malign influence and leave him out of the side.

The message finally struck home in 1993 as Botham waged an impressive publicity-led campaign for his reselection for the England side to take on the Aussies. Given that England had played poorly in India that winter, a change in personnel was likely, but would picking an ailing thirty-eight-year-old really be a step forward? Botham bowled well at the start of the season in a meaningless game for the Duchess of Norfolk's XI against Australia at Arundel, taking two for twenty-nine in ten tidy overs. To Botham, this was evidence that he still held the Indian sign over the Australians. This was absurdly naive. Sadly, the unworldly Ted Dexter was crass in remarking that it looked as though the Aussies were trying to play Botham into the Test team. An off the cuff joke it might have been, and the underlying point that the game proved nothing was a good one, but it was still grossly insulting to a figure of Botham's stature.

Botham was no longer good enough to play Test cricket, but he continued to play for Durham in the hope the call might come. It's true that England were in trouble again against Australia that summer, but it was time to move on. If changes had to be made, bring in some youngsters, not those whose day had gone. Sadly, Botham was starting to resemble those old stagers who knew it all whom he'd despised in his earlier career. The time had come for him to look to the future. Ironically, it was Dexter who offered him the chance to take a place in the England set-up, asking him to lead an England 'A' side on a brief visit to Holland in July. Sure, this was not the big time he'd been used to, but as a service to English cricket and a first toe in the water towards a coaching position in the hierarchy, it had potential. Botham refused, complaining in his book that Dexter had asked him to go on a 'clog-dancing mission'. This was hardly the action of a patriot who wanted to do all he could to help the development of the national side and the spread of the game of cricket.

Perhaps Botham had come fully to embody Ralph Waldo Emerson's view of heroism: 'self-trust is the essence of heroism ... [it is] scornful of petty calculations and scornful of being scorned. It persists; it is of an undaunted boldness and a fortitude not to be wearied out. Its jest is the littleness of common life ... heroism is obedience to a secret impulse of an individual's character.' This was Ian Botham, it had always been so, but as his career wound down it seemed more the case than ever. His greatest admirers were often angered by England's poor use of his gifts and equally saddened by his own refusal or inability to settle down to the hard work that even the greats must do, produce the weight of runs of which he was capable, and demand inclusion as a specialist batsman. That did not appeal.

Botham was an artist, not an artisan. If he had been the intrepid adventurer in his early days, he was to adopt another of W.G.'s mantles, that of the great impresario. People flocked to watch any game in which he was involved because they knew they would see a cameo of Botham's greatness. That seemed to be enough for him, to dazzle briefly and then retire to the seclusion of the dressing room to prepare himself for *A Question Of Sport*, a speaking tour, or a pantomime. Again, like W.G., his very presence was enough for many; perhaps also like W.G., he came to believe that he was bigger than the game.

Certainly it's easier to make out a case that the Pakistani series of 1987 should have been his last. His back surgery of 1988 prolonged his useful life as a county cricketer but he was left short of Test quality since he seemed unwilling or unable to score the runs required of him. If Test matches are there to be won, if they are the supreme test of national sporting fortitude, the best side needs to be selected. Botham did not meet those requirements any longer. He knew the end was coming, and it frustrated him. He joined the long list of cricketers to be niggled by Dermot Reeve – nothing strange in that – but this irascibility was more pointed, more heartfelt, no longer just part of the act. According to Reeve's autobiography, 'Ian was beginning to be under pressure for his all-rounder spot in the England team [when] we had our spat in 1990 ... he hadn't made the England tour party to the West Indies in '89/90 and that had hurt him ... he was still having to rack up some performances to get back in the England side.' That pressure rattled him. A characteristically unorthodox knock from Reeve against Worcestershire was ended by Botham who, on dismissing him, roared, 'Go on, fuck off.' Reeve's typically succinct rejoinder was, 'You've had your day, mate.'

Reeve was right, closer to the truth than Botham would have liked. Even so, his competitive instinct helped him to fight off all comers for far longer than was necessary or good for English cricket. Just as he had overshadowed Mike Gatting early in his career, so the shadow of his legend has loomed large over those who have looked to replace him. That's a mighty long list now. Phil DeFreitas was the first real contender, but he was a good bowler who was well short of Test class with the bat. Dermot Reeve himself could have been effective in the Test arena, might even have made a good England captain, but few rated his all-round skills highly enough to give him an extended opportunity. That much is also true of Dominic Cork, though his batting shows some promise and he may yet become a genuine international all-rounder. Like Reeve, he has the bloody-mindedness of Botham, a fierce determination to win and to impose himself on the opposition. Never overawed, his problem may be that which beset Botham: as England's only regular wicket taker, he is in danger of being bowled into the ground, his useful life shortened. Darren Gough is similar to Cork in terms of quality and the two could forge a useful new-ball partnership for England. If both stay fit and in form, the two together might equal Botham as batsman. That's always been the problem post 1985 – England need two players to replace him. Perhaps the man most affected by the Botham legend has been Chris Lewis. If any English all-rounder could come close to Botham, it is him. A great natural talent, Lewis's toughest opponent seems to be himself. There has been many a false dawn in his career when it seems he has finally established himself only for him to fall out of the picture once again. The pressure of expectation always seems to be too much for a player who should be dominating the England side in an attack with Cork, Gough, Tufnell and one other, guaranteeing that England could bat usefully down to number nine.

Despite Botham's detrimental though wholly innocent effect on those that would follow, many players have benefited from playing alongside him. Phil Neale is particularly bullish about the impact he had on Worcestershire once he arrived at New Road:

His presence was important. He came here because he knew we were a good side and that he wouldn't have to carry us. His arrival meant we went from being a picturesque little club playing nice cricket in a cosy little atmosphere but which hadn't won anything in a while, to a club that was looking for success. Suddenly Ian came and the press came with him. That's a double edged thing, we had to be careful about what we said, but also it attracted attention that the others thrived on. That got a number of our lads into the England side. When Ian got injured in 1988, it looked like a crippling blow because we looked on him as a main part of the side but the guys came in and filled the hole – Martin Weston deputised superbly well. People had thought Ian's arrival meant the end for him but he played his best cricket while Ian was at the club and related very well to him. I know Ian had a very positive influence on guys like him and Stuart Lampitt. In that season, though he couldn't play, he was very supportive and a positive influence about the dressing room. The thing that struck me was Ian was totally committed and very focused on Worcestershire being successful. He was the first to get a plan in the mind about how the season would go – which games we ought to win, where we'd need to work hard, he was determined that we would be successful.

At England level, the Botham effect was less obvious on the field, but his presence had an impact nonetheless. Tony Lewis, writing in the *Daily Telegraph*, noted that

> these days [his] cricket is as much aura as reality. When he was recalled at The Oval [in 1991] a golden glow settled on the England dressing room ... it was Robin's return to Sherwood Forest. The lesser merry men gathered around him and heard words devoid of apprehension, loaded with self-confidence and found themselves thrust to the centre of the country's news media concern ... 'Both' was back, all would be well now ... his batting these days lacks continuity because he struggles to find the linking strokes between defence and thundering hits ... at his best he often picked up singles by turning the straight ball to leg but now there are false messages from eye to the body and the strokes are sometimes flawed ... although the terrific assaults of 1981 may never be repeated and though he is unlikely to get five wickets in a Test innings again, Ian Botham is a cricketer who makes things happen.

That perhaps is the most fitting epitaph for Botham's cricketing career. He made glorious things happen, the unexpected, the thoroughly impossible. To him, the impossible was commonplace so it is not surprising that he felt he could go on repeating those feats ad infinitum. Consequently his time with Durham was an unhappy one. We were faced with the dispiriting sight of this colossus blaming others for not realising he could still beat the Aussies when, by his own admission, it was an effort just to get out of bed.

Having brought down the curtain, and with cricket finally out of his life, Botham needed new battles to fight.

His court case against Imran bore the hallmarks of a man who needed to vanquish a foe once again; perhaps that litigation was used to suppress the withdrawal symptoms that all greats suffer once they leave the stage. Certainly he has a pronounced sense of injustice and a desire to right any perceived wrongs, but given that courtroom decisions are every bit as uncertain as events on a cricket field, he was ill advised to fight an alleged libel published in a small circulation magazine. Better by far to have laughed off such risible accusations of racism – would Viv Richards have a racist as his closest friend? – and meaningless jibes about his lack of breeding. They meant nothing to anyone but Botham and his fellow litigant, Allan Lamb. Few had seen the article, fewer still believed it. More unwise still was Botham's attack on an article appearing under Imran's name in the *Sun* which accused all of England's great bowlers, and most of those in the rest of the world, of cheating at one time or another, though none was actually named. Botham felt this to be a smear and acted, while Trueman, Statham, Bedser, Tyson, Snow, Willis, Lillee, McKenzie, McDermott, Hall, Holding, Ambrose, Walsh *et al* laughed off Imran's charges as too contemptible to be worthy of comment. Appropriately enough for such a risible and unnecessary case, the trial itself often degenerated into farce over the course of its thirteen days in Court 13. Among the moments of prime comedy there was Allan Lamb unable to tell the difference between 'condemning' and 'condoning', Brian Close refusing to confirm that Geoff Boycott was an honest man, and Boycott attempting verbally to lay into Close and narrowly avoiding facing contempt of court charges.

Botham's pride may have been wounded by Imran's apparent accusations but his failure to let sleeping dogs lie cost him dearly. With Imran securing the services of George Carman QC in his defence, it was obvious that Botham would not be given an easy ride. During his fourteen-hour spell in the witness box, all the sordid tabloid stories of the past twenty years were unearthed in a squalid and thoroughly distasteful attempt to blacken his character, putting himself and his family life under the microscope yet again, a process that must have been painful but one which he must have expected. His performance was persuasive, making it perfectly clear that the sanctity of his reputation was paramount and that not just he but his parents, his wife and his children had all been hurt by Imran's comments. Even so, it did little to show why he felt he had had to resort to legal action, especially since Imran had offered to publish a full letter of apology in *The Times*, one which would have exonerated Botham and would have severely damaged the standing of his opponent.

In the course of the trial, perhaps Botham got the vindication he wanted without getting the result – rather like scoring a hundred but finishing up on the losing side. Certainly Imran was forced to recant on his accusations that he was a cheat for having put together a lengthy video which purported to show members of the English team wilfully altering the condition of a ball; he withdrew it from evidence once Botham and David Gower took the stand to refute his accusations. This meant that the defence of 'justification' had collapsed, this after Imran had called a number of star witnesses – Mike Atherton, Derek Pringle, David Lloyd, Lloyd actually doing more for Botham's case by discounting all the tales of ball tampering that he'd recounted in a book as 'stories. And good 'uns!' – to back up his theory that tampering was widespread in the game.

With this central plank of Imran's defence disappearing

beneath him, the result of the trial seemed a foregone conclusion. There was genuine amazement when the jury finally found in favour of Imran since he had now admitted that Botham was no cheat. After days of semantic argument centring around what might or might not be defined as 'cheating' within the laws of the game, and with little time given over to the possibly more important accusations of racism beyond emotional denials of the charge from the Botham and Lamb camps, it appeared that the jury still couldn't see what all the fuss was about. If their verdict meant anything at all, it seemed to say that all those involved should have known better and not wasted their time, that if Imran had indeed impugned the integrity of Lamb and Botham, they should have been men enough to accept a suitably fulsome apology, shake hands and leave it at that. The final word on the whole affair would be Botham's, a comment he made on the second day when Carman asked why he had failed to sue the Sunday news-papers over the Lindy Field story. Having pointed out that he hadn't the means to take on the tabloids, he added, 'at the end of the day, they were just fish-and-chip wrapping'. Perhaps the unconscious irony of that statement was not lost on the jury.

In the final analysis, competition was in Botham's blood. It was that which made him great, it was that which was his downfall. He turned the competitive instinct into an art form, that was his gift, yet it left him tainted. He was unfortunate to live in an era when everything is played out under the microscopic gaze of the media; back in the 1950s he'd have been loved as a cavalier playboy like Denis Compton. Truth be told, he *was* loved by the majority of the English cricketing public. The sermons he attracted in the tabloids were forgotten as another lofty drive dropped into the members' enclosure for six. He gave so many people such extraordinary pleasure that perhaps he should have been indulged his wilder moments. Yet sport has come to mean too much, games are taken out of all proportion to their worth. If England win a meaningless one day match in Madras, they are the finest side the world's ever seen. If they lose a similar game two days later in Calcutta, they are a disgrace to the nation and should be brought home immediately. Neither response is intelligent, neither is true, neither is helpful. Under such ludicrous pressures it's small wonder that volatile young men go off the rails. Forty years ago, if Keith Miller got Compton's wicket with a full toss in front of a full house in Melbourne with the Ashes riding on it, both men would have laughed at the preposterousness of it all. The crowd would have applauded, would have revelled in their enjoyment. Botham brought that enjoyment back to cricket. While he was winning, all was well, but when he smiled at his demise in a Test in Christchurch – caught by fluke off a full-blooded shot – he was castigated for his couldn't-care-less attitude; in the 1950s he'd have been cherished as a character. Now, he was a 'mixed blessing' for the game, a yob. Isn't that absurd? For the sake of himself and his family, Botham may be better off without cricket. For all his faults, cricket is still immeasurably the poorer without him.

CHAPTER EIGHT

Angels in the Architecture

Who Is The Greatest?

The perennial question which surrounded Botham's years at the top concerned his position among the great all-rounders – did he compare with Keith Miller, was he in the same class as Garfield Sobers? Cricket has changed so rapidly over the last twenty post-Packer years that such judgements are impossible to make; there is more cricket played today, under different circumstances and under different pressures. All we can safely say is that Botham would have been successful in Miller's era just as Miller would be a hit today. The more sensible comparison is surely with the other three great all-rounders who played in Botham's era. Who was the greatest – Ian Botham, Imran Khan, Kapil Dev or Richard Hadlee? To consider the question in 1980 would have been the work of a moment, for Botham was the undisputed number one. As time passed, Botham slipped down the field. All four left the game around the same time in the early 1990s, by which time he had the weakest credentials of any of them, playing for England more on reputation than results, while the others remained true champions.

Any such argument must be a subjective one and there will be as many different views as there are people. As a starting point, it's useful to look at their comparative statistics with bat and ball. Each meets the all-rounder criteria. In their prime they would have deserved selection for the national side as either batsman or bowler, with Hadlee perhaps the only borderline case, his batting never quite as robust as that of the others, though it should be pointed out that in a crisis he regularly made crucial runs. Each has won games for his country with bat and ball.

	TESTS	INNS	N.O.	RUNS	H.S.	AVGE	100s	50s
Botham	102	161	6	5200	208	33.55	14	22
Hadlee	86	134	19	3124	151*	27.16	2	15
Imran	88	126	25	3807	136	37.69	6	18
Kapil	131	184	15	5248	163	31.05	8	27

	BALLS	RUNS	WKTS	AVGE	STRIKE	BEST	5WI	10WM
Botham	21,815	10,878	383	28.40	56.96	8/34	27	4
Hadlee	21,918	9612	431	22.30	50.85	9/52	36	9
Imran	19,458	8258	362	22.81	53.75	8/58	23	6
Kapil	27,740	12,867	434	29.65	63.92	9/83	23	2

Each numbers among the greatest cricketers his nation has ever produced. Each would grace virtually any side in the history of the game. But who is the greatest of the four?

Kapil Dev is in many ways the most unlikely of the quartet. Until his arrival on the scene in 1978/79, the very idea of the Indians unleashing a highly successful quick bowler was quite laughable. Opening bowlers were there simply to take the shine off the ball so that spinners such as Bishan Bedi and Bhagwat Chandrasekhar could get on to beguile for over after over; the sight of military medium trundlers such as Abid Ali taking the new ball in a Test match rarely struck terror into the opposing openers. On the featherbed pitches regularly produced throughout India's Test match history right up until the Golden Jubilee of 1979/80, fast bowling was a back-breaking, heart-breaking business. It was an occupation that was fruitless and few took up the challenge. Those that did generally had short careers. In consequence, at home on turning pitches, India were a formidable force, the attacking thrust of their opponents blunted by the surfaces upon which they toiled. Away from home, however, they were perpetually vulnerable. Unused to playing fast bowling, their batsmen could often be unhinged by belligerence; Trueman's destruction of them at Headingley in 1952 was a case in point, the punch-drunk tourists collapsing to 0 for 4, the worst ever start to a Test match innings. Just prior to Kapil's arrival on the scene, India's tour to the West Indies in 1975/76 was plagued by injury inflicted by Clive Lloyd's lightning fast pacemen. The nadir came at Sabina Park when the Indian second innings closed for ninety-seven with only five wickets down, captain Bedi insisting that there were no more batsmen fit enough to take to the crease – he had declared at 306 for 6 in the first innings as a protest against intimidatory bowling which had caused both Gaekwad and Patel to retire hurt, while Viswanath broke a finger in getting out.

If the batsmen were at sea against the quicks, when India

took to the field they would often find themselves bowling on tracks tailor made for seam and swing bowlers, offering nothing for the spinners. Once Kapil Dev arrived in Indian sides, home teams could no longer produce fast pitches knowing they were free from any retaliation. He turned the prevailing logic on its head and was the single most important reason for India enjoying its most consistently successful period in Test cricket throughout the 1980s and into the 1990s. In addition, it was his charismatic leadership and dynamic batting that captured the World Cup in 1983, surely the most popular win until Sri Lanka's success on the subcontinent in 1996.

In his early career, Kapil was a constant threat to the batsmen, his bowling a whirl of activity and aggression unusual among the traditionally gentle Indian sides. Though a smile was rarely far from his face, Kapil could bowl like a demon, hurrying up to the wicket and hurling down deliveries that were distinctly nippy. It was his misfortune that India lacked an equally potent threat from the other end. Ghavri was a useful foil, but just how much more dangerous would Kapil have been had he been partnered by the current pairing of Javagal Srinath and Venkatesh Prasad, two men clearly inspired by Kapil's example? As it was, batsmen were happy just to keep Kapil out, attempting to score their runs at the other end; this was certainly the case in matches held beyond India's sunny clime where colleagues like Shastri or Doshi were equally threatening with the turning ball. The benefit Kapil did enjoy was that he had less competition in the side and more opportunity to bag lots of wickets – if no one else in the side could break through, then he would eventually. In England's 633 for 5 at Edgbaston in 1979, for example, Kapil got all five wickets. As his strike rate illustrates, he had to do a lot more bowling to get his victims, a combination of batsmen's caution and his having to play a high proportion of matches on fairly lifeless pitches.

As a batsman, there were few more pleasing sights than Kapil Dev in full flow. He allied a typically wristy Indian approach to deceptive physical power, his wiry frame uncoiling like a spring to clatter the ball to the boundary. Those who saw it can never forget his batting at Lord's in 1990. India, with their last pair at the crease, required twenty-four to avoid the follow on after Gooch had made his magnificent 333. Facing a new over from Hemmings, the first two deliveries brought no runs. Then, as if suddenly aware of the vulnerability of his partner at the other end, Kapil launched into four quite monumental hits, each sending the ball sailing over the boundary ropes, saving the follow on in a manner none could have imagined possible. It was a feat that would even have stretched Botham in 1981. As David Frith remarked, 'Kapil could touch the sublime in carefree batsmanship'. Certainly few have ever batted with his abandon on such a regular basis.

He and Botham are similar in many ways. Both had a tendency to play from the heart at times when they might have been better advised to play from the head. Yet as Botham proved, such a tendency is often the root of genius; to ignore convention, trust yourself and give free rein to the spirit can create moments of pure magic. Kapil did that most memorably in 1983 in a Prudential World Cup game at Tunbridge Wells. Choosing to bat first against Zimbabwe, India crashed to 17 for 5 with Gavaskar, Patil, Amarnath, Srikkanth and Yashpal Sharma all out. Given that the opposition were relative minnows, the sensible course for Kapil would have been to try to bat out the fifty-five overs with the help of his colleagues, shielding them and not taking any undue risks, looking to post a target of 150 or so. Instead he thrashed 175, a tournament record, as India reached 266 to make qualification for the next stage a formality. It was an innings that transformed the tournament and did as much as anything to capture the trophy. Only those who fit Emerson's definition of heroism could perform so irresponsibly in conventional terms and yet be so successful.

Like Botham, Kapil had his detractors. Certainly he was not as incisive a bowler in his latter years when he seemed to be continuing partly because there was no replacement on the horizon, and partly to accumulate yet more records. He bagged forty-five of his wickets against Sri Lanka, then a relatively weak nation – this equates to Botham picking up scalps in the Packer period, though Botham took far more wickets than that. Yet picking up cheap wickets against poor opposition is not the formality it sometimes appears; you still need to be a fine bowler regularly to get five or six wickets in an innings. Poor sides might represent an easier foe, but they still have to be beaten. If we look at Kapil's displays against the West Indies, they are exemplary, and indicate he was a considerable bowler. Of course, Kapil did more bowling than the other three and so would expect to get more wickets. His strike rate is the poorest of the four, but given that he often played on lifeless pitches in India, that's to be expected. It should be remembered too that Botham's strike rate was built up in his first forty Tests and that the rest of his career was far less dramatic. At a time when Botham should have been benefiting from the accumulated wisdom of experience, he was often bowling like a drain. The other three seldom did so, cutting their cloth according to their physical well-being, letting brain do the work that had formerly been the preserve of brawn.

In that regard Kapil, like Imran and Hadlee, had a physical advantage over Botham. Where Botham was a naturally large framed man, one who was always going to fill out into a bulky individual, the others were more wiry. If that gave Botham the greater reserves of stamina which allowed him to bowl long spells, it also put a greater strain on him as he got older. Bowling quick is a debilitating business and the extra weight he naturally carried gave his lower body a pounding. It also made it harder for him to maintain the superb action he had before he had matured fully, placing additional stress on that perpetually fragile back. Kapil remained a naturally lithe figure and was therefore better able to maintain his fitness and so his form. As Botham's star burst into the heavens in a blaze of glory only to extinguish itself as swiftly, Kapil's burned with a consistent intensity, lighting up the sky long after Botham had become yesterday's man. Yet in terms of performances over a career it is almost impossible to separate Botham and Kapil Dev. Their records are similar, their feats stupendous, their achievements equally immense – for Botham's regular destruction of Australia, read Kapil hauling India into the modern age.

Sir Richard Hadlee is a different matter altogether, the only one of the four who might struggle to call himself a genuine all-rounder. As fierce a striker of the ball as any of the others, it was as one of the very greatest bowlers of all time that he truly made his reputation; in that sense, he is the only one of the four who might not get in a World XI as an all-rounder, yet the only one who would make it on the strength of just one of the two disciplines. Surely he would be the first choice for the best quick bowler of the 1980s, Malcolm Marshall perhaps his worthiest challenger for that crown. In his *Wisden* appreciation of Hadlee in 1991, Don Mosey termed him 'the most intelligent fast bowler the world has seen'. David Frith selects him of all the great all-rounders in history 'to bowl for my life'. These are judgements from the game's historians that are worthy of respect; they're yet more remarkable when you consider Hadlee's early years in Test cricket were not wildly successful. It wasn't until the start of the 1980s, some seven years after his debut, that Hadlee began to construct his wonderful figures. To that stage he'd played twenty-six Tests and taken 107 wickets at a cost of thirty. The rest of his career saw him capture 324 wickets in sixty Tests at a cost of just 19.7, an astonishing performance given that he was playing for one of the weakest Test nations over that period. Like Kapil, he was short of the very best support, though the likes of Chatfield and Cairns were reliable performers, more threatening than India's seamers. As New Zealand matured as a side in the 1980s, picking up victories all around the world, men like Martin Crowe and John Wright deserve great credit for the invaluable part they played. Essentially, though, Hadlee carried the hopes of the New Zealand team on his shoulders. It's no surprise that his best batting often came when the side was either in trouble or urgently seeking to press home an advantage. If New Zealand won a Test, it was fair to assume that another sterling performance from Hadlee was at the root of it all. Certainly, he was *the* decisive factor in more Tests and over a greater period of time than Botham could ever lay claim to.

It's become a cliché that Botham was the greatest competitor in the cricketing world, but does that bear scrutiny? Certainly his desire, his will to win, was staggering, but did that make him the greatest? Hadlee was every bit as determined. Although the acuity of Botham's cricketing brain is not in doubt, it was often clouded by the red mists of competition, the need to bounce a batsman out or hit a bowler out of the attack. On occasion such tactics worked, but as he aged they worked less frequently, ended more depressingly. Hadlee, on the other hand, rarely allowed himself to be consumed by the frenzied atmosphere of a Test match. Instead he drew back from the emotions of the day, concentrating, always concentrating, on the job in hand. He probed for weaknesses in a batsman, searched through his filing system to recall modes of dismissal, looked for the ones and twos when he was batting to break up the field before he hit out, turning the game into a science rather than an art form. In that sense he outstrips Botham and Kapil Dev. Yet in terms of the all-rounder debate, one has to question his performance as a batsman. The most interesting statistic is that, like his bowling, his batting improved with age. Surely that is the hallmark of a great all-round cricketing mind rather than just a gifted all-round cricketer? Hadlee never sold himself short. He stretched his gifts to the absolute maximum, which is all that can be asked of any player.

Botham is perhaps the hardest to judge. Undeniably he was the most heroic, the most theatrical, the easiest to warm to or take offence against. If your prime motivation in watching cricket was to be entertained, Botham was your man. Whether he was playing superbly or in the lowest trough of form, life was never dull while he was around. His early runs and wickets were often taken against poor or weakened sides, but they were taken nevertheless, voraciously so. In addition, it's perhaps his misfortune that he played against poorer sides when at his best. If a full strength West Indian or Australian side had toured England in 1979, maybe Botham would have shredded their batting orders too. It's unfortunate that those games are still relatively fresh in the memory and we remember the weakened state of the opposition. How many other epic displays have been given in such circumstances? Hutton's 364 at the Oval in 1938 was achieved on a perfect pitch against a bowling attack in which only Tiger O'Reilly could truly be called great – the back-up of Waite, McCabe, Barnes and Fleetwood-Smith was not awe-inspiring, especially on that blameless surface. Sobers was equally fortunate in the Pakistani attack that toiled against him in vain at Sabina Park in 1957/58 when he eclipsed Hutton, only Fazal Mahmood a worthy adversary. So let's not be too quick to condemn Botham for the heinous crime of being too good for the opposition. Much of the case against him rests on his performances against the West Indies. Throughout the 1980s, the West Indies provided the supreme test. This is how the four fared against them with bat and ball:

	TESTS	INNS	N.O.	RUNS	H.S.	AVGE	100s	50s
Botham	20	38	1	792	81	21.40	0	4
Hadlee	10	15	3	389	103	32.42	1	1
Imran	18	33	5	775	123	27.68	1	3
Kapil	25	39	4	1,079	126*	30.82	3	4

	BALLS	RUNS	WKTS	AVGE	STRIKE	BEST	5WI	10WM
Botham	3,609	2,146	61	35.18	59.16	8/103	3	0
Hadlee	2,506	1,124	51	22.04	49.13	6/50	4	1
Imran	3,488	1,695	80	21.19	43.60	7/80	6	1
Kapil	4,639	2,216	89	24.90	52.12	9/83	4	1

If these comparisons tell us anything, it is that against the best side in the world Botham was the only one to be systematically reduced to the role of mere mortal in both departments of the game. Hadlee's performance is significantly better than his career averages, while Kapil and Imran were both more successful bowlers against the West Indies compared with their overall career figures. Looked at in these cold statistical terms, Botham looks ineffective. But, of course, Disraeli was right and if these statistics don't actually lie, they need to be viewed in the light of mitigating circumstances.

As a bowler, Botham never faced the West Indies when at his fittest, all his games against them coming in the wake of his back problems. His tours to the Caribbean were beset with problems, some of his own making, others not. Whoever was at fault, it is only fair to concede that his run ins with the press would have had an egregious effect on the form of the most thick skinned individual and so the tabloids must take some of the blame for his under achieving in the West Indies. Most damaging, perhaps, he played in an England side that regularly lacked the fibre to fight back against the West Indians, sapping even his morale. The sides that took the field under Gower against the West Indies often seemed rudderless ships. For all his gifts, Gower was palpably unsuited to the role of leading England against the West Indies; once things were going badly for them, no one seemed able to take responsibility, to marshal the troops and instigate a fightback. Certainly in the West Indies the pitches were very poor indeed and the home bowling extremely fearsome, but to lose ten straight Tests was woeful. Like rabbits caught in the headlights, England were regularly run down by the oncoming juggernaut driven by Vivian Richards. As England's most explosive cricketer, Botham should have been the one to produce the goods under pressure, but so demoralised was the side as a whole and so big a part did the soap opera of his life play in that demoralisation, it was beyond even him. The Lord's Test of 1984 was a case in point: he took eight West Indian victims in the first knock, his highest score against them of eighty-one in the second. Yet with the West Indians facing a stiff target of 342 in the fourth innings, Botham and his colleagues bowled with all the discipline of an alcoholic village green eleven to be beaten out of sight by nine wickets. So strong was the psychological hold the West Indies had on England that even Botham could not escape its grip.

It's equally true to say that for deep-rooted historical reasons, the West Indians prize victory over England more than any other, even when England are in dire straits and clearly no match for them. Under Lloyd and then Richards, they attacked England's weaknesses ruthlessly and never offered a moment's respite. Yet despite this convincing barrage of excuses, we must still face the fact that Botham's performances against the West Indies were desperately ordinary. Taking that on board, all the evidence still suggests that Botham's greatest moments – in 1978 against Pakistan, in 1979/80 against India, and then against the

Australians in 1981 – were a little overrated. The nature, as much as the scale, of his achievements tended to sweep people away in the heat and glory of the moment; cooler analysis indicates that Botham, although England's greatest ever all-rounder, may not have been foremost of this quartet.

Perhaps Botham's greatest failing in comparison with the others was his attitude of no surrender, the very attitude that had launched his career. He had to score quickly, hit hard, bowl fast, even when the ability was no longer quite there, even if circumstances argued that he should show caution. There were some glimpses of him batting with the required measure of responsibility – Sydney in 1979, the Oval in 1987, Edgbaston in 1989 – but these were relatively few and far between. Botham genuinely believed that he would best serve his team by playing according to type. For a time when he was young, fully fit and incredibly strong, that worked supremely well. Later, he needed to keep a check on his temperament but rarely managed to do so. Had Botham been endowed with Hadlee's calculating brain, his appetite for hard work off the field, his desire to probe for weaknesses and to maximise his gifts, his figures would be yet more awesome than they are; if you could weigh the natural talents of all four on a set of kitchen scales, they would tip in the Englishman's favour. The talent was there to the end, but the appetite for the basics waned. In the West Indies in 1985/86, for example, his one good performance came when he was told that he'd been on the verge of losing his place in the side. If that said anything, it was that as you get older, natural talent isn't enough. The reflexes slow, the eye dims, you need to work harder at your game. Botham seemed to feel he was still twenty-one.

John Arlott once said of Botham that he didn't realise what a complicated game cricket was and that that was at the root of his success. He played in an uncomplicated way – a gleeful swing of the bat, a wholehearted delivery, an improbable leap to grasp a dazzling slip catch. That was wonderful while it lasted, but once injury robbed him of his zip he needed to go back to the drawing board. Temperamentally, he could not seem to do so. He still had to try to bounce players out when he was no more threatening than an ordinary medium pacer. If he'd followed the Gooch regimen to keep in trim, remodelled his action and bowled at a reduced pace, he could still have been a top class bowler, following the example of Lillee or Hadlee. As it was, Botham played with the heart more than the head and couldn't, or wouldn't, change. That attitude gave us Headingley 1981; it also gave us the second innings at Lord's in 1984 when Gordon Greenidge humbled him. That was Botham, the glorious and the grotesque. That was what made him the most unpredictable cricketer of the four, one of the most exciting ever. Yet in some ways, Botham wasn't the great cricketer of folklore, certainly not in performance terms beyond his initial four-year explosion; a man like Bradman, a true legend of the game, earned that status year after year by performances on the field, so too did Headley, Trueman, Sobers, Richards, Border and the like. Botham was as much a phenomenon as he was a cricketer, legendary for his impact on the world as much as for his deeds on the field. That made him a great competitor, wonderful theatre, a potential match winner, but not a wholly reliable performer.

The acid test comes when selecting the World XI to play the invading Martians for the future of the earth. If selections relate to career performances, then I don't believe

Botham should be the first choice all-rounder from these four. That honour must surely go to Imran Khan, Botham's *bête noire*, particularly if one allows that Hadlee would be selected purely on the strength of his bowling. Imran and Botham again have a lot in common: both are extremely charismatic characters on and off the field; each has his admirers who will defend him to the hilt; each is capable of opening the mouth before the brain is fully engaged, leading himself into trouble; each has done a huge amount of valuable charity work, Botham for leukaemia research, Imran for the construction of a specialist cancer hospital in Pakistan. Time and again, though, the two have crossed swords, going right back to their first Test encounters in England in 1982, an ill tempered series that the Pakistanis felt was stolen from them by poor, or in their eyes malicious, English umpiring. Given that the English have been complaining about the standard of Pakistani umpiring, with good reason, since we first set foot in their country, the Pakistanis had every right to question one or two dubious decisions that went England's way. However, even though the hairline decisions may have tilted the balance in a tight three-Test series, Imran did himself little good in the eyes of the sporting world by bemoaning the fact time and again. It suggested he was lacking in sportsmanship, failing to look closely at his own side's shortcomings and preferring to blame others for an unacceptable defeat. On the field, that series was a modest one for Botham but one in which Imran was superb – 212 runs at fifty-three and twenty-one wickets at 18.6 compared with Botham's 163 runs at twenty-seven and eighteen wickets at 26.6. Never mind the cricket though, the real feature of the series was the animosity that threatened to engulf Anglo-Pakistan relations – a boil that continued to fester until good relations were restored by Wasim Akram and Mike Atherton in 1996 – and a rivalry which developed between Imran and Botham that apparently seethes to this day.

If Imran was unchivalrous in 1982, Botham was crass in 1984, making comments about Pakistan that he was soon to regret. Living as he does in a country that still regards Bernard Manning as a comedian, it's understandable that Botham should have made a feeble joke about his mother-in-law in relation to the standard of accommodation on offer to tourists in Pakistan. It was not meant offensively for in England it passed without comment, such was the everyday nature of the jibe, but it was nonetheless a stupid thing to say. Though Pakistani hotels may not measure up to those in the west, the people are hospitable and genuinely welcoming, something which is far more important and which should be appreciated by those who visit. Not only were Botham's comments offensive, they were rude to his hosts; more important still, since there are many people of Pakistani origin who live in this country and have to deal with the oppressive weight of casual racism every day, it's vital that public figures such as Botham do nothing to stoke those fires, however inadvertently. If it was easy to see why Botham thought nothing of the comment at the time, it was just as reasonable that the Pakistanis should take offence against these flippant remarks. Even so, as an educated man and one with wide experience of British culture, Imran should have been able to rise above the jibe, to treat it as a contemptible irrelevance, and he should not have responded at any time. His comments that painted Botham as a racist in *India Today* were unworthy – racists rarely send messages of support to anti-apartheid rallies as Botham has done. Imran's accusations did far more damage to his reputation than that of Ian Botham, not least because it made him seem petty, while the worst that can be said about Botham was that his initial off the cuff remark was thoughtless.

Ball tampering is another issue altogether. Imran's admission that he did occasionally scratch the side of the ball and lift the seam must inevitably take the shine off some of his performances as a bowler, but equally we must respect his claims that these were the isolated incidents he described them as. As a genuinely hostile fast bowler, he often measured up to the standards set by Hadlee and Lillee. Incisive with the new ball, he could be every bit as penetrative with the old, pioneering that latest bowling innovation, reverse swing. He taught his successors well too. The advent of reverse swing in recent years and the ability of the Pakistani bowlers, notably Wasim Akram and Waqar Younis, to make the old ball deviate prodigiously has been viewed with suspicion, yet as Derek Pringle explained in 1995's *Wisden*, it is no surprise that such a skill should emanate from the subcontinent: 'A perfect example of man's triumph over an unhelpful environment ... playing on grassless pitches of low bounce with hard, bare outfields, where cricket balls rapidly deteriorate, Pakistan's bowlers developed a method of swinging an old ball. It requires a creation of opposites on the ball's surface, a kind of Yin and Yang effect where one side is kept smooth and damp while the other is allowed to roughen but is kept scrupulously dry.' As Jack Bannister pointed out in the 1993 almanack 'remember that Wasim and Waqar have played in county cricket but no other Lancashire or Surrey bowler has suddenly developed the ability to swing the old ball so much ... even more significantly, the Pakistan support bowler Aqib Javed has not benefited anything like as much from any so-called doctoring'. Perhaps we should accept that the two are quite exceptional bowlers. No one suggested that Bob Massie tampered with the ball when he took sixteen wickets on his debut at Lord's in 1972, or when Botham himself made the ball go like a boomerang at Lord's in 1978 against Pakistan. These were natural but uncommon occurrences. Perhaps Imran and then Waqar and Wasim have learned how to control the freakish? Given that English bowlers such as Darren Gough are now reverse swinging the ball, perhaps we can accept that it is a new addition to the quick bowler's armoury and congratulate the Pakistanis. As Bannister continued, 'any genuine innovation in sport is fascinating to watch'; we should note too that Shane Warne, prior to his recent injury, seemed able to develop a completely new kind of delivery almost each year, so it is possible to revolutionise the fundamentals of the game. Therefore, in the absence of any firm evidence to the contrary, we should admire the ingenuity of Imran and his colleagues rather than castigate them.

Yet the Pakistanis continue to upset Botham more than any other cricketing nation. It must be significant that he decided to opt out of touring just in time to ensure that he missed the World Cup, held in India and Pakistan in 1987, and then the England tour of Pakistan in 1987/88. Perhaps this was nothing more than mere coincidence, yet it certainly suggested that the problem was not physical. Botham was willing to put up with the rigours of an Australian winter but not another jaunt into Asia. His weariness with the press pack was obviously the major factor in his decision making, but from a Pakistani perspective, it looked calculated and ungracious. Little wonder that the Pakistanis were always keen to put one over on him, something in which they often succeeded.

In the face of such resolve, it was inevitable that Botham would be sucked into controversy. It is true that Pakistan have at times been an annoying side to play against. They have their superficial irritants like the hyperactive Javed Miandad, they have been known to appeal overzealously, Salim Yousuf being a prime culprit at Headingley in 1987, but it is Imran who really seemed to get under Botham's skin. Perhaps it was Imran's patrician streak, his assumption of aristocratic bearing that simply got up Botham's egalitarian nose. Perhaps, as with Viv Richards, Botham was unnerved by an opponent who represented a superior force, a talent greater than his own. Certainly in that rain-ruined 1987 series, Imran held the upper hand as Pakistan won the only completed game of the rubber. Scoring a magnificent century at the Oval, Imran totalled 191 runs at forty-eight and took twenty-one wickets at twenty-two, Botham responding with 232 runs at thirty-three and seven wickets at sixty-two. It was clearly Imran's series, one in which he installed himself as perhaps the premier all-rounder. He'd long been seen as a superb opening bowler, but in the latter stages of his career in particular he became one of the finest technicians in the world with the bat, combining an enviable ability to dominate the best attacks with the intelligence and craft to combat top class bowling on helpful wickets. He was good enough to get into a strong Pakistani side purely as a batsman on a number of occasions when he was troubled by injuries that prevented him bowling, and responded to crises with a cool head.

Yet more valuable – and most remarkable of all, the feature that sets him apart from Kapil, Hadlee and Botham – was his skill as a captain. Learning from his own shortcomings when touring England in 1982, he rarely allowed himself to become flustered by events subsequently, displaying a great ability to calm the volatile talents that surrounded him. His presence in the middle was a steadying influence that allowed his team to make best use of their substantial gifts. In its report of the 1987 tour of England, *Wisden* reported that 'without Imran's leadership, or his ability as a player, such triumphs [as Pakistan's first series victory in England, having previously achieved a similar first in India] would not have been celebrated'. As a skipper, he followed Clive Lloyd's lead and presided over a dressing room that had often been beset by quarrels and feuds; just as the West Indies had sometimes been weakened by internal strife, so Pakistan were oft wounded by internecine conflict. Like Lloyd, Imran gave strong leadership, setting standards and imposing a sensible level of discipline on a hitherto undisciplined side. This was powerfully illustrated in a Test match at Headingley in 1987. His wicketkeeper Salim Yousuf claimed a catch off Botham when he'd clearly dropped the ball first. *Wisden* notes that Botham 'reacted angrily, and umpire Palmer had to be quick to separate them. Imran also acted smartly, dressing down Yousuf in no uncertain manner.' Too many captains would defend the indefensible on their own side – Miandad did so when Aqib Javed showed dissent to umpire Palmer at Old Trafford in 1992, for example. As a mature cricketer, Imran refused to let himself be blind to his own side's inadequacies of temperament.

It was Imran's strength of purpose and of character that carried Pakistan to victory in the World Cup of 1992, the final glorious swansong for both himself and Botham. Both had distinguished tournaments, Botham rousing himself to heights that had long seemed beyond him, fired by the dream of winning the World Cup, performing supremely in almost all of England's eight qualifying games. More impressive still was Imran who transformed a bedraggled outfit into potential winners with his now legendary exhortation to his men to fight like the cornered tiger. Having been mauled by the West Indies, skittled out by England for seventy-four in a game ended by rain, beaten heavily by India, and thoroughly outplayed by the South African novices, qualification for the semi-finals seemed an unlikely pipe dream at best. Imran's career was heading for an ignominious end, yet he rallied his side to beat Australia and Sri Lanka with ease, before New Zealand were brushed aside to seal a semi-final showdown against the same opposition. By now, they were looking like the team to beat and a solid victory in Auckland put them through to the final to be held under the lights in Melbourne.

England, asked to field by Imran, started well with Pringle taking two early wickets. But it was Imran with a sensible, then explosive, seventy-two who took the game away from them, the Pakistanis posting 249 as Botham toiled through seven overs to take one wicket – ironically that of Imran – for forty-two. Succeeding as pinch hitter through the tournament, Botham opened with Gooch. With just six on the board, Botham was caught behind for nought off Wasim Akram, causing Aamir Sohail to wonder aloud why he hadn't sent his mother-in-law in to bat instead. When Stewart followed fifteen runs later and then Hick and Gooch fell in quick succession, the game was up. Though expensive, Imran had the satisfaction of taking the last wicket when Richard Illingworth succumbed with England twenty-two runs behind. Imran's role was a deep and decisive one. His leadership along with his exhilarating play had transformed a beaten side into world champions; in its way, his achievement ranked with Botham's rearrangement of the Ashes series in 1981. It offered final confirmation, were it needed, that this was a very substantial cricketer indeed. Since Imran was a great captain when Botham clearly was not, he must shade Botham, Hadlee and Kapil Dev in the cricketing argument, and claim his place as the greatest of these four eminent all-rounders.

Is that a volcano erupting on Alderney?

CHAPTER NINE

Out of Time

Where Do We Go From Here?

Now that Ian Botham has played his final game, what will be his role for the rest of his working life? It may be that he has already stumbled across it. The ventures into pantomime might have seemed crazy at the time, but they were hugely successful; when he appeared in *Cinderella* at Wimbledon in the winter of 1994/95, he helped make it London's most profitable panto of the season. Oh yes he did. Despite reviews that pointed out that he was as wooden as the stage, the kids loved seeing him and he loved working with them; after all, he was the biggest kid in the place. Nevertheless, an actor's life was not for Botham on the incontrovertible grounds that he can't act. Speaking tours were much more his line, allowing him to capitalise on the goodwill won over his spell on *A Question Of Sport* where he and Bill Beaumont became a much loved double act, accorded the warmth usually reserved for the likes of Morecambe and Wise. Their honest good humour and obvious enjoyment of the show made it one of the BBC's great success stories of recent years. The two bowed out at the top, perhaps sensibly allowing new blood to revitalise an old formula, with the consequence that their shows will always be remembered with affection.

A Question Of Sport was the ideal vehicle for Botham, for it allowed him to relax and be himself in front of the TV cameras, an excellent grounding for a future career in television journalism, the avenue he is now pursuing with Sky Sports. How much longer he remains with them is a question that can only be answered by the authorities at Lord's for any role that he might take up as a national selector would require him to step down. That would be ironic, for Botham used *A Question Of Sport* as a platform from which to launch his unsuccessful bid for elevation to the selection committee in 1996. That particular scramble for power was marked by its almost surreal nature, a comedy of errors that left English cricket looking rather stupid – though that's by no means a rare experience. Following the dismal World Cup showing, Botham was proposed as a selector by Surrey and Derbyshire ensuring that a ballot was necessary. Illingworth supported the ageing Brian Bolus and Fred Titmus before the latter's withdrawal, then giving his blessing to John Edrich's candidature. The field eventually expanded to include Chris Cowdrey, Kim Barnett, Graham Gooch, David Graveney and Geoff Miller prior to a mid-April election. The TCCB members found it incumbent upon them to remind the counties that the full-time media work of one candidate was incompatible with his election. It was inevitable thereafter that Botham would fail to gain election, the panel eventually being made up of Gooch and Graveney along with new coach David Lloyd and Chairman Ray. Indeed Graveney might have been installed as chairman had not the Professional Cricketers' Association for whom he worked forced him to stand down from the contest. The whole sorry mess unfolded in the pages of the press over several weeks making sense to few and saddening many, notably those who supported Botham. However, there was much sense in Alan Lee's column in *Wisden Cricket Monthly* once the results were announced. Noting that Botham 'would be utterly miscast as a selector', he went on to point out that his supporters 'beat the drum for his election without any explanation of how their man was going to alter the habits of a lifetime for a job that involves all the detail, observation and analysis that he detests'. Lee's analysis was quite correct. Never a great watcher of the game, the very idea of Botham trawling the country for fresh new talent was hard to credit.

In order to counter that particular impression, Botham launched his latest book, *The Botham Report* in 1997, his blueprint for the game, modestly subtitled 'What Is Wrong With English Cricket – And How I Intend To Put It Right'. Given that Botham has no official role in the game's upper echelons, the idea that Botham will wave a magic wand and restore English cricket to its former greatness is a thoroughly misleading one. Without power, he is left to lead the cheers and the boos from the sidelines, impotent, firing broadsides through the tabloids he detests. Nevertheless, his report into the game's ills has its moments, the more so as it deals with cricket in greater depth than his autobiography did.

By the book's very nature, it has to be provocative and apocalyptic – his view that Sky will pull out of English cricket in due course if England fail to win is unrealistic. For all England's failings, the Test grounds are still full, there is still great interest in the game, cricket is still entrenched in our culture. Although that should not breed complacency, it makes claims of imminent bankruptcy look absurd. Equally, it might be said that we are just now beginning to see the benefits both of four-day cricket and of Mike Atherton's leadership. As Botham admits, England did well in the West Indies in 1993/94 when Atherton led a very young side. He returned to find that Illingworth had taken over the reins and reversed the drive for youth by reinstating Gatting, Emburey and Gooch at various stages, paving the way for defeat in Australia. Gradually however, Atherton has regained control and is working with a far more sympathetic selection committee. As younger players are given a run in the side we have seen players such as Hussain, Thorpe and Caddick emerge as genuine Test match cricketers. There is real cause for some optimism where England's future is concerned which Botham is a little loath to credit.

The iniquities and inadequacies of the game's leaders over the last dozen years have been well documented in numerous publications in recent years, yet even now, some of the decisions taken are quite astonishing. Certainly Botham exposes the flaws in leadership with obvious relish, settling a few old scores along the way, but this is no mere grudge match. Whatever his faults, he is genuinely concerned at what is happening to the English cricket team and to the game at domestic level. His feeling for the mental and physical well-being of the players is equally touching, again making it perfectly clear that had Botham's energy been harnessed for the good of the team as England vice captain in his latter days, results might have been considerably better. His fellow-feeling for the trials and tribulations undergone by Mark Taylor, and the tribute to him which accompanies it, has a great deal of warmth, unusual in one caricatured as an inveterate, simple-minded Aussie-basher.

But it is his arguments regarding the burn-out factor for England's bowlers that carry the greatest conviction and weight. For those on the outside, the catalogue of pills, injections, medicines and strappings that get a quick bowler through an English season is a real eye-opener. If a race-horse trainer were to subject his charges to the maulings that Angus Fraser, Darren Gough, Dominic Cork *et al* struggle through every year, he'd have the RSPCA permanently camped in his yard. There can be no question that these players are remorselessly overworked by county and country, asked to travel ludicrous distances from one game to the next, often driving themselves, and consigned to stay in second-rate hotels without the proper facilities required by top-class athletes. If the spectators sometimes wonder why our cricketers aren't always built in the lithe lines of footballers or sprinters, it's because they're not treated in the same way and because their lifestyle from April to September makes it virtually impossible to train in any sensible fashion. How can it be that professional sportsmen are required to drive themselves from one engagement to the next: do Chelsea travel up to Newcastle for a Premiership game in half a dozen different cars like a Sunday morning side, Zola and Vialli meeting up for a bite to eat at a service station on the M1 along the way? It's a preposterous way to behave. County cricketers are like a rock band on tour throughout the summer so why not line up the same luxury coaches that allow players to relax, to sleep, watch TV or whatever they want to do while reaching their destination refreshed and ready for the next game?

From reaching the conclusion that our top men are overworked, it is but a short step to contracting the England team to the ECB, thereby allowing the England selectors to pick and choose what county fixtures their charges appear in. In principle, this is an undeniably sound argument for it is the England team which subsidises the rest of our domestic cricket, and therefore everything should be done to further that cause. However, that argument is undermined to a degree by looking at the amount of cricket our senior players will then get. As Botham admits when dismissing the idea of a transfer market in the game, Test players will play so little domestic cricket they'd have no value. How, then, does a player work out a deficiency in his game if not by time spent out in the middle? Net practice is valuable, but it is under the microscope of match pressure that a player's game faces its fiercest scrutiny. Equally, if an England squad of, say, fifteen players is taken out of the game at the start of the season and plays few county games, what will that do to the standard of the County Championship? As with the argument over overseas players, ridding the game of its greatest exponents does little for standards. Imagine Surrey playing without Butcher, Stewart, Thorpe and the Hollioakes. There are more than a few bowlers who would fancy their chances of picking up wickets against a side sending out a second string batting line-up. But what would be the value of that? And what of Surrey itself? Although county cricket is easily dismissed as anachronistic and meaningless today, each club is under increasing pressure from the members to produce results, perfectly illustrated by the many and varied upheavals at Warwickshire, Yorkshire, Surrey, Sussex, Lancashire and Derbyshire in recent years. You must also ask why the counties would put money into nursery schemes to find good young players in the knowledge that if they do, those kids will be whisked away into England colours within a couple of seasons. The other contradiction is obvious. As a leading protagonist for divisional championships in both four- and one-day cricket, how does that square with his avowed desire to reduce travelling for our players? At present counties are locked together for five days for a county game followed by a Sunday League match. With separate divisions, that administrative simplicity is lost. Middlesex might play Durham in a Second Division County Championship match then find themselves speeding down the motorway to play Surrey at the Oval the following day in a First Division Sunday League game.

Surely though English cricket, now under new management with the introduction of Lord MacLaurin, can find a place for the most charismatic player of his generation? One would like to think so, but it begs the very tough question of just what that place should be. Over recent years, English cricket has been overwhelmed with supposedly messianic figures who were there to cure all our ills and take the national side to the peaks of the game. Peter May, Ted Dexter and Raymond Illingworth all started their reigns as chairman of selectors amid a blaze of optimistic publicity only to have their hopes dashed once they took office – each one was heralded as the 'people's choice', much as Botham has been. Given that these three were all eminent men with acute cricketing brains, one has to wonder if they were at fault or whether they were asked to operate within the fabric of an unworkable system. A little of both is the case, for the English cricket season is so designed that it seems impossible for us to unearth a fast bowler who can stay fit in body and mind for long enough to make an enduring impact on the Test scene. That has been our greatest failing since Bob Willis bowed out of international cricket in 1984. Devon Malcolm has threatened to replace him on occasion, but woefully insensitive handling and Malcolm's own inconsistency meant that his promise never fully came to fruition. Left to his own devices, told to think of nothing but bowling fast and taking wickets, Malcolm would surely have become the centrepiece of England's attack and our record would have been significantly improved over recent years. Yet like Hick, he is always the scapegoat for England's failings. The tragedy is that he has been the only England fast bowler of note in more than a decade. Clearly, then, there is something wrong with the system that will bedevil anyone who is linked with the fortunes of the national side, and Botham is correct in pointing that out.

He is just as correct to draw attention to our archaic administration, the cavalier way in which the game's sponsors have been treated, to prove that the game has been run by people out of touch with the modern world. One cameo from *The Botham Report* is revealing. During the Ashes series of 1997, David Graveney, chairman of selectors, was under the misapprehension that Devon Malcolm hadn't bowled much in the early weeks of the season. It wasn't until he contacted Kim Barnett at Derbyshire that he was informed Malcolm had sent down 200 overs by the start of June! Graveney can hardly be faulted, given that he clocks up thousands of miles a year watching England's hopefuls all over the country. He scarcely has time to digest all the county scoreboards on a day-by-day basis, especially if that means finding the right newspaper to give him the right information. But this is the age of technology, an age where even cricket scoring is done on computer. It cannot be beyond the means of the ECB to give the selectors their own laptop computer and to e-mail them a statistical database on a daily basis, giving full scoreboards, averages etc., for the season as a whole. Surely that would make sense? If English cricket wants to approach the new millennium in good shape, it needs to embrace its technology.

Equally, what the May, Dexter and Illingworth years have shown us is that England need a backroom staff of men who are closer to the players' age rather than those who played most of their cricket nearly thirty years ago. However shrewd they might have been when it comes to the basic disciplines of the game, they are too divorced from an era where cricket has evolved at a bewildering pace. Anyone who played the game in the pre-Packer era can have little idea of the different pressures today's players face. I reiterate that that doesn't make the current shape of cricket better or worse than it was in 1956, 1966 or 1976, but it is a dramatically different shape. One-day cricket was almost unheard of when Illingworth led England for the last time in 1973 – he actually played just three such internationals, managing one win, one defeat and one no-result, the full hand. His disdain for such matches is obvious and he was obviously shocked by the public backlash which attended England's dismal one-day form in South Africa and then the World Cup in 1996; to him, these games seemed unimportant. Illingworth was clearly out of touch with the public and it is they to whom he is finally accountable.

Botham is, of course, still revered by much of the cricketing public and significant sections of the tabloid press, including the *Mirror* for whom he contributes a column. He was scathing in his criticism of the English performances in the World Cup, suggesting that for the first time he wanted to see England humbled in the hope that changes might be made. These were the opening salvoes in Botham's own bid for the premiership in English cricket, a long campaign that rumbled on into the early weeks of the 1996 season. In the revised paperback edition of his autobiography, he pushed his claims for Illingworth's job, while making the point that England should be coached by players like Lamb, Gower, Boycott, Gooch and himself. That England need leadership from a man closer to the players' own experience is undeniable, an argument that will prove to be irresistible over the coming years. At the same time, one needs to question the names he puts forward.

Boycott, for example, is a fine technician who clearly knows the game inside out and has helped many English players informally. However, as one who makes his living from the media and who is not afraid to offer vigorous criticism of what he sees as poor cricket in front of the nation, he is not wildly popular with the players.

Lamb, Gower and Botham were all exorcised from the English set-up in part because they were felt to be a disruptive influence by Dexter, Stewart and Gooch – though Botham was ostensibly dropped from the West Indies tour of 1989/90 on the grounds of poor form, that was a handy excuse. The selectors wanted to change direction. It is a matter of opinion as to whether or not that was a necessary decision or not. However, one must remember that the 1980s for England was not one long period of constant success – memories of that decade are too often swayed by thoughts of Headingley in 1981. But let's remember, too, the West Indian blackwashes of 1984 and 1985/86 and the 4–0 defeat in 1988. There were series defeats at the hands of New Zealand in 1983/84 and 1986 along with a drawn rubber in 1987/88, losses to India in 1981/82 and 1986, to Pakistan in 1983/84, 1987 and 1987/88. These were not the glory years they've been portrayed as. What made the 1980s special was beating Australia in 1981, 1985 and 1986/87. Even then, they hammered us in return in 1979/80 and

1989, also winning in 1982/83. Our great players in these less than distinguished years were Botham, Gower, Lamb, Gooch and Gatting, with Botham's own record standing as played 102, won 35, lost 30, drawn 37, not as great as memory alone might suggest, though rapturous statistics in the light of England's recent offerings. Interestingly, post-1982, his record is played 48, won 11, lost 21, drawn 16, suggesting that perhaps lifestyle had got in the way of the cricket. Given that the Gooch/Stewart partnership bore some fruit in the West Indies before fitness training became a wearisome obsession, the loss of Botham and Gower was not the grievous blow it might have appeared.

But of course they do represent a wealth of experience which should be tapped in some way, even if only in an advisory capacity alongside a different kind of coach, one who is open to new methods and the latest techniques for maximising an individual's performance on the field. A modern, forward-thinking coach is desperately important if England are to progress. David Lloyd's appointment was a step in the right direction, presenting the players with someone on the same wavelength, someone who understood the demands of the game as it was played in 1997. In tandem with Mike Atherton, he looks to be building on the work that Graham Gooch had done in his time as England skipper. If Gower's demise came more swiftly and far less graciously than was necessary, Gooch, Dexter and Stewart were right in calling time on 'the champagne set'. Men like Botham, Lamb and Gower were great players, relying on flair, instinct, natural timing. They had gifts beyond the ordinary and consequently they could get away with a few late nights and still perform well. Equally, they were around at the right time, for now such licence could not be given to players.

Touring was not quite so intensive even six or seven years ago and England's away matches were not captured live on television as they are by Botham's current employers, Sky. A poor performance on the other side of the world was criticised but rarely put under the spotlight as it is today. The rewards have grown enormously, but so have the pressures. Those who are merely very good players need to work harder than a Gower or a Botham did at their peak. Sure, they need a drink or two in the evening to unwind, but equally they need to adopt a highly focused and rigorously professional attitude to what is an increasingly professional game – when England won the football World Cup under Alf Ramsey in 1966, the players barely had a drink in two months of intense work so in these more handsomely rewarded days, it's surely not too much to ask our cricketers to do likewise? The foundations laid by Gooch have borne fruit in the determined and utterly committed approach of men like Mike Atherton and Alec Stewart. Dermot Reeve made the point in *Winning Ways* that 'Goochy had difficulty understanding why others in the team lacked his dedication and desire to succeed ... I was impressed with the way he led by example and trained so hard. Goochy was quite right to say that times had changed, that you couldn't have a good night out and then expect to turn it on at full power in a vital game. He felt you had to treat your body like an engine, putting the best oil in it, with regular services ... he loved a laugh, enjoyed a drink at the right times and encouraged the players fully.' In *The Botham Report*, however, Botham continues to have a schizophrenic approach to Gooch, praising him for his captaincy record, at least until 1992, then criticising Gooch for trying to mould individuals into a team. Yet surely that was an important factor in the improved results?

The very best coaches in the game recognise the importance of a team approach to solving problems on the field. Look at the seismic advances made by the South Africans in a very short time under the eye of Bob Woolmer. He is not afraid to admit he is still learning about the game, is not dogmatic, fosters a good team spirit and is ready to encourage the players to express themselves. His is an original mind capable of lateral thinking. He employs nutritionists, dieticians, medical experts on every form of physical fitness. Botham himself seems unimpressed by this aspect of the modern game and though he would like to be involved in the England set-up, he also admits that 'I don't see myself strutting around the nets in a tracksuit.' Comments like that suggest that he has learned little from the advances made by Australia and South Africa in recent years and that he is living in as much of a time warp as Illingworth ever was. The lackadaisical days have gone. Australia win so regularly not simply because they have good players but because they work hard and fight for one another. It's a cliché to say that the Aussies are as fresh at the end of a long day as they are at the start, but it happens to be true. The Waughs, Taylor, Elliott *et al* are all capable of playing the very long innings that Test cricket demands because their concentration does not waver with fatigue. Their bowlers can be relied upon to bowl with the same control in the final session as they did in the first. As a team, they are fiercely fit for they have recognised that the last thirty minutes of a day are every bit as important as the first thirty. Much of that comes down to preparation, something at which Botham was poor.

Since Botham was impatient with some of Gooch's methods, it seems unlikely that he would be the best man to deal with the differing demands of players. Just as

Gooch could not deal with Gower's relaxed attitude to his cricket, Botham seems unhappy with those who are keen to get into the best physical shape, who turn fitness into a fetish or who have their own attitude to getting ready for a game. Therefore, instead of having a hands-on role elsewhere, Botham would surely be of most use in a motivational role. He is still a commanding figure in the game. He could be an extremely useful supporting player alongside a supremo figure like Lloyd or Dermot Reeve – now that would be a pairing! But it would need to be a supporting role, for the number one position is not one to which he is suited. Equally interesting in the light of Botham's ambitions is his assertion in *The Botham Report* that 'we are, after all, in the entertainment business'. But are we? Is entertaining always compatible with winning? When the West Indians ruled cricket and bowled twelve overs of chin music an hour, was that always thrilling? When Viv Richards was in full flow it was, but not when yet another Colin Croft bouncer from a no-ball thudded into the keeper's gloves and he began the long trudge back to his mark. And had Mike Atherton been more inclined to entertain the paying spectators in Johannesburg in 1995/96, would he have saved the Test match? If Botham created a thrilling England side that lost every series 5–0, would it pack the grounds? Alternatively, if he produced a team of grinders that won every series 5–0 would the grounds be empty? Now, more than ever, the national side has to win first, ask questions later. Recall the last Olympics. There was plenty of entertainment from Roger Black, Jonathan Edwards, Denise Lewis and the rest of our athletes, but the debate centred around our inability to win gold medals. Sadly, winning is the be all and end all of international sport these days, and anyone who thinks sport is in the entertainment business does not understand spectators' motivation.

The position as the Illingworth-styled supremo is not one that would suit him, though predictably he writes that 'I believe in a one man band'. It would be astonishing if he did not, for that was very much the way he played the game. There is also a great deal of sense in that argument, in saying that Illingworth was the wrong man in the right job. But the job is not for Botham who continues to lack analytical flair. His sentiments towards Gooch are contradictory, as is his attitude to Lord MacLaurin. Castigating him for the ill-conceived, ill-thought out and illogical conference system he put forward for the County Championship, within nine pages of *The Botham Report*, he then suggests that all the measures in MacLaurin's blueprint illustrate that here is a man of rare vision. Botham is by nature a man of great passions, emotional, enthusiastic, committed but not necessarily with the cool, clear head that the supremo role demands.

Just as important, such a position could do him harm. Botham is a team player but his popular image is too big for the wider world to accept him as simply that. The selection committee would be cast as Botham and Botham would be cast as the selection committee. That much is inescapable. Equally, although he has a good mind for the game, he has rarely shown much aptitude for scouring the country for players, sitting down to watch a game ball-by-ball as a selector must. Still respected by the public, a stint as the face of English cricket might harm that reputation and consequently his commercial well-being; after all, although England are scarcely world-beaters at present, just who are the names lurking in county cricket that might transform them into a side capable of winning regularly all around the globe? Botham could help pick a side; sadly he couldn't be transported back to his early twenties. Raymond Illingworth went from being the eminence grise of English cricket to being an object of derision in just eighteen months. Wouldn't the same fate befall Botham? Recall the captaincy years, if one needs evidence of the fickle nature of both the media and the public. After his years in the job, Ray Illingworth is now in effective retirement. No longer wanted as a commentator, the *Express* is the only outlet for his views. If things go badly with Botham at the helm, where would that leave him? Botham's retort would be that with him in command, such results would not come about, but is that realistic? Isn't it more accurate to say that, our improving fortunes notwithstanding, whoever leads England in the next eighteen months is looking down the barrel of a gun?

There are good players in English cricket, many of whom are under achieving. Darren Gough, for example, looked a top class Test match prospect just two years ago, but since then injury and loss of form have come his way. Dominic Cork had a decidedly average second season in Test cricket, bowed down by overwork. What of Chris Lewis, Mark Ramprakash, Phil Tufnell? These men, along with established players such as Atherton, Stewart and Thorpe, offer a nucleus of talent that should at least make England hard to beat. Why then were they so easily swept aside by Australia after such a great start – they could as easily have lost the series 5–1 as 3–2 – why was the 1996 World Cup such a disaster, why have England slipped down the world rankings? Perhaps Botham might be able to get the very best out of these men by his mere presence, but if he was seen to be associated with losers, might not the lucrative speaking tours and advertisements dry up? Would

Sky want him back if his tenure ended in ignominy? If nothing else, it would end all the arguments as to who is the greatest that fly back and forth between himself and Ray Illingworth, but perhaps Botham is better off leaving that unanswered.

Clearly the selection of Ray Illingworth as English manager and chairman of selectors was, in hindsight, a mistake. His blunt public pronouncements for many years on TV must have rankled with those who came under his stewardship. Allowing him to write regular newspaper columns on the players he'd picked and discarded was incredibly stupid – that's something that might affect Botham in due course. It's little wonder that Robin Smith, for example, fell away so badly once Illingworth was installed, having had to listen to his trenchant criticism of his technique for a number of years. Equally, his treatment of Angus Fraser and Devon Malcolm was less than inspirational. More than anything else, Illingworth seemed an anachronism. He wanted a side that could win the Ashes as they were fought for in 1972.

Botham is close to falling into the same trap. His impatience for authority has been well documented. He has always wanted to do things his own way, but might that way not be out of date too? Think back to that quotation from Peter Roebuck's *It Sort Of Clicks* when discussing Botham's captaincy of Somerset: 'he had a vision of a beautiful world where he and his mates, arriving in eccentric clothes to upset the fuddy-duddies, would laugh and drink the nights away, and then storm around defeating all the conventional types with their managers and their serious faces'. It didn't work then and it certainly could not work now. It may be prosaic, but good, successful cricket is built upon masses of hard work – Brian Lara is a regular visitor to the nets whatever his form.

Other dangers lurk for Botham in his work for the *Mirror* and for Sky Sports. Though informally co-opted into the England think-tank for the winter tour of Zimbabwe and New Zealand, he was caught off guard at times when donning his broadcasting hat. During the First Test against New Zealand in Auckland in 1996/97 during a particularly torpid piece of English cricket when Cork and Gough were unable to score the quick runs required, Botham was asked about England's game plan. His reply made it clear that he was unimpressed, wondering aloud whether a game plan existed. Commenting on Sky's coverage, Roy Hattersley noted in the *Express* that on the first day when England bowled poorly 'there was the constant implication that in their fast bowling days, Bob Willis and Ian Botham would have run through the New Zealanders before lunch'. Like Boycott before him, Botham may soon have to choose between commentary and country lest he make his position with the latter untenable with remarks made for the benefit of his paymaster.

One thing is perfectly clear: he's unlikely to fit in with the Lord's hierarchy, so a job with the newly established ECB seems like a non-starter. Botham would clearly love to put something back into the game and transform the England side into winners, but is that the best job for him given his outside interests? Cricket is about to undergo the greatest revolution in its history. Just as football and rugby have been irrevocably changed by Murdoch's television millions, so too will cricket. It's amazing in many ways that the current structure of Test cricket has stayed intact for so many years for, essentially, it's utterly meaningless. A beautiful absurdity. We play against one country one year, another the next but, an Ashes series apart, what's the point? Where does it lead? Arguments go on about who are the World Champions, but no one can ever prove it conclusively. Every other sport leads inexorably to a supreme final, be it a World Cup, an Olympic Games or whatever. Test matches lead nowhere. A World Championship of Test cricket is the inevitable next step if it is to survive as the most important form of the game.

When this revolution comes, the game will be turned upside down by money, the old structures swept away. The players will become superstars, as important as Shearer, Cantona or Gullit. We will watch cricket on TV all the year round from all over the world, beamed to us at odd times from odd locations to maximise the profitability for the TV companies that will underwrite the game. Change will come so quickly and in such dramatic fashion that the Packer revolution will seem mild by comparison and the experience of those who played in the 1980s will be as redundant to the new realities as those who played in the 1960s are to today. When that day comes – and it is not far off – professionalism will be vital and an era of charismatic personalities will be consigned to the dustbin of history, a delightful eccentricity from a forgotten age. The personalities will be off the field since the faceless players will be worked so hard and will be so determined to stay at the top that they won't have the time or the freedom to get involved in the kind of escapades that Gower or Botham or Miller or Compton or Sobers or Benaud did. Great personalities will be needed to front the programmes, to remind us of a time when sport was fun, when there were laughs to be had, when it wasn't all a matter of life and death. What will be required are heroes of the past who have a ready wit, are comfortable in front of the camera, who have shown themselves to have a genuine rapport with the public, someone to whom they respond warmly. Now *that* sounds like a job for Ian Botham.

POSTSCRIPT

Walk This Way
Leukaemia Research

It's a pretty sad reflection of the times in which we live that when a public figure tries to do something for a worthwhile cause, the first question that's asked is always 'What's in it for them?' Admittedly, plenty of celebrities have tried to cash in on causes over the years, turning their apparent charitable concern into one glorious photo opportunity to further their own careers. The public has a right to be cynical about it all, but that doesn't mean that every good turn is done in the hope of boosting an ego or raising a profile.

It must be conceded that when the plans for his great John o' Groats to Land's End walk were first unveiled in 1985, Ian Botham was not at his most universally popular. The New Zealand/Pakistan tour of 1983/84 had been a disaster on and off the field. The great Botham had not overcome the West Indians in the home series of 1984. His press was unflattering and he was surrounded by an unpleasant atmosphere, almost one of decay. It was something he could not dispel however hard he tried. His critics leapt upon the walk idea as evidence that he was trying to bribe his way back into the public affection; unable to charm them on the field any longer, the yob was pretending to have a conscience. Given that Botham had already been quietly helping the cause for eight years and has subsequently pounded his way across thousands of miles and raised millions for leukaemia research, perhaps those critics are proud of their contribution.

Had they taken the trouble to find out the reasons for Botham's interest in the subject, they'd have found they were deeply rooted. It dated back to the summer of 1977 when he'd picked up an injury while fielding in the Australian second innings of the Fourth Test at Headingley. Standing on the ball in his attempt to field it, he managed to break a bone in his left foot. Unaware of that at the time, he ignored the injury and continued to bowl, further aggravating the damage. Back in Taunton after the game he went to the local Musgrove Park Hospital for further treatment, passing through the children's ward while he was there. It was then that he was informed that two of the children, who looked right as rain to the naked eye, had little time left. Struck down by leukaemia, they were incurable. Already in a highly emotional state himself since Kath was in the final days of her pregnancy with Liam, Botham was stunned by this news, news of a disease that, like so many of us back then, he'd barely heard of. With his own child about to be born, his mood could be summed up as 'there but for the grace of God go my family'.

His initial response was typically generous. On hearing that the annual party for the children had been cancelled, he handed over fifty pounds to make sure it would go ahead. Many would have left it at that, happy to have made some contribution, unsure of what to do next until all thoughts of the disease were pushed out of mind by the demands of day to day living. Given the frantic lifestyle that Botham lived, it would be excusable for him to have forgotten all about it in a matter of months. But that is not his way. Certainly he can be arrogant and rude at times, but equally he is a committed father and, when approached in the right way, cannot do enough for those he chooses to help. When you take into account everything else that was going on in his life, he was surely one of the greatest charity fundraisers of the 1980s, and while the sums raised can't quite compare with Live Aid, the amount of work he and Kath undertook in arranging the night-marish itineraries that attended the walks, organising help from local businesses and so on, compares with that done by Sir Bob Geldof. Perhaps both the Bothams deserved that kind of recognition too.

Where the walks are concerned, Botham deserves every last word of praise that he has received. Of course the walks have done his reputation no harm, but that was never a consideration. Had he been solely interested in looking after his battered public image, he could easily have engaged the services of a media guru, had a make-over, appeared contrite at his failings and come out the other end smelling of roses. That would have required virtually no effort on his part and might even have earned him some lucrative new commercial contracts. That would have been an easy option, one guaranteed to succeed. Instead, he did what he wanted to do and stuff the consequences. When, on the eve of a vitally important Test match tour to the West Indies, someone as busy as Ian Botham gives up a month of his life to walk the length of Britain, he deserves to be taken seriously, deserves to be taken at face value. That alone underlined that he was interested in the cause. In its way, this was a more remarkable effort than anything he'd ever done on the field of play, far more heroic in its scale and purpose, the more so since the huge physical effort might even have taken its toll on his performance on the cricket field, laying him open to criticism from all sources.

That first long trudge through October and November 1985 lasted thirty-five days amid a whirl of publicity. A 'Who's Who' of English cricket accompanied him at one stage or another, Jack Bannister filing an on the spot report for *Wisden Cricket Monthly* which demonstrated just how badly Botham had been misunderstood over the years:

> his treatment of the crowd was exemplary, with the very young and the aged receiving special consideration ... a woman approached him and stuffed a £10 note in one hand and a scribbled note in the other. He read it and silently handed it to me. It read 'My little one has got it. For God's sake, keep going' ... on Day 34 Botham still had enough instinct for the right action at the right time to present an old lady in an invalid chair with a long-stemmed red carnation ... he struck chords of empathy with the public, young and old alike, which will reverberate for a long while.

In the face of those reactions, it's hard to see how anyone could criticise him as self-serving.

His need for new challenges – substitute Headingleys – is detailed elsewhere. If there was any selfish motive involved in his fundraising walks, it was in providing him with another mighty challenge. The leukaemia walk, created out of a genuine passion to help the helpless, was another Headingley. It was a classic example of his core philosophy: nothing is impossible. If Botham can imagine it, he can turn it into reality. After a year when the press had scarcely been off his back, who else would emerge from the security and privacy of his own home and lay himself out in the open before the public for the greater part of five weeks? The reaction was impossible to predict; given the level of media hostility towards him, he could have been ignored, booed, attacked, he could have had things thrown at him, failed to raise any money and been made to look ridiculous. Instead he swept the whole country along with him, manipulating the newspapers that had victimised him so remorselessly over the years.

Hardbitten journalists were among the first to fall under the Pied Piper's latest spell, dispelling any lingering thoughts that this was a glorified PR exercise. They were swept along on the rising tide of public feeling, responding to Botham as the rest of the country did. Even when the novelty had worn off five years later, commentators such as the *Mail on Sunday*'s Patrick Collins were sufficiently touched by Botham's obvious feeling for the cause that they filed glowing reports about less glamorous walks such as the East Coast March from Aberdeen to Ipswich. Catching up with him in Grimsby, Collins reported one of the local mayor's attendants saying 'He's got his critics has Ian Botham, but after this, I shan't have a word said against him.' 'For what it's worth,' added Collins, 'neither shall I. There are those who suspect that Botham has used these walks to enhance his frequently dubious image. After attempting to match his stride on a single 25-mile, six-hour slog, I can give the lie to that cynicism.' Botham himself pointed out that 'sure it's a struggle. I mean, after about an hour every day, my hands start swelling incredibly and my feet feel like they don't belong to me. But I get a good rest every night and I'm ready next morning. It's got to be done, hasn't it?' When Collins remarked that the Test team was about to depart for Australia, Botham offered a stunning rejoinder: 'Not for me, mate. I don't want it any more. I wouldn't swop this for anything.'

The first walk, John o' Groats to Land's End, raised a sum not far short of £1,000,000 from a slew of donations and was indicative of the Botham determination to make a difference in the face of a terrible disease. It was a genuinely inspiring, genuinely heroic effort that allowed the whole country to take part in what became a moral crusade in the mould of Live Aid. Aside from the mind-boggling statistics of the walk itself, it did represent a welcome opportunity for Botham to meet the people and to change the public perception of him in the wake of the constant drug allegations. The Ian Botham that we saw on the charity walk was the real man, warts and all. There were the moments when his temper got the better of him, striking out at a police officer who, fortunately, made nothing of the incident, understanding that physical exhaustion can play havoc with perspective. There were the moments of bravado – running thirty-six miles in bursts, turning somersaults on the road. There were the moments of generosity, tenderness and genuine communication with the people. There were the moments designed purely for the crowds: finishing the walk in top hat and tails, leaping into the Atlantic off Land's End. There was the spirit of camaraderie that existed between Botham and his fellow walkers, Alan Border's brother John, journalist Chris Lander and Mancunian businessman Phil Rance, men who took Botham at face value and who wanted nothing from him but his friendship, a spirit which carried them through to their goal.

Inevitably, efforts were made to rain on his parade. One freelance journalist made unsubstantiated allegations that Botham and friends had been smoking pot. Since the quartet had had a police escort virtually every step of the way and had been mobbed wherever they went, it was difficult to see how they could possibly have got away with any such thing. The charge was investigated by police and quickly dismissed out of hand. It must have saddened Botham though to see his generous enterprise sullied by such pettiness. And while not wishing to condone the use of illegal substances, even if the four *had* been fuelled by any or every soft drug on the list, those leukaemia sufferers who have been helped by the walk would not have cared less.

This trek up and down the country, along with further walks such as Belfast to Dublin, around the Channel Islands, the East Coast March detailed above, from Land's End to Margate, or retracing Hannibal's journey across the Alps, have swelled the coffers for the cause. In truth, Botham is far better suited to this role than that of an international cricketer in the media age. He is a bigger spirit than the staid game of cricket can handle. He is a bolder man than the little world of opinion formers can bear. He has a mission, he has ambitions, he has the common touch. It requires an indomitable and generous spirit to undertake anything as ostensibly impossible as his charity walks. That humanity can spill over, his exuberance can cause difficulties in a world of petty regulations, while his sense of certainty in everything that he does can lead him into trouble on the occasions when he hasn't got it right. When he is out of touch he resembles a dinosaur, for everything he does is on such a grand scale. Mistakes look worse just as triumphs seem unimaginably enormous. He has got many things wrong in his time but he's got far more things right. Still his generosity shines through the occasionally surly demeanour he adopts when discussing cricket. In New Zealand he had his head shaved, an action which according to Sky Sports managed to raise £50,000 for charity. That's a mark of his open and giving nature and also a tribute to his enduring legend. Who else would have raised £5,000, never mind £50,000, from such a simple action?

Ian Botham will always have his critics. He pretends to ignore them but his willingness to take legal action against those whom he feels have transgressed illustrates his surprisingly thin skin. Botham, above all, wants to be loved by the people, wants to rekindle the flame of affection that he felt throughout his golden years. That may well be beyond him for those were the headiest of days. He would be better served by far to draw satisfaction from his deeds. Forget the runs, catches and wickets. When he gets to bed at night, he need only recall that the leukaemia research laboratories in Glasgow have been named in his honour as a tribute to his tireless fundraising activities. That is enough for any man. No one who could react so spontaneously and vigorously to an anonymous disease could be anything but a very great man. The last word on that score goes to Vivian Richards: 'he responds, he's human, he's not a plastic guy'.

CHRONOLOGY

24/11/55	Born in Heswall, Cheshire – weight 10lb 1oz.
1969	Debut for Somerset Under 15s.
1971	Plays for the South West in the English Schools' Under 15 cricket festival, Liverpool.
8/71	Has trial for Lord's groundstaff and is invited back for the following year.
1972	Spends summer on Lord's groundstaff.
1973	Invited to return to Lord's, but spends most of the summer playing for Somerset Second Eleven.
2/9/73	Makes Somerset debut versus Sussex at Hove in John Player League. Scores two, bowls three overs (0/22) and takes one catch to dismiss Tony Greig.
8/5/74	First class debut for Somerset against Lancashire at Taunton. Scores thirteen, bowls three overs for fifteen, catches Jack Simmons.
27/5/74	Takes first first class wicket, Gloucestershire's Dunstan.
12/6/74	Struck in the face by an Andy Roberts bouncer but still guides Somerset to victory in Benson & Hedges quarter-final against Hampshire.
26/6/74	Meets Kathryn Waller at the Benson & Hedges Cup semi-final at Leicester.

13/7/74	Maiden first class fifty, fifty-nine against Mike Brearley's Middlesex at Taunton.
9/74	Completes debut season with 441 runs and thirty wickets in first class cricket.
9/75	Season of improvement sees him finish with 584 runs and sixty-two wickets.
31/1/76	Marries Kathryn Waller.
3/8/76	Maiden first class hundred, 167 not out against Nottinghamshire at Trent Bridge.
26/8/76	Makes international debut against West Indies in one day international at Scarborough. Scores one, bowls three overs for twenty-six, takes wicket of Lawrence Rowe.
9/76	Ends season with 1022 runs and sixty-six wickets.
Winter 76/7	Spends winter on Whitbread scholarship in Australia.
28/7/77	Test match debut versus Australia at Trent Bridge. Takes 5/74 in first innings, first Test wicket being Greg Chappell. Scores twenty-five in only innings. England win by seven wickets.
26/8/77	Son Liam is born.
9/77	Completes season with two Test caps and selection for winter tour to Pakistan and New Zealand. Scores 738 runs and takes eighty-eight wickets in season.
Winter 77/8	Plays all three Tests against New Zealand. Scores maiden hundred, 103, in second game at Christchurch – runs Boycott out in second

innings on Willis's instructions. Also takes eight wickets in match. Gets a further five and another fifty in third game. Returns home as England's number one all-rounder.

4/78   Selected as one of *Wisden*'s Five Cricketers of the Year.

19/4/78   Takes hat-trick for MCC against Middlesex – Radley, Barlow, Featherstone, all bowled.

6/78   Scores two centuries and takes thirteen wickets in home series against Pakistan. At Lord's, becomes first man to score a hundred and take eight wickets in an innings in Test history.

8/78   Takes twenty-four wickets in home series against New Zealand.

9/78   Ends season with selection for Australian tour.

10/78   Injures hand by putting it through glass in a revolving door at a pub in Epworth. Unfit at start of tour to Australia.

Winter 78/9   Scores 291 runs and takes twenty-three wickets in triumphant series for England.

3/2/79   Daughter Sarah is born.

23/6/79   Plays in defeated England side in Prudential World Cup Final against West Indies.

6/8/79   Takes 100th Test wicket when Brearley catches Gavaskar at Lord's. Completes feat in two years, nine days, a new record. It is his nineteenth Test.

20/8/79   Scores 99 before lunch for England against India at Headingley.

30/8/79   Reaches 1000 Test runs in his twenty-first Test.

Records the fastest ever Test match double of 1000 runs and 100 wickets.

8/9/79 Plays in Somerset side that wins Gillette Cup at Lord's, beating Northamptonshire by forty-five runs. It is Somerset's first ever trophy.

9/9/79 Helps Somerset clinch John Player League with victory over Nottinghamshire at Trent Bridge.

Winter 79/80 Tours Australia with England and tops bowling averages, third in batting averages. England play the Golden Jubilee Test in India on their way home. Botham scores a hundred, takes six wickets in first innings and seven in second, an unparalleled individual performance.

4/80 Sustains back injury during game versus Oxford University.

5/80 Appointed England captain.

24/5/80 Registers highest career score, 228 not out in 184 minutes against Gloucestershire at Taunton.

28/5/80 First match as England captain, Prudential Trophy game at Headingley. West Indies win by twenty-four runs. England win second game at Lord's on 30/5, Botham hitting the winning runs.

30/5/80 Appointed captain for first two Tests against West Indies.

4/6/80 Stopped for speeding by police.

5/6/80 Leads England in a Test match against West Indies at Trent Bridge. Scores a total of sixty-one runs and has match figures of four for ninety-eight. England lose by two wickets.

12/8/80	England lose West Indian series by one game to nil.
30/8/80	Assaulted by MCC members during suspension of play in Centenary Test.
1/9/80	Appointed England captain for tour of West Indies. Is ordered to lose weight.
23/12/80	Involved in a night club incident in Scunthorpe. Comes to aid of friend, Joe Neenan of Scunthorpe United, but is later charged with assault. Is later acquitted.
15/2/81	On rest day of First Test in Trinidad, Botham suggests that if England don't get a draw 'heads will roll'. England lose by an innings.
2/81	Robin Jackman's visitor's permit is revoked in Guyana. The Second Test is cancelled and tour placed in jeopardy.
14/3/81	Ken Barrington dies of a heart attack in Barbados.
18/3/81	Shell-shocked England lose Third Test by 298 runs.
15/4/81	Series ends in two–nil defeat, England salvaging draws in last two games. Botham ends series with seventy-three runs at ten and fifteen wickets at thirty-three – tops bowling averages.
4/81	Jostles Henry Blofeld at Nassau airport following disagreement over a press article.
5/81	Appointed England captain for Australian

	series on match by match basis.
8/6/81	England lose Prudential Trophy series by two to one.
21/6/81	England lose First Test by four wickets.
7/7/81	Botham registers pair at Lord's in drawn Second Test. Returns to pavilion to stony silence. Resigns captaincy.
21/7/81	Completes innings of 149 not out as England win Third Test at Headingley having followed on, first such Test match occurrence since 1894/95.
25/7/81	Plays in Somerset side that wins Benson & Hedges Cup, beating Surrey at Lord's by seven wickets.
2/8/81	Takes five wickets for one run in final burst to seal victory in Fourth Test at Edgbaston.
15/8/81	Scores century in Fifth Test to clinch series win at Old Trafford, described as one of the finest innings ever.
31/8/81	Dismisses Rodney Marsh to claim 200th Test wicket at the Oval. Completes ten wickets in a Test match for the final time.
1/9/81	Man of the Series versus Australia: 399 runs at thirty-six, thirty-four wickets at twenty-one.
23/9/81	Is cleared of charges relating to Neenan incident on 23/12/80.
12/81	Voted BBC Sports Personality of the Year.
Winter 81/2	Tours India under Keith Fletcher. Tops batting averages with 440 runs at fifty-five. On 1

December, completes 2000 runs in Tests.
Fastest ever double double – forty-two Tests.
On 22 January 1982 scores the fastest ever
century on Indian soil against Central Zone
at Indore – fifty minutes, forty-eight balls.

13/3/82	Sends message of support to anti-apartheid rally in Trafalgar Square.
17/5/82	Crashes two Saab motor cars in a celebrity race day at Thruxton.
9/7/82	Completes highest Test score, 208, versus India at the Oval. Fastest ever Test double hundred in balls received – 220.
24/7/82	Plays in Somerset side which retains the Benson & Hedges Cup with a nine wicket win over Nottinghamshire.
Winter 82/3	Tours Australia. On 12 November reaches 3000 runs in fifty-fifth Test. Otherwise, an ordinary tour as England lose the Ashes. Is fined £200 by tour manager Doug Insole for comments about Australian umpires.
6/83	Defies TCCB attempts to end his *Sun* column.
22/6/83	Plays in England side beaten by India in Prudential World Cup semi-final.
25/8/83	Scores last Test century on home soil, 103, against New Zealand at the Oval.
3/9/83	Captains Somerset side that wins the NatWest Bank Trophy at Lord's, beating Kent by twenty-four runs.
24/11/83	Appointed as Somerset's captain.
Winter 83/4	Tours with England in New Zealand and

Pakistan. Tour is marred by newspaper allegations regarding drug taking by England players. Botham decides to sue the *Mail on Sunday*. Returns home early from Pakistan for a knee operation. While in hospital, gives an interview in which he says Pakistan 'is the kind of place to send your mother-in-law for a month, all expenses paid'. Is subsequently fined £1000 by TCCB.

4/84   Begins first season as Somerset captain – it is also his benefit year.

2/7/84   Reaches 4000 runs in his sixty-ninth Test.

3/7/84   Ends most personally successful Test against West Indies – eighty-one and 8/103 – on the losing side at Lord's. On final day, bowls twenty overs for 117 runs.

26/7/84   Announces he will be unavailable for England's winter tour of India.

7/84   Arrives late for his benefit game at Sparkford, Club captain Graham Reeve complains about Botham's attitude and makes it clear he will not be welcome in future.

9/8/84   Takes his 300th wicket in his seventy-second Test, the first man to complete 4000 runs and 300 wickets.

9/84   Completes first season as county captain. Somerset are seventh in the Championship, quarter-finalists in the two cup competitions, and thirteenth on Sundays.

31/12/84   Police search Botham's Epworth home and find a small quantity of cannabis.

14/2/85   Pleads guilty to possession of cannabis at
               Scunthorpe Magistrates Court. Is fined £100.

3/85   Engages Tim Hudson as manager.

1/7/85   Dismisses Australia's Graeme Wood at Lord's
               to become England's greatest wicket taker in
               Tests.

13/7/85   Has argument with Umpire Whitehead during
               Trent Bridge Test. Given severe warning about
               future conduct by TCCB.

26/7/85   Scores fastest hundred of the season against
               Warwickshire at Edgbaston in forty-nine
               minutes. Registers twelve sixes in his innings
               of 138 not out.

8/85   It's announced that his 1984 benefit season
               raised £90,822, a Somerset record.

9/85   Completes season with a world record of eighty
               sixes in the summer. Season ends with
               Somerset bottom of County Championship.

8/10/85   Botham resigns the Somerset captaincy.

13/11/85   Daughter Rebecca is born.

10 & 11/85   First marathon walk in aid of leukaemia
               research from John o' Groats to Land's End.

Winter 85/6   Tours West Indies with England. Tour is
               dogged by further press allegations concerning
               drugs and extra-marital affairs. Botham
               manages 168 runs at seventeen and eleven
               wickets at forty-nine. Prior to Fourth Test
               comes close to being dropped for the first time
               since 1977/78. Ends series with 354 wickets,
               one behind Dennis Lillee.

22/1/86	A portrait of Botham by John Bellany is unveiled in the National Portrait Gallery, the first cricketer to be so honoured since W.G. Grace. The portrait receives a mixed reaction.
3/86	Sacks Tim Hudson as manager.
5/86	Is made a vice president of Scunthorpe United.
18/5/86	In a *Mail on Sunday* article, Botham confesses that he has used pot in the past.
29/5/86	TCCB ban Botham from cricket from 29 May until 31 July, on the grounds of bringing the game into disrepute with his newspaper article, denying in the past that he had used cannabis and making public pronouncements without the clearance of his county.
2/8/86	Returns to first class cricket against Worcestershire at Weston-super-Mare.
3/8/86	Scores 104 not out from sixty-six balls in sixty-four minutes.
21/8/86	Returns to Test cricket against New Zealand at the Oval. Dismisses Bruce Edgar with first ball. Eleven balls later, dismisses Jeff Crowe to become the leading wicket taker in Test match history.
25/8/86	Hits the second fastest half century in Test history. Takes twenty-four from one over off Derek Stirling to equal the Test record set by Andy Roberts off Botham in 1980/81.
8/86	Viv Richards and Joel Garner are informed their playing contracts with Somerset will not be renewed. Botham threatens to leave unless

they are reinstated.

9/86	A new waxwork of Botham is unveiled at Madame Tussaud's.
10/86	Announces that he will spend the next three winters playing for Queensland.
8/11/86	Special General Meeting of Somerset CCC backs the cricket committee. Richards and Garner are not reinstated. Botham says he will leave the club on the expiry of his contract on 31/12/86.
Winter 86/87	Tours Australia with England. During First Test on 15/11/86, registers last Test match century. In the Second Test, he captures his 100th catch in Tests on 3/12/86, the eighth outfielder to do so. In the Fourth Test, takes 5/41 on 26/12/86, his final fivewicket haul in Tests. *Wisden* notes that he has been an excellent influence on the side and has gone out of his way to help the younger players throughout the tour.
10/1/87	Signs a contract to play for Worcestershire.
4/87	Walks 150 miles from Belfast to Dublin in aid of leukaemia research.
25/4/87	Makes Championship debut for Worcestershire in a two-wicket win over Kent at New Road.
8/8/87	Concedes 217 runs from fifty-two overs against Pakistan at the Oval, the most conceded by any Englishman in Tests.
10/8/87	Scores his 5000th run in his ninety-fourth Test.

13/9/87	Scores sixty-one as Worcestershire clinch the Refuge Assurance League by beating Northamptonshire at Worcester. In the final four games, Botham and Tim Curtis share four century partnerships.
Winter 87/8	Plays for Queensland in Australia. Helps them reach the Sheffield Shield final. An altercation on the flight to the final in Perth ends with Botham's brief arrest. Following defeat in the final, Queensland terminate Botham's three-year contract after just one season.
4/88	Walks from Perpignan to Turin in the footsteps of Hannibal in aid of leukaemia research.
20/5/88	Botham finally bows to his back injury. He announces that he requires an operation to fuse two vertebrae and will miss the remainder of the season. He is an important influence in the dressing room as Worcestershire win the County Championship and retain the Refuge Assurance League.
14/12/88	Taken to Chelsea police station to answer charges of assault on one Kevin James Batten. Charges withdrawn, though not before the allegations make the front page of the *Sun*. They make an out of court settlement.
15/4/89	Botham returns to first class cricket, playing for Worcestershire against MCC.
2/7/89	Is struck in the face by a drunken youth in an unprovoked attack in a Northampton pub.
31/8/89	Botham helps Worcestershire retain the County Championship by beating Gloucestershire at

New Road.

9/89   Following an indifferent season, Botham is
              omitted from England's party to tour West
              Indies. His failure to make the party is
              overshadowed by the dropping of David
              Gower, England captain throughout the
              previous summer.

5/11/89   Appears on BBC Radio's Desert Island Discs.

14/7/90   Plays in Worcestershire team beaten in the
              Benson & Hedges Cup Final by Lancashire.

11/90   Walks 630 miles in twenty-six days from
              Aberdeen to Ipswich in aid of leukaemia
              research.

Winter 90/91 Takes part in *Jack & The Beanstalk*
              pantomime at Bradford Alhambra.

14/7/91   Plays in Worcestershire team that beat
              Lancashire by sixty-five runs in the Benson &
              Hedges Cup Final.

9/91   Announces that he will to move Durham for
              their inaugural Championship season in 1992.

15/9/91   Ends Worcestershire career by playing in the
              team that beats Lancashire by seven runs to
              win the Refuge Assurance Cup.

9/91   Is selected for England tour to New Zealand
              and then Australia for the Benson & Hedges
              World Cup series. Is given permission to join
              the tour late so that he may discharge his
              commitments to the Bournemouth pantomime,
              Jack & The Beanstalk.

6/2/92   Plays his 100th Test, against New Zealand in

Wellington.

25/3/92 Plays in the England side that loses the World Cup Final to Pakistan by twenty-two runs.

25/4/92 Makes his first class debut for Durham against Leicestershire in their inaugural Championship match at Durham University. Takes Durham's first Championship wicket when he dismisses Nigel Briers.

29/4/92 Scores 105 on Durham debut. It is their first Championship century.

13/6/92 Is appointed OBE in the Queen's Birthday Honours.

21/6/92 Completes his final Test match for England at Lord's as they lose to Pakistan by two wickets. Scores two and six, takes none for nine and holds two catches. His final record is 102 Tests, 5200 runs at 33.55 with fourteen centuries. He has 383 wickets at a cost of 28.40. He has also held 120 catches, an English record he holds with Lord Cowdrey.

24/8/92 He plays his final game in England colours, the Fifth Texaco Trophy game against Pakistan at Old Trafford, a game England win by six wickets. Botham bowls eleven overs for forty-three runs and does not bat. His one day record is 116 games, 2113 runs at 23.2, thirty-six catches and 145 wickets at 28.54.

10/92 Walks 546 miles from Land's End to Margate in aid of leukaemia research.

11 & 12/92 Appears on a speaking tour in the UK with Viv Richards – 'The King & I'.

Winter 92/93	Takes part in *Jack & The Beanstalk* pantomime in Stockport.
2/93	Takes the 'King & I' show to Australia.
18/7/93	Announces his immediate retirement from the game during Durham's match with the touring Australians.
19/7/93	Completes his final first class game by keeping wicket in the final over without pads or gloves. His final first class figures are 402 matches, 19,399 runs at 33.97 with thirty-eight centuries. He held 354 catches and took 1171 wickets at 27.22.
Winter 93/4	Takes part in *Dick Whittington* pantomime in Bath.
Winter 94/5	Takes part in *Cinderella* pantomime in Wimbledon.
3/95	Goes on speaking tour with Allan Lamb – 'Beef & Lamb In A Stew'.
5/95	Joins Sky Sports as commentator and analyst.
4/96	Accepts nomination as England selector. Fails to get elected to panel.
15/7/96	Begins the first of thirteen days in the Royal Court of Justice, taking action against Imran Khan for alleged libels in the *Sun* and *India Today*.
31/7/96	Trial ends. On both counts, the jury find in favour of Imran by a majority of 10–2. Later, Botham and Lamb decide to appeal against the decision.
11/96	Further speaking tour with Lamb – 'Balls 'n'

all'.

Winter 96/7 Works alongside David Lloyd in an informal coaching and motivational capacity on England's tour of Zimbabwe and New Zealand.

TEST MATCH STATISTICS

Below is a match by match summary of Ian Botham's Test career. The left hand column details all of his Test match victims, mode of dismissal, and his full bowling analysis for each innings. The right column gives similar details of his batting performances, indicating his score, how he was out, and who dismissed him. For example, in his first game at Trent Bridge in 1977 he took the wickets of Chappell, Walters, Marsh, Walker and Thomson, taking five for seventy-four in the first innings and none for sixty in the second. When he batted, he scored twenty-five before being bowled by Max Walker.

ENGLAND VS AUSTRALIA AT TRENT BRIDGE
July 28, 29, 30, August 1, 2, 1977. England won by 7 wkts.

G.S. Chappell	bowled	19	20–5–74–5	b Walker	25
K.D. Walters	c Hendrick	11	25–5–60–0		
R.W. Marsh	lbw	0			
M.H.N. Walker	c Hendrick	0			
J.R. Thomson	c Knott	21			

ENGLAND VS AUSTRALIA AT HEADINGLEY
August 11, 12, 13, 15, 1977. England won by an innings and 85 runs.

D.W. Hookes	lbw	24	11–3–21–5	b Bright	0
K.D. Walters	c Hendrick	4	17–3–47–0		
R.W. Marsh	c Knott	2			
M.H.N. Walker	c Knott	7			
J.R. Thomson	bowled	0			

ENGLAND VS NEW ZEALAND AT BASIN RESERVE
February 10, 11, 12, 14, 15, 1978. New Zealand won by 72 runs.

J.G. Wright	lbw	55	12.6–2–27–2	c Burgess b Hadlee	7
S.L. Boock	bowled	4	9.3–3–13–2	c Boock b Hadlee	19
M.G. Burgess	c Boycott	6			
D.R. Hadlee	c Roope	2			

ENGLAND VS NEW ZEALAND AT LANCASTER PARK
February 24, 25, 26, 28, March 1, 1978. England won by 174 runs.

M.G. Burgess	c Roope	29	24.7–6–73–5	c Lees b Boock	103
B.E. Congdon	lbw	20	7–1–38–3	not out	30
W.K. Lees	c Miller	0			
R.O. Collinge	c Edmonds	32			
E.J. Chatfield	c Edmonds	3			
R.O. Collinge	c Miller	0			
S.L. Boock	c Taylor	0			
E.J. Chatfield	lbw	6			

ENGLAND VS NEW ZEALAND AT EDEN PARK
March 4, 5, 6, 8, 9, 10, 1978. Match drawn.

R.W. Anderson	c Gatting	17	34–4–109–5	c Edwards b Collinge	53
M.G. Burgess	c Randall	50	13–1–51–0		
B.E. Congdon	c Miller	5			
J.M. Parker	lbw	14			
R.J. Hadlee	c Roope	1			

ENGLAND VS PAKISTAN AT EDGBASTON
June 1, 2, 3, 5, 1978. England won by an innings and 57 runs.

Mudassar Nazar	c and b	14	15–4–52–1	c Qasim b Liaquat	100
			17–3–47–0		

ENGLAND VS PAKISTAN AT LORD'S
June 15, 16, 17, 19, 1978. England won by an innings and 120 runs.

Mudassar Nazar	c Taylor	10	5–2–17–0	b Liaquat	108
Haroon Rashid	bowled	4	20.5–8–34–8		
Talat Ali	c Roope	40			
Wasim Raja	c and b	1			
Wasim Bari	c Taylor	2			
Sikander Bakht	c Roope	1			
Iqbal Qasim	bowled	0			
Javed Miandad	c Gooch	22			

ENGLAND VS PAKISTAN AT HEADINGLEY
June 29, 30, July 1, 3, 4, 1978. Match drawn.

Haroon Rashid	c Brearley	7	18–2–59–4	lbw Sarfraz	4
Sadiq Mohammad	c Brearley	97			
Wasim Raja	lbw	0			
Sarfraz Nawaz	c Taylor	4			

ENGLAND VS NEW ZEALAND AT THE OVAL
July 27, 28, 29, 31, August 1, 1978. England won by 7 wkts.

G.P. Howarth	c Edmonds	94	22–7–58–1	c Bracewell b Boock	22
R.W. Anderson	c Taylor	2	19–2–46–3		
J.G. Wright	lbw	25			
M.G. Burgess	lbw	7			

ENGLAND VS NEW ZEALAND AT TRENT BRIDGE
August 10, 11, 12, 14, 1978. England won by an innings and 119 runs.

B.A. Edgar	c Taylor	6	21–9–34–6	c Hadlee b Boock	8
R.W. Anderson	lbw	19	24–7–59–3		
M.G. Burgess	c Taylor	5			
B.E. Congdon	c Hendrick	27			
G.N. Edwards	c Taylor	0			

R.J. Hadlee	c Gooch	4
B.E. Congdon	c Brearley	4
B.L. Cairns	lbw	0
R.J. Hadlee	c Taylor	11

ENGLAND VS NEW ZEALAND AT LORD'S
August 24, 25, 26, 28, 1978. England won by 7 wkts.

J.G. Wright	c Edmonds	17	38–13–101–6	c Edgar b Collinge	21
M.G. Burgess	lbw	68	18.1–4–39–5		
B.E. Congdon	c Emburey	2			
R.W. Anderson	bowled	16			
R.J. Hadlee	c Brearley	0			
G.P. Howarth	c Taylor	123			
B.A. Edgar	bowled	4			
J.G. Wright	bowled	12			
J.M. Parker	c Taylor	3			
M.G. Burgess	c Hendrick	14			
R.O. Collinge	bowled	0			

ENGLAND VS AUSTRALIA AT WOOLLOONGABBA
December 1, 2, 3, 5, 6, 1978. England won by 7 wkts.

K.J. Hughes	c Taylor	4	12–1–40–3	c Maclean b Hogg	49
R.M. Hogg	c Taylor	36	26–5–95–3		
A.G. Hurst	c Taylor	0			
P.M. Toohey	lbw	1			
R.H. Hogg	bowled	16			
A.G. Hurst	bowled	0			

ENGLAND VS AUSTRALIA AT WACA GROUND
December 15, 16, 17, 19, 20, 1978. England won by 166 runs.

11–2–46–0	lbw Hurst	11
11–1–54–0	c Wood b Yardley	30

ENGLAND VS AUSTRALIA AT MELBOURNE CRICKET GROUND
December 29, 30, 1978, January 1, 2, 3, 1979. Australia won by 103 runs.

K.J. Hughes	c Taylor	0	20.1–4–68–3	c Darling b Higgs	22
G.N. Yallop	c Hendrick	41	15–4–41–3	c Maclean b Higgs	10
J.A. Maclean	bowled	8			
G.M. Wood	bowled	34			
R.M. Hogg	bowled	1			
K.J. Hughes	c Gower	48			

ENGLAND VS AUSTRALIA AT SYDNEY CRICKET GROUND
January 6, 7, 8, 10, 11, 1979. England won by 93 runs.

| P.M. Toohey | c Gooch | 1 | 28–3–87–2 | c Yallop b Hogg | 59 |
| G. Dymock | bowled | 5 | | c Wood b Higgs | 6 |

ENGLAND VS AUSTRALIA AT ADELAIDE OVAL
January 27, 28, 29, 31, February 1, 1979. England won by 205 runs.

A.R. Border	c Taylor	11	11.4–0–42–4	c Wright b Higgs	74
P.H. Carlson	c Taylor	0	14–4–37–1	c Yardley b Hurst	7
B. Yardley	bowled	28			
W.M. Darling	c Willis	15			
W.M. Darling	bowled	18			

ENGLAND VS AUSTRALIA AT SYDNEY CRICKET GROUND
February 10, 11, 12, 14, 1979. England won by 9 wkts.

P.M. Toohey	c Taylor	8	9.7–1–57–4	c Carlson b Yardley	23
P.H. Carlson	c Gooch	2			
G.N. Yallop	c Gower	121			
A.G. Hurst	bowled	0			

ENGLAND VS INDIA AT EDGBASTON
July 12, 13, 14, 16, 1979. England won by an innings and 83 runs.

C.P.S. Chauhan	c Gooch	4	26–4–86–2	b Dev	33
Kapil Dev	lbw	1	29–8–70–5		
A.D. Gaekwad	c Gooch	15			
G.R. Viswanath	c Taylor	51			
M. Amarnath	lbw	10			
Kapil Dev	c Hendrick	21			
S. Venkataraghavan	lbw	0			

ENGLAND VS INDIA AT LORD'S
August 2, 3, 4, 6, 7, 1979. Match drawn.

C.P.S. Chauhan	c Randall	2	19–9–35–5	b Venkataraghavan	36
A.D. Gaekwad	c Taylor	13	35–13–80–1		
Kapil Dev	c Miller	4			
Yashpal Sharma	c Taylor	11			
B. Reddy	lbw	0			
S.M. Gavaskar	c Brearley	59			

ENGLAND VS INDIA AT HEADINGLEY
August 16, 17, 18, 20, 21, 1979. Match drawn.

13–3–39–0	c Ghavri b Venkataraghavan	137

ENGLAND VS INDIA AT THE OVAL
August 30, 31, September 1, 3, 4, 1979. Match drawn.

S.M. Gavaskar	c Bairstow	13	28–7–65–4	st Reddy b Venkataraghavan	38
G.R. Viswanath	c Brearley	62	29–5–97–3		
K.D. Ghavri	c Bairstow	7			
B. Reddy	c Bairstow	12			
S.M. Gavaskar	c Gower	221			
Yashpal Sharma	lbw	19			
Yajurvindra Singh	lbw	1			

ENGLAND VS AUSTRALIA AT WACA GROUND
December 14, 15, 16, 18, 19, 1979. Australia won by 138 runs.

B.M. Laird	lbw	0	35–9–78–6	c Toohey b Thomson	15
A.R. Border	lbw	4	45.5–14–98–5	c Marsh b Lillee	18
G.S. Chappell	c Boycott	19			
R.J. Bright	c Taylor	17			
D.K. Lillee	c Taylor	18			
G. Dymock	bowled	5			
K.J. Hughes	c Miller	4			
P.M. Toohey	c Taylor	3			
R.W. Marsh	c Gower	4			
R.J. Bright	lbw	12			
J.R. Thomson	bowled	8			

ENGLAND VS AUSTRALIA AT SYDNEY CRICKET GROUND
January 4, 5, 6, 8, 9, 1980. Australia won by 6 wkts.

K.J. Hughes	c Taylor	18	17–7–29–4	c Chappell b Pascoe	27
A.R. Border	c Gooch	15	23.3–12–43–0	c Wiener b Chappell	0
D.K. Lillee	c Brearley	5			
G. Dymock	c Taylor	4			

ENGLAND VS AUSTRALIA AT MELBOURNE CRICKET GROUND
February 1, 2, 3, 5, 6, 1980. Australia won by 8 wkts.

K.J. Hughes	c Underwood	15	39.5–15–105–3	c Marsh b Lillee	8
G. Dymock	bowled	19	12–5–18–1	not out	119
A.A. Mallett	lbw	25			
R.B. McCosker	lbw	2			

ENGLAND VS INDIA AT WANKHEDE STADIUM
February 15, 17, 18, 19, 1980. England won by 10 wkts.

S.M. Gavaskar	c Taylor	49	22.5–7–58–6 lbw Ghavri	114
S.M. Patil	c Taylor	30	26–7–48–7	
Yashpal Sharma	lbw	21		
Kapil Dev	c Taylor	0		
N.S. Yadav	c Taylor	8		
D.R. Doshi	c Taylor	6		
R.M.H. Binny	lbw	0		
G.R. Viswanath	c Taylor	5		
S.M. Patil	lbw	0		
S.M. Gavaskar	c Taylor	24		
S.M.H. Kirmani	c Gooch	0		
Yashpal Sharma	lbw	27		
N.S. Yadav	c Taylor	15		

ENGLAND VS WEST INDIES AT TRENT BRIDGE
June 5, 6, 7, 9, 10, 1980. West Indies won by 2 wkts.

A.I. Kallicharran	bowled	17	20–6–50–3	c Richards b Garner	57
A.M.E. Roberts	lbw	21	16.4–6–48–1	c Richards b Roberts	4
J. Garner	c Lever	2			
I.V.A. Richards	lbw	48			

ENGLAND VS WEST INDIES AT LORD'S
June 19, 20, 21, 23, 24, 1980. Match drawn.

C.G. Greenidge	lbw	25	37–7–145–3 lbw Garner	8
D.L. Haynes	lbw	184		
D.L. Murray	c Tavare	34		

ENGLAND VS WEST INDIES AT OLD TRAFFORD
July 10, 11, 12, 14, 15, 1980. Match drawn.

A.I. Kallicharran	c Knott	13	20–6–64–3	c Murray b Garner	8

| I.V.A. Richards | bowled | 65 | | lbw Holding | 35 |
| D.L. Murray | bowled | 17 | | | |

ENGLAND VS WEST INDIES AT THE OVAL
July 24, 25, 26, 28, 29, 1980. Match drawn.

| I.V.A. Richards | c Willey | 26 | 18.2–8–47–2 | lbw Croft | 9 |
| J. Garner | c Gatting | 46 | | c Greenidge b Garner | 4 |

ENGLAND VS WEST INDIES AT HEADINGLEY
August 7, 8, 9, 11, 12, 1980. Match drawn.

| C.G. Greenidge | lbw | 34 | 19–8–31–1 | c Richards b Holding | 37 |
| | | | | lbw Marshall | 7 |

ENGLAND VS AUSTRALIA AT LORD'S
August 28, 29, 30, September 1, 2, 1980. Match drawn.

| K.J. Hughes | lbw | 84 | 22–2–89–0 | c Wood b Pascoe | 0 |
| | | | 9.2–1–43–1 | | |

ENGLAND VS WEST INDIES AT QUEEN'S PARK OVAL
February 13, 14, 16, 17, 18, 1981. West Indies won by an innings and 79 runs.

| M.A. Holding | lbw | 26 | 28–6–113–2 | lbw Croft | 0 |
| J. Garner | lbw | 4 | | c Holding b Richards | 16 |

ENGLAND VS WEST INDIES AT KENSINGTON OVAL
March 13, 14, 15, 17, 18, 1981. West Indies won by 298 runs.

E.H. Mattis	lbw	16	25.1–5–77–4	c Murray b Holding	26
A.M.E. Roberts	c Bairstow	14	29–5–102–3	c Lloyd b Roberts	1
M.A. Holding	c Gatting	0			

J. Garner	c Bairstow	15
D.L. Haynes	lbw	25
C.H. Lloyd	lbw	66
A.M.E. Roberts	c Bairstow	0

ENGLAND VS WEST INDIES AT ST JOHN'S
March 27, 28, 29, 31, April 1, 1981. Match drawn.

D.L. Haynes	c Downton	4	37–6–127–4	c Lloyd b Croft	1
H.A. Gomes	c Gower	12			
E.H. Mattis	c Butcher	71			
D.A. Murray	c Boycott	1			

ENGLAND VS WEST INDIES AT SABINA PARK
April 10, 11, 12, 14, 15, 1981. Match drawn.

M.A. Holding	c Downton	0	26.1–9–73–2	c Greenidge b Marshall	13
C.E.H. Croft	c sub	0		c Garner b Holding	16

ENGLAND VS AUSTRALIA AT TRENT BRIDGE
June 18, 19, 20, 21, 1981. Australia won by 4 wkts.

G.F. Lawson	c Gower	14	16.5–6–34–2	b Alderman	1
A.R. Border	c and b	63	10–1–34–1	c Border b Lillee	33
G.N. Yallop	c Gatting	6			

ENGLAND VS AUSTRALIA AT LORD'S
July 2, 3, 4, 6, 7, 1981. Match drawn.

J. Dyson	c Gower	7	26–8–71–2	lbw Lawson	0
A.R. Border	c Gatting	64	8–3–10–1	b Bright	0
T.M. Chappell	c Taylor	5			

ENGLAND VS AUSTRALIA AT HEADINGLEY
July 16, 17, 18, 20, 21, 1981. England won by 18 runs.

G.M. Wood	lbw	34	39.2–11–95–6	c Marsh b Lillee	50
K.J. Hughes	c and b	89	7–3–14–1	not out	149*
G.N. Yallop	c Taylor	58			
A.R. Border	lbw	8			
G.F. Lawson	c Taylor	13			
R.W. Marsh	bowled	28			
G.M. Wood	c Taylor	10			

ENGLAND VS AUSTRALIA AT EDGBASTON
July 30, 31, August 1, 2, 1981. England won by 29 runs.

R.J. Bright	lbw	27	20–1–64–1	b Alderman	26
R.W. Marsh	bowled	4	14–9–11–5	c Marsh b Lillee	3
R.J. Bright	lbw	0			
D.K. Lillee	c Taylor	3			
M.F. Kent	bowled	10			
T.M. Alderman	bowled	0			

ENGLAND VS AUSTRALIA AT OLD TRAFFORD
August 13, 14, 15, 16, 17, 1981. England won by 103 runs.

A.R. Border	c Gower	11	6.2–1–28–3	c Bright b Lillee	0
R.J. Bright	c Knott	22	36–16–86–2	c Marsh b Whitney	118
D.K. Lillee	c Gooch	13			
K.J. Hughes	lbw	43			
T.M. Alderman	lbw	0			

ENGLAND VS AUSTRALIA AT THE OVAL
August 27, 28, 29, 31, September 1, 1981. Match drawn.

G.M. Wood	c Brearley	66	47–13–125–6	c Yallop b Lillee	3
M.F. Kent	c Gatting	54	42–9–128–4	lbw Alderman	16
K.J. Hughes	hit wicket	31			
R.J. Bright	c Brearley	3			

T.M. Alderman	bowled	0
M.R. Whitney	bowled	4
M.F. Kent	c Brearley	7
R.W. Marsh	c Gatting	52
R.J. Bright	bowled	11
D.M. Wellham	lbw	103

ENGLAND VS INDIA AT WANKHEDE STADIUM
November 27, 28, 29, December 1, 1981. India won by 138 runs.

G.R. Viswanath	c Boycott	8	28–6–72–4	c Gavaskar b Doshi	7
S.M. Patil	lbw	17	22.3–3–61–5	c Azad b Dev	29
S.M. Gavaskar	c Taylor	55			
Kapil Dev	c Taylor	38			
D.B. Vengsarkar	c Tavare	5			
S.M. Gavaskar	c Taylor	14			
S.M. Patil	lbw	13			
G.R. Viswanath	c Taylor	37			
D.R. Doshi	bowled	7			

ENGLAND VS INDIA AT KARNATAKA STATE C.A. STADIUM
December 9, 10, 12, 13, 14, 1981. Match drawn.

| K. Srikkanth | c Gooch | 65 | 47–9–137–2 | c Madan b Doshi | 55 |
| S.M.H. Kirmani | lbw | 9 | | | |

ENGLAND VS INDIA AT FEROZ SHAH KOTLA
December 23, 24, 26, 27, 28, 1981. Match drawn.

| G.R. Viswanath | bowled | 107 | 41–6–122–2 | c Azad b Madan | 66 |
| Kapil Dev | c Gooch | 16 | | | |

ENGLAND VS INDIA AT EDEN GARDENS
January 1, 2, 3, 5, 6, 1982. Match drawn.

| D.B. Vengsarkar | c Taylor | 70 | 27–8–63–2 | c Gavaskar b Dev | 58 |

S.M.H. Kirmani   bowled   10   11–3–26–0   c Yadav b Doshi   31

ENGLAND VS INDIA AT CHIDAMBARAM STADIUM
January 13, 14, 15, 17, 18, 1982. Match drawn.

Yashpal Sharma   c Tavare   140   31–10–83–1   c Kirmani b Shastri   52
                                        8–1–29–0

ENGLAND VS INDIA AT GREEN PARK
January 30, 31, February 1, 3, 4, 1982. Match drawn.

Pranab Roy   bowled   5   25–6–67–1   st Kirmani b Doshi   142

ENGLAND VS SRI LANKA AT SARAVANAMUTTU STADIUM
February 17, 18, 20, 21, 1982. England won by 7 wkts.

S. Wettimuny   c Taylor   6   12.5–1–28–3 b De Mel   13
L.R.D. Mendis   lbw   17   12–1–37–0
G.R.A. De Silva   c Emburey   12

ENGLAND VS INDIA AT LORD'S
June 10, 11, 12, 14, 15, 1982. England won by 7 wkts.

G.A. Parkar   lbw   6   19.4–3–46–5 c Malhotra b   67
                                                    Madan
G.R. Viswanath   bowled   1   31.5–7–
                                        103–1
S.M. Gavaskar   bowled   48
Madan Lal   c Tavare   6
D.R. Doshi   c Taylor   0
Kapil Dev   c Cook   89

ENGLAND VS INDIA AT OLD TRAFFORD
June 24, 25, 26, 27, 28, 1982. Match drawn.

G.R. Viswanath   c Taylor   54   19–4–86–1   b Shastri   128

ENGLAND VS INDIA AT THE OVAL
July 8, 9, 10, 12, 13, 1982. Match drawn.

D.B. Vengsarkar	c Edmonds	6	19–2–73–2	c Viswanath b Doshi	208
S.M. Patil	c sub	62	4–0–12–0		

ENGLAND VS PAKISTAN AT EDGBASTON
July 29, 30, 31, August 1, 1982. England won by 113 runs.

Mudassar Nazar	lbw	0	24–1–86–2	b Imran	2
Mohsin Khan	c Willis	26	21–7–70–4	lbw Tahir	0
Mudassar Nazar	lbw	0			
Mansoor Akhtar	c Taylor	0			
Mohsin Khan	lbw	35			
Wasim Bari	c Taylor	12			

ENGLAND VS PAKISTAN AT LORD'S
August 12, 13, 14, 15, 16, 1982. Pakistan won by 10 wkts.

Mansoor Akhtar	c Lamb	57	44–8–148–3	c Mohsin b Qadir	31
Haroon Rashid	lbw	1	7–0–30–0	c Sarfraz b Mudassar	69
Imran Khan	c Taylor	12			

ENGLAND VS PAKISTAN AT HEADINGLEY
August 26, 27, 28, 30, 31, 1982. England won by 3 wkts.

Mohsin Khan	c Taylor	10	24.5–9–70–4	c sub b Sikander	57
Mudassar Nazar	bowled	65	30–8–74–5	c Majid b Mudassar	4
Abdul Qadir	c Willis	5			
Ehteshamuddin	bowled	0			
Mansoor Akhtar	c Randall	39			
Zaheer Abbas	lbw	4			
Javed Miandad	c Taylor	52			
Majid Khan	c Gower	10			
Imran Khan	c Randall	46			

ENGLAND VS AUSTRALIA AT WACA GROUND
November 12, 13, 14, 16, 17, 1982. Match drawn.

| A.R. Border | c Taylor | 8 | 40–10–121–2 | c Marsh b Lawson | 12 |
| R.W. Marsh | c Cook | 0 | 6–1–17–0 | b Lawson | 0 |

ENGLAND VS AUSTRALIA AT WOOLLOONGABBA
November 26, 27, 28, 30, December 1, 1982. Australia won by 7 wkts.

J. Dyson	bowled	1	22–1–105–3	c Rackemann b Yardley	40
K.J. Hughes	c Taylor	0	15.5–1–70–0	c Marsh b Thomson	15
R.W. Marsh	c Taylor	11			

ENGLAND VS AUSTRALIA AT ADELAIDE OVAL
December 10, 11, 12, 14, 15, 1982. Australia won by 8 wkts.

J. Dyson	c Taylor	44	36.5–5–112–4	c Wessels b Thomson	35
K.C. Wessels	c Taylor	44	10–2–45–1	c Dyson b Yardley	58
B. Yardley	c Gower	38			
J.R. Thomson	c and b	3			
K.C. Wessels	c Taylor	1			

ENGLAND VS AUSTRALIA AT MELBOURNE CRICKET GROUND
December 26, 27, 28, 29, 30, 1982. England won by 3 runs.

A.R. Border	bowled	2	18–3–69–1	c Wessels b Yardley	27
J. Dyson	c Tavare	31	25.1–4–80–2	c Chappell b Thomson	46
J.R. Thomson	c Miller	21			

ENGLAND VS AUSTRALIA AT SYDNEY CRICKET GROUND
January 2, 3, 4, 6, 7, 1983. Match drawn.

K.C. Wessels	c Willis	19	30–8–75–4	c Wessels b Thomson	5
K.J. Hughes	c Cowans	29	10–0–35–1	lbw Thomson	32
G.F. Lawson	c and b	6			
J.R. Thomson	c Lamb	0			
K.C. Wessels	lbw	53			

ENGLAND VS NEW ZEALAND AT THE OVAL
July 14, 15, 16, 17, 18, 1983. England won by 189 runs.

J.G. Bracewell	c and b	7	16–2–62–4	b Hadlee	15
R.J. Hadlee	c and b	84	4–0–17–0	run out	26
B.L. Cairns	c Lamb	2			
E.J. Chatfield	c Willis	0			

ENGLAND VS NEW ZEALAND AT HEADINGLEY
July 28, 29, 30, August 1, 1983. New Zealand won by 5 wkts.

| | | | 26–9–81–0 | c Howarth b Cairns | 38 |
| | | | 0.1–0–4–0 | c Howarth b Coney | 4 |

ENGLAND VS NEW ZEALAND AT LORD'S
August 11, 12, 13, 15, 1983. England won by 127 runs.

M.D. Crowe	bowled	46	20.4–6–50–4	lbw Cairns	8
E.J. Gray	c Lamb	11	7–2–20–1	c Coney b Chatfield	61
B.L. Cairns	c Lamb	5			
I.D.S. Smith	c Lamb	3			
J.G. Wright	c Taylor	12			

ENGLAND VS NEW ZEALAND AT TRENT BRIDGE
August 25, 26, 27, 28, 29, 1983. England won by 165 runs.

| T.J. Franklin | c Smith | 2 | 14–4–33–1 | lbw Snedden | 103 |
| | | | 25–4–73–0 | c Edgar b Gray | 27 |

ENGLAND VS NEW ZEALAND AT BASIN RESERVE
January 20, 21, 22, 23, 24, 1984. Match drawn.

J.G. Wright	c Cook	17	27.4–8–59–5	c Crowe b Cairns	138
B.A. Edgar	c Taylor	9	36–6–137–1		
G.P. Howarth	c Gower	15			
R.J. Hadlee	c Gatting	24			
I.D.S. Smith	lbw	24			
J.J. Crowe	lbw	3			

ENGLAND VS NEW ZEALAND AT LANCASTER PARK
February 3, 4, 5, 1984. New Zealand won by an innings and 132 runs.

| M.D. Crowe | c Tavare | 19 | 17–1–88–1 | c Chatfield b Cairns | 18 |
| | | | | c Crowe b Boock | 0 |

ENGLAND VS NEW ZEALAND AT EDEN PARK
February 10, 11, 12, 14, 15, 1984. Match drawn.

| | | | 29–10–70–0 | run out | 70 |

ENGLAND VS PAKISTAN AT NATIONAL STADIUM
March 2, 3, 4, 6, 1984. Pakistan won by 3 wkts.

| Zaheer Abbas | c Lamb | 0 | 30–5–90–2 | c Ramiz b Qadir | 22 |
| Abdul Qadir | c Lamb | 40 | | b Tausif | 10 |

ENGLAND VS WEST INDIES AT EDGBASTON
June 14, 15, 16, 18, 1984. West Indies won by an innings and 180 runs.

| C.H. Lloyd | c Pringle | 71 | 34–7–127–1 | c Garner b Harper | 64 |
| | | | | lbw Garner | 38 |

ENGLAND VS WEST INDIES AT LORD'S
June 28, 29, 30, July 2, 3, 1984. West Indies won by 9 wkts.

| C.G. Greenidge | c Miller | 1 | 27.4–6–103–8 | c Richards b Baptiste | 30 |

H.A. Gomes	c Gatting	10	20.1–2–117–0	lbw Garner	81
D.L. Haynes	lbw	12			
C.H. Lloyd	lbw	39			
I.V.A. Richards	lbw	72			
P.J.L. Dujon	c Fowler	8			
R.A. Harper	c Gatting	8			
J. Garner	c Downton	6			

ENGLAND VS WEST INDIES AT HEADINGLEY
July 12, 13, 14, 16, 1984. West Indies won by 8 wkts.

| | | | 7–0–45–0 | c Dujon b Baptiste | 45 |
| | | | | c Dujon b Garner | 14 |

ENGLAND VS WEST INDIES AT OLD TRAFFORD
July 26, 27, 28, 30, 31, 1984. West Indies won by an innings and 64 runs.

| D.L. Haynes | c Cowans | 2 | 29–5–100–2 | c Garner b Baptiste | 6 |
| P.J.L. Dujon | c Downton | 101 | | c Haynes b Harper | 1 |

ENGLAND VS WEST INDIES AT THE OVAL
August 9, 10, 11, 13, 14, 1984. West Indies won by 172 runs.

C.G. Greenidge	lbw	22	23–8–72–5	c Dujon b Marshall	14
I.V.A. Richards	c Allott	8	22.3–2–103–3	c Marshall b Garner	54
P.J.L. Dujon	c Tavare	3			
R.A. Harper	bowled	18			
M.A. Holding	lbw	0			
M.D. Marshall	c Lamb	12			
D.L. Haynes	bowled	125			
M.A. Holding	lbw	30			

ENGLAND VS SRI LANKA AT LORD'S
August 23, 24, 25, 27, 28, 1984. Match drawn.

S.A.R. Silva	lbw	8	29–6–114–1	c sub b John	6
S. Wettimuny	c Gower	13	27–6–90–6		
R.S. Madugalle	bowled	3			
R.L. Dias	lbw	38			
A. Ranatunga	lbw	0			
L.R.D. Mendis	c Fowler	94			
A.L.F. De Mel	c Ellison	14			

ENGLAND VS AUSTRALIA AT HEADINGLEY
June 13, 14, 15, 17, 18, 1985. England won by 5 wkts.

C.J. McDermott	bowled	18	29.1–8–86–3	b Thomson	60
S.P. O'Donnell	lbw	0	33–7–107–4	b O'Donnell	12
G.M. Ritchie	bowled	46			
G.M. Wood	c Lamb	3			
A.R. Border	c Downton	8			
S.P. O'Donnell	c Downton	24			
G.F. Lawson	c Downton	15			

ENGLAND VS AUSTRALIA AT LORD'S
June 27, 28, 29, July 1, 2, 1985. Australia won by 4 wkts.

K.C. Wessels	lbw	11	24–2–109–5	c Ritchie b Lawson	5
D.C. Boon	c Downton	4	15–0–49–2	c Border b Holland	85
G.M. Ritchie	lbw	94			
W.B. Phillips	c Edmonds	21			
A.R. Border	c Gooch	196			
A.M.J. Hilditch	c Lamb	0			
G.M. Wood	c Lamb	6			

ENGLAND VS AUSTRALIA AT TRENT BRIDGE
July 11, 12, 13, 15, 16, 1985. Match drawn.

| G.M. Wood | c Robinson | 172 | 34.2–3–107–3 | c O'Donnell b McDermott | 38 |
| G.F. Lawson | c Gooch | 18 | | | |

S.P. O'Donnell   c Downton   46

ENGLAND VS AUSTRALIA AT OLD TRAFFORD
August 1, 2, 3, 5, 6, 1985. Match drawn.

D.C. Boon	c Lamb	61	23–4–79–4	c O'Donnell b McDermott	20
W.B. Phillips	c Downton	36	15–3–50–0		
G.R.J. Matthews	bowled	4			
G.F. Lawson	c Downton	4			

ENGLAND VS AUSTRALIA AT EDGBASTON
August 15, 16, 17,19, 20, 1985. England won by an innings and 118 runs.

G.M. Wood	c Edmonds	19	27–1–108–1	c Thomson b McDermott	18
A.M.J. Hilditch	c Ellison	10	14.1–2–52–3		
S.P. O'Donnell	bowled	11			
C.J. McDermott	c Edmonds	8			

ENGLAND VS AUSTRALIA AT THE OVAL
August 29, 30, 31, September 2, 1985. England won by an innings and 94 runs.

G.M. Wood	lbw	22	20–3–64–3	c Phillips b Lawson	12
A.M.J. Hilditch	c Gooch	17	17–3–44–3		
D.R. Gilbert	bowled	1			
G.M. Wood	bowled	6			
K.C. Wessels	c Downton	7			
W.B. Phillips	c Downton	10			

ENGLAND VS WEST INDIES AT SABINA PARK
February 21, 22, 23, 1986. West Indies won by 10 wkts.

R.B. Richardson	lbw	7	19–4–67–2	c Patterson b Marshall	15

| J. Garner | c Edmonds | 24 | | b Marshall | 29 |

ENGLAND VS WEST INDIES AT QUEEN'S PARK OVAL
March 7, 8, 9, 11, 12, 1986. West Indies won by 7 wkts.

| B.P. Patterson | c Gooch | 9 | 9.4–0–68–1 | c Richardson b Marshall | 2 |
| | | | | c Payne b Marshall | 1 |

ENGLAND VS WEST INDIES AT KENSINGTON OVAL
March 21, 22, 23, 25, 1986. West Indies won by an innings and 30 runs.

| P.J.L. Dujon | c sub (Slack) | 5 | 24–3–80–1 | c Dujon b Patterson | 14 |
| | | | | c Dujon b Garner | 21 |

ENGLAND VS WEST INDIES AT QUEEN'S PARK OVAL
April 3, 4, 5, 1985. West Indies won by 10 wkts.

P.J.L. Dujon	c Downton	5	24.1–3–71–5	b Holding	38
I.V.A. Richards	lbw	87	3–0–24–0	c Gomes b Marshall	25
R.A. Harper	lbw	21			
M.A. Holding	bowled	25			
B.P. Patterson	c Downton	3			

ENGLAND VS WEST INDIES AT ST JOHN'S
April 11, 12, 13, 15, 16, 1986. West Indies won by 240 runs.

| C.G. Greenidge | bowled | 14 | 40–6–147–2 | c Harper b Garner | 10 |
| I.V.A. Richards | c Gooch | 26 | 15–0–78–0 | b Harper | 13 |

ENGLAND VS NEW ZEALAND AT THE OVAL
August 21, 22, 23, 25, 26, 1986. Match drawn.

B.A. Edgar	c Gooch	1	25–4–75–3	not out	59
J.J. Crowe	lbw	8	1–0–7–0		
J.V. Coney	c Gooch	38			

ENGLAND VS AUSTRALIA AT WOOLLOONGABBA
November 14, 15, 16, 18, 19, 1986. England won by 7 wkts.

C.D. Matthews	c Gatting	11	16–1–58–2	c Hughes b Waugh	138
M.G. Hughes	bowled	0	12–0–34–1		
D.C. Boon	lbw	14			

ENGLAND VS AUSTRALIA AT WACA GROUND
November 28, 29, 30, December 2, 3, 1986. Match drawn.

G.R. Marsh	c Broad	15	22–4–72–1	c Border b Reid	0
			7.2–4–13–0	c Matthews b Reid	6

ENGLAND VS AUSTRALIA AT MELBOURNE CRICKET GROUND
December 26, 27, 28, 1986. England won by an innings and 114 runs.

G.R. Marsh	c Richards	17	16–4–41–5	c Zoehrer b McDermott	29
A.R. Border	c Richards	15	7–1–19–0		
T.J. Zoehrer	bowled	5			
C.J. McDermott	c Richards	0			
M.G. Hughes	c Richards	2			

ENGLAND VS AUSTRALIA AT SYDNEY CRICKET GROUND
January 10, 11, 12, 14, 15, 1987. Australia won by 55 runs.

	23–10–42–0	c Marsh b Taylor	16
	3–0–17–0	c Wellham b Taylor	0

ENGLAND VS PAKISTAN AT OLD TRAFFORD
June 4, 5, 6, 8, 9, 1987. Match drawn.

Javed Miandad	c French	21	14–7–29–1	c Wasim b Tauseef	48

ENGLAND VS PAKISTAN AT LORD'S
June 18, 19, 20, 22, 23, 1987. Match drawn.

	Did not bowl	c Miandad b Wasim	6

ENGLAND VS PAKISTAN AT HEADINGLEY
July 2, 3, 4, 6, 1987. Pakistan won by an innings and 18 runs.

Did not bowl	c Yousuf b Mudassar	26
	c Mudassar b Mohsin	24

ENGLAND VS PAKISTAN AT EDGBASTON
July 23, 24, 25, 27, 28, 1987. Match drawn.

Ijaz Ahmed	lbw	20	48–13–121–1	c and b Wasim	37
Salim Malik	c and b	17	20.3–3–66–2	c Mohsin b Wasim	6
Ijaz Ahmed	bowled	11			

ENGLAND VS PAKISTAN AT THE OVAL
August 6, 7, 8, 10, 11, 1987. Match drawn.

Ramiz Raja	bowled	14	52–7–217–3	b Qadir	34
Mudassar Nazar	c Moxon	73		not out	51
Salim Malik	c Gower	102			

ENGLAND VS AUSTRALIA AT EDGBASTON
July 6, 7, 8, 10, 11, 1989. Match drawn.

G.R. Marsh	lbw	42	26–5–75–1	b Hughes	46

ENGLAND VS AUSTRALIA AT OLD TRAFFORD
July 27, 28, 29, 31, August 1, 1989. Australia won by 9 wkts.

G.R. Marsh	c Russell	47	24–6–63–2	b Hohns	0
D.M. Jones	bowled	69		lbw Alderman	4

ENGLAND VS AUSTRALIA AT TRENT BRIDGE
August 10, 11, 12, 14, 1989. Australia won by an innings and 180 runs.

30–4–103–0	c Waugh b Hohns	12

ENGLAND VS WEST INDIES AT THE OVAL
August 8, 9, 10, 11, 12, 1991. England won by 5 wkts.

R.B. Richardson	c Stewart	20	11–4–27–1	hit wkt b Ambrose	31
P.V. Simmons	c Lewis	36	16–4–40–2	not out	4
C.B. Lambert	lbw	14			

ENGLAND VS SRI LANKA AT LORD'S
August 22, 23, 24, 26, 27, 1991. England won by 137 runs.

R.S. Mahanama	c Russell	2	10–3–26–1	c Mahanama b Ramanayake	22
			6–2–15–0		

ENGLAND VS NEW ZEALAND AT BASIN RESERVE
February 6, 7, 8, 9, 10, 1992. Match drawn.

C. L. Cairns	c Russell	33	14–4–53–1	c Cairns b Su'a	15
J.G. Wright	c Russell	0	8–1–23–2	lbw Patel	1
B.R. Hartland	lbw	19			

ENGLAND VS PAKISTAN AT EDGBASTON
June 4, 5, 6, 7, 8, 1992. Match drawn.

19–6–52–0	

ENGLAND VS PAKISTAN AT LORD'S
June 18, 19, 20, 21, 1992. Pakistan won by 2 wkts.

5–2–9–0	b Waqar	2
	lbw Waqar	6

TEST MATCH BATTING & BOWLING RECORDS

BATTING BY OPPONENTS

Oppt	Tests	Inns	N.O.	Runs	H.S.	AvgE	100s	50s
Australia	36	59	2	1673	149*	29.35	4	6
India	14	17	0	1201	208	70.65	5	5
New Zealand	15	23	2	846	138	40.29	3	4
Pakistan	14	21	1	647	108	32.35	2	3
Sri Lanka	3	3	0	41	22	13.67	0	0
West Indies	20	38	1	792	81	21.40	0	4
TOTAL	**102**	**161**	**6**	**5200**	**208**	**33.55**	**14**	**22**

BATTING BY CAPTAIN

Capt	Tests	Inns	N.O.	Runs	H.S.	Avge	100s	50s
Brearley	26	38	2	1489	149*	41.36	7	3
Gower	21	35	0	933	85	26.66	0	6
Willis	18	31	0	1276	208	41.16	4	5
Botham	12	21	0	276	57	13.14	0	1
Gatting	10	15	2	480	138	36.92	1	2
Fletcher	7	9	0	453	142	50.33	1	4
Gooch	5	7	1	81	31	13.50	0	0
Boycott	3	5	1	212	103	53.00	1	1
TOTAL	**102**	**161**	**6**	**5200**	**208**	**33.55**	**14**	**22**

BOWLING BY OPPONENTS

Oppt	Balls	Runs	Wkts	Strike	Avge	5WI	10WM	Best
Australia	8479	4093	148	57.29	27.65	9	2	6/78
India	3371	1558	59	57.14	26.41	6	1	7/48
New Zealand	3284	1500	64	51.31	23.44	6	1	6/34
Pakistan	2491	1271	40	167.27	57.18	2	0	8/34
Sri Lanka	581	310	11	52.82	28.18	1	0	6/90
West Indies	3609	2146	61	59.16	35.18	3	0	8/103
TOTAL	**21,815**	**10,878**	**383**	**56.96**	**28.40**	**27**	**4**	**8/34**

BOWLING BY CAPTAIN

Capt	Balls	Runs	Wkts	Strike	Avge	5WI	10WM	Best
Brearley	6690	2815	150	44.60	18.77	15	4	8/34
Gower	4421	2680	74	59.74	36.22	5	0	8/103
Willis	3958	2133	61	64.89	34.97	3	0	5/46
Botham	2211	1158	35	63.17	33.09	0	0	4/77
Gatting	1601	811	19	84.26	42.68	1	0	5/41
Fletcher	1592	725	20	79.60	36.25	1	0	5/61
Gooch	534	245	7	76.29	35.00	0	0	2/23
Boycott	808	311	17	47.53	18.29	2	0	5/73
TOTAL	**21,815**	**10,878**	**383**	**56.96**	**28.40**	**27**	**4**	**8/34**

BIBLIOGRAPHY

Benaud, Richie, *On Reflection* (Collins, 1984)

Benaud, Richie, *The Appeal Of Cricket* (Hodder & Stoughton, 1995)

Botham, Ian & Peter Smith, *The Incredible Tests 1981* (Pelham, 1981)

Botham, Ian & Ian Jarrett, *Botham Down Under* (Collins, 1983)

Botham, Ian & Peter Roebuck, *It Sort Of Clicks* (Collins, 1986)

Botham, Ian & Peter Hayter, *My Autobiography: Don't Tell Kath* (Collins, 1995)

Boycott, Geoff & Terry Brindle, *Opening Up* (Arthur Barker, 1980)

Chappell, Greg & David Frith, *The Ashes '77* (Angus & Robertson, 1977)

Close, Brian & Don Mosey, *I Don't Bruise Easily* (Futura, 1979)

Coleman, Ray, *John Ono Lennon* (Sidgwick & Jackson, 1984)

Collins, Patrick, *The Sportswriter* (Virgin, 1996)

Doust, Dudley, *Ian Botham The Great All-rounder* (Granada, 1981)

Eagar, Patrick, *Botham* (Kingswood Press, 1985)

Gooch, Graham & Frank Keating, *My Autobiography* (Collins, 1995)

Gower, David & Martin Johnson, *The Autobiography* (Fontana, 1993)

James, C.L.R., *Beyond A Boundary* (Stanley Paul, 1963)

Lamb, Allan & Jack Bannister, *My Autobiography* (Collins, 1996)

Lee, Alan, *Lord Ted* (Vista, 1996)

Martin-Jenkins, Christopher, *The Jubilee Tests* (MacDonald & Jane's, 1977)

McDonald, Trevor, *Viv Richards: The Authorised Biography* (Sphere, 1984)

McLellan, Alastair, *The Enemy Within* (Blandford, 1994)

Murphy, Patrick, *Botham: A Biography* (J.M. Dent & Sons, 1988)

Reeve, Dermot & Patrick Murphy, *Winning Ways* (Boxtree, 1996)

Richards, Viv & David Foot, *Viv Richards* (World's Work, 1979)

Roebuck, Peter, *Slices of Cricket* (George Allen, 1982)

Roebuck, Peter, *It Never Rains ...* (George Allen, 1984)

Roebuck, Peter, *Ashes To Ashes* (Heinemann, 1987)

Roebuck, Peter, *From Sammy To Jimmy* (Partridge Press, 1991)

Savidge, Michele & Alastair McLellan, *Real Quick* (Blandford, 1995)

Sobers, Sir Garfield & Ivo Tennant, *The Changing Face Of Cricket* (Ebury Press, 1996)

Steen, Rob, *David Gower: A Man Out Of Time* (Gollancz, 1995)

Trueman, Fred, *Ball Of Fire* (J.M. Dent, 1976)

West, Peter & Wendy Wimbush, *The Battle For The Ashes* (*Daily Telegraph*, 1987)

Willis, Bob & Alan Lee, *Diary Of A Cricket Season* (Pelham, 1979)

Willis, Bob & Alan Lee, *The Captain's Diary* (Collins, 1984)

Wisden Cricketers' Almanack   *The Times*
Wisden Cricket Monthly   *Daily Telegraph*
The Cricketer   *Mail on Sunday*
                                 Guardian

INDEX